DAILY ⊚ NEWS

presents

Jets: Broadway's 30-Year Guarantee

SPORTS PUBLISHING INC.
www.SportsPublishingInc.com

Coordinating Editors: Joseph J. Bannon, Jr. and Joanna L. Wright
Editor: Susan M. McKinney
Book Design, Production Coordinator: Jennifer L. Polson
Dustjacket Design: Terry N. Hayden
Photo Editors: Eric Meskauskas and Angela Troisi
Proofreader: David Hamburg

ISBN: 1-58261-016-9
Library of Congress Number: 98-89632

Printed in the United States.

www.SportsPublishingInc.com

ACKNOWLEDGMENTS

As the final seconds of Super Bowl III ticked down in Miami on January 12, 1969, the *Daily News* was there to record history. The upstart AFL Jets had made good on Joe Namath's bold guarantee of victory over the heavily favored NFL Baltimore Colts. Headlines in the *Daily News* the next day screamed, **SUPERDUPER!** and **JETS SUPER CHAMPS**. The *Daily News* was also there nine months later when the World Champion Jets swamped the New York Giants in the preseason Yale Bowl—to many New Yorkers the *real* Super Bowl.

Chronicling the Jets' super season took hard work and dedication from hundreds of people at the *Daily News*. The efforts of the many reporters, columnists, editors, executives, photographers, librarians, and illustrators were all essential in bringing the Jets' historic season to the pages of the newspaper. Among those who were instrumental in bringing this project to life were Les Goodstein and Ed Fay, who provided enthusiastic support and access to the paper's unmatched resources; John Polizano and Jonathan Moses, who encouraged our work and contributed their business and legal expertise; Eric Meskauskas, Angela Troisi, Bill Martin and Vincent Panzarino, who guided us through the paper's photographic archives; Faigi Rosenthal and Dawn Jackson, who helped us pore through the *Daily News* library files; and Lori Comassar and Lenore Schlossberg, who once again made sure we got all the assistance we needed.

From the *Daily News* sports pages, we specifically want to acknowledge the contributions of Larry Fox, Norm Miller and Dan Farrell. Space limitations preclude us from thanking all the other writers and photographers whose work appears in this book. However, wherever available, we have preserved the writers' bylines and the photographers' credits to ensure proper attribution for their work.

At Sports Publishing Inc., we are grateful for the never-ending support of Jennifer Polson, Susan McKinney, Terry Hayden, Bret Kroencke, Victoria Parrillo, Terrence Miltner and David Hamburg. And finally, to Hall of Famer Don Maynard, whose great catches not only made the Super Bowl season possible, but who was generous enough to share some of those memories with us.

Joanna L. Wright
Joseph J. Bannon, Jr.
Coordinating Editors

CONTENTS

Forward vi

Preseason Change of Ownership 1

Preseason 8

Game 1 20

Game 2 28

Game 3 36

Game 4 44

Game 5 50

Game 6 58

Game 7 66

Game 8 74

Game 9 84

Game 10 92

Heidi Aftermath 100

Game 11 108

Clinch 120

Game 12 128

Game 13 136

Game 14 144

Playoff Preview 152

First Round Playoffs 158

AFL Championship 164

Super Bowl Hype 176

Super Bowl III 186

Super Bowl Celebration 198

Epilogue 210

FOREWORD

From the year of 15 knee operations in 1967 came the New York Jets of 1968. Everyone anticipated a great year. Training camp went smoothly, and before we knew it we were finished with the exhibition games and it was time to travel to Kansas City to open the regular season against the Chiefs.

Kansas City was always a tough team. We knew if we could beat the Chiefs, it would be clear that we had the makings of a good team. Late in the game, we were able to control the ball for the final five minutes to preserve the victory. The win increased our confidence and got us off to a quick start.

We played well throughout the season, losing only three games. The first loss was to the Buffalo Bills—their only win all season. Our third loss that year is one of the more famous games in football history—the Heidi game. With just over a minute to play, the network switched from the Jets-Raiders game to the movie *Heidi*. When the network switched, we were leading the Raiders by three points, but Oakland came back and scored two touchdowns in less than a minute to beat us.

When the regular season ended, the Jets were 11-3. We were on to the toughest and most important game in our team's history. In order to get to the Super Bowl, we had to win the AFL championship game, a rematch against the Oakland Raiders. The pressure was on, and all the players did a great job. Offense, defense and special teams all came through, and we defeated the Raiders and earned our shot at the world championship.

We were now off to the Orange Bowl in Miami and the first true Super Bowl. Our game with the Colts on January 12, 1969 marked the first time that the championship game between the NFL and the AFL was officially called the Super Bowl.

Our time in Miami was fairly low key. We adhered to the same routine and practice schedule as we did when preparing for home games in New York. The two weeks went by quickly, and the waiting was soon over. We were the champions of the AFL, and it was time to prove ourselves to the NFL and the rest of the world.

The game and all the events and exposure surrounding it were unreal. To some degree, the entire country had stopped in order to participate in this great event. The odds and point spreads were the highest you could imagine. Both teams had great support from their fans, although some were louder or more vocal than others. And of course, Joe Namath issued the guarantee that has become as famous as the game itself.

When the game was over and we had won, there were a few people who did not consider our victory an upset. Most people, however, were "shocked," and remained that way for years to come. On that Sunday afternoon, we secured our place in history in one of the greatest football games America has ever seen.

Don Maynard

JETS' NEW PREZ DIES AT 66

— Story on Page 84

Pretty, as You Please. Jockey Bobby Ussery keeps Pretty Bug along the rail and in front of the pack as the field thunders into stretch in first race at Big A yesterday. Pretty Bug needled in with a $7.80 payoff. Then, in the second race, Ron Turcotte booted Tradesman ($8.40) home for a $48.20 daily double.

NEWS photo by John Tresilian

Ringo Stars. Ringo, a mostly St. Bernard, is certified a canine hero by Mayor William Fuller in Euless, Tex., as his master, Randy Saleh, 2, looks on. When Randy wandered into heavy traffic, Ringo ran into street, warned oncoming cars, saving his master's life. —*Story on page 26*

UPI Telephoto

Ugh! More Rain? Ever wonder what happened to hoola hoops? Well, a member of the American Indian Thunderbird Dancers has found a good use for them. He's dancing for a lunchtime audience at Chase Manhattan Plaza in financial district. But will it bring some rain?

NEWS photo by John Pedin

**New York City Mayor Lindsay and Jets owner Phil Iselin.
(News photo by Vincent Riehl)**

The months preceding the New York Jets' 1968 season were anything but calm, with club leadership changing hands three times in two months. Jets giant Sonny Werblin sold his share of the organization to partners Donald Lillis, Leon Hess, Townsend B. Martin and Philip Iselin for $2 million. The flamboyant Werblin was credited with putting the Jets on the map with the acquisition of players like Joe Namath and his fight to save the AFL.

Soon after, Donald Lillis took over as president and chief executive officer of the Jets, but this was short-lived, as he passed away just two months after he was named Werblin's successor. The torch was finally given to Philip Iselin, and the Jets were ready for the upcoming season.

Is Sonny's Future in Sunny Miami?

by Gene Ward
Daily News

The sports world may have lost its most dynamic promoter when David (Sonny) Werblin sold his $23^1/_3$ percent interest in the Gotham Football Club, but he'll be back. That's a promise he made in an exclusive disclosure to *The News* yesterday.

That is all Sonny would say — nothing as to where or when — following a news leak Tuesday night that revealed he finally had agreed to sell his share in the Jets to partners Donald Lillis, Leon Hess, Townsend B. Martin and Phil Iselin for $2 million.

The negotiations had been under way in a strained atmosphere for three months, with the partners offering to sell their respective shares (Hess and Martin, 23 1/3 percent; Lillis, 20 percent; Iselin, 10 percent) to Werblin or to buy him out. Sonny would have had to raise something like $9 million and he couldn't swing it.

As for continuing in pro football, he long ago expressed a keen interest in the Miami Dolphins.

Why had the sunshine gone out of the job of masterminding the Jets for Sonny?

There are several answers. His partners were irked at being left out of the limelight. They wanted more say in the operation of the team, but Sonny couldn't see it that way. He told them the prerequisite for success in any business operation, and most particularly a sports franchise, was one-man control.

At least two of the partners were in favor of taking their profits and getting out.

The old Harry Wismer Titan franchise in the AFL had cost the Werblin group $1 million; now it is appraised at between $11 and $12 million.

It was Sonny Werblin who put life into the AFL by getting together the syndicate which gave the league its strong New York anchor franchise. Then he came up with Joe Namath, the first of football's fantastic bonus players, and thereby gave the game a whole new image.

Next, he used his television savvy to assemble the NBC package, which saved the AFL in its war with the NFL.

It also led to the merger which, in itself, is ironic because Sonny wanted no part in joining forces with the other league.

Sonny Werblin is a lone wolf. Either he runs the show or the show goes on without him, minus the high-octane quality of his promotional genius.

We're all going to miss Sonny Werblin around our town.

SONNY SELLS INTEREST IN JETS TO FOUR PARTNERS

Sonny Werblin has sold his share of the Jets to his four partners, one of the partners confirmed last night. "The deal has been made," Townsend B. Martin said. "We offered Sonny a price and he accepted. There will be four equal partners and Don Lillis will be the new president."

Weeb Ewbank will remain as GM and head coach "as far as I know," Martin said. He added that he knew nothing of rumors to try to persuade Vince Lombardi to leave the Packers to coach the Jets.

Along with Martin and Lillis, the other two partners are Philip H. Iselin and Leon Hess. Martin did not disclose the amount paid to Werblin for his "little better than 20 percent" of the team.

Sad Parting for Werblin & Co.

by Larry Fox
Daily News

In the same office building from which he and his partners first ran the Jets in happier days, Sonny Werblin yesterday signed away his share of the club.

The transaction whereby Werblin's 23 1/3 percent of the club was bought by his four partners for an estimated $2 million was completed in the 660 Madison Ave. offices of attorney Arnold Grant. Grant is the lawyer of Donald C. Lillis, who succeeds Werblin as president and chief executive officer of the Jets.

A couple of years ago the Jets moved their offices three blocks downtown to 595 Madison. Werblin is expected to move out over the weekend. He's been cleaning out his files since early this week.

"I feel badly . . . and he must too. He broke those offices in," Lillis said.

Lillis plans to complete the takeover a week from Monday, June 3.

"I'm tired," he confessed. "It's been hectic. I'm going to Chicago and then I'll take a long Memorial Day weekend before I move in and go to work."

Lillis, Werblin and the other partners—Leon Hess, Phil Iselin and Townsend Martin—were present for the signing ceremony in the attorney's office. When it was all over, Lillis announced: "It's all done. The stock is in the box and it's official."

Approval of the stock transfer had been obtained by the AFL President Milt Woodard in a telephone poll of league owners Wednesday night. The only formality is for Woodard himself to approve the "structure of ownership," when it's forwarded to him. This is virtually automatic.

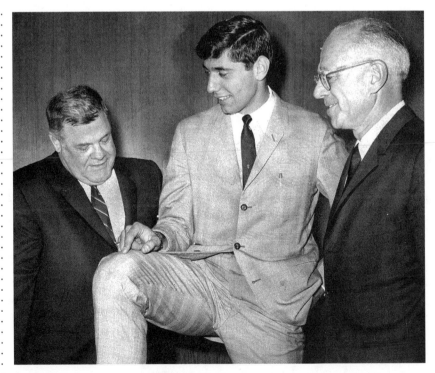

Joe Namath (center), coach Weeb Ewbank (l.) and owner Dave (Sonny) Werblin (r.). Namath displays his now famous knee. (News photo by Tom Baffer)

Lillis, Jets' Prexy, 66, Dies of Heart Attack

by Larry Fox
Daily News

Donald C. Lillis, president and chief executive officer of the Jets, died in a Rhode Island hospital yesterday morning, but at the Hofstra training camp in Hempstead, L.I., his football team went about its regular routine.

"Mr. Lillis would have wanted it that way. That's the kind of man he was," said Weeb Ewbank, coach and general manager of the Jets. "Of course, we're all shocked by what happened and we'll decide later what to do on Friday, the day of the funeral."

Lillis, 66, had been in ill health for several months. In the last year he had been hospitalized for emphysema and just two weeks ago, underwent an emergency appendectomy.

Cause of death was listed as a heart ailment, but it was the other illnesses that had worn down the energetic executive.

Phil Iselin, vice president and treasurer of the Jets, said no decision would be made on naming a new chief executive "until the board of directors meets sometime in the near future."

President of Monmouth Park Jockey Club, Iselin appears most likely to be given the task of chief operating officer. The other partners are Townsend B. Martin, chairman of the board, and Leon Hess, secretary.

Lillis' previous interest in sports had been as president of Bowie Race Course. He retired from that post a couple of years ago after reviving that once-failing track with the introduction of winter racing. His major business interests had been as a limited partner in Bear, Stearns & Co. and as a member of the New York Stock Exchange. He was chairman of the board of the Nuclear Corporation of America and chairman of the executive board of the National Can Co.

ISELIN, JETS PRESIDENT, WANTS AFL CROWN

August 7, 1968—Philip H. Iselin, one of the "silent" partners who bought Sonny Werblin's Jet stock, yesterday was named president and chief executive officer of the AFL club. Iselin replaces the late Don Lillis, who passed away last month.

In other management moves, Leon Hess, who'd been executive secretary under Lillis, becomes vice president. Arnold M. Grant, who was general counsel of the corporation, becomes secretary-treasurer. Richard L. Barovick, a new member of the board of directors, was named to the newly-created post of assistant secretary, with Townsend B. Martin remaining as chairman of the board.

"It's both an honor and a challenge to become president of the Jets," Iselin said. "It is an honor because the Jets are a good team with excellent personnel and a good coaching staff, backed by skilled and hard-working men and women in the front office.

"It is a challenge, because we want to give our loyal fans a championship team. It is our number one goal — to make the New York Jets champions of the American Football League and the first representatives of the AFL to win the Super Bowl.

New Jets owner Phil Iselin. (Daily News photo)

New York Jets
1968 AFL Regular-Season Schedule

Date	Opponent	Location
September 15, 1968	Kansas City Chiefs	Kansas City, Missouri
September 22, 1968	Boston Patriots	Birmingham, Alabama
September 29, 1968	Buffalo Bills	Buffalo, New York
October 5, 1968	San Diego Chargers	Shea Stadium, New York
October 13, 1968	Denver Broncos	Shea Stadium, New York
October 20, 1968	Houston Oilers	Houston, Texas
October 27, 1968	Boston Patriots	Shea Stadium, New York
November 3, 1968	Buffalo Bills	Shea Stadium, New York
November 10, 1968	Houston Oilers	Shea Stadium, New York
November 17, 1968	Oakland Raiders	Oakland, California
November 24, 1968	San Diego Chargers	San Diego, California
December 1, 1968	Miami Dolphins	Shea Stadium, New York
December 8, 1968	Cincinnati Bengals	Shea Stadium, New York
December 15, 1968	Miami Dolphins	Miami, Florida

Joe Namath

News photo by Dan Farrell

As the 1968 pre-season opened, the Jets were poised to make big news both on and off the field. The night life and love life of the AFL's brightest star, Jets quarterback Joe Namath, were a constant source of fan and media attention. On the field, the Jets were preparing for a title run. However, injury was the key theme in the Jets' pre-season. After missing the first two pre-season games, a recovering Joe Namath took on the Falcons in his collegiate state of Alabama. With teammates Emerson Boozer, Pete Lammons, John Schmitt, Don Maynard, and Bob Talamini on the sidelines due to injuries, Namath and the Jets still managed a 27-12 victory. While the Jets were optimistic about Namath's knees, they were not so sure about Boozer's. Emerson Boozer, it was felt by many, was an essential piece to the Jets' puzzle, and without him the previous year, the Jets had been shut down.

At the end of the pre-season, the Packers and the Rams were the favorites to win the NFL championship of 1968, while the Jets, Chiefs, and Raiders were among the leaders in the AFL. In a little-noticed player trade, the Baltimore Colts picked up reserve quarterback Earl Morrall from the New York Giants.

Namath Set for First Test Back in 'Bama Country

by Norm Miller
Daily News

Joe Namath, finally rendered fit by the miracles of modern medicine and his own will power, exposes his gimpy knees in his first exhibition venture of '68 tonight when the Jets take on the NFL Falcons at Birmingham, Alabama.

Satisfied that the pain in his left knee, which kept him sidelined in the Jets' first two pre-season games, has diminished considerably after two cortisone shots. Namath will start at QB tonight. Coach Weeb Ewbank would like him to play at least a half, and longer if Joe feels up to it.

The return to the country where he was a college hero and the challenge of meeting an NFL trial may have hastened the healing process in Namath's knee. He worked out for about 45 minutes in 98 degree weather at Legion Stadium after his arrival yesterday.

Joe Namath works out at Shea Stadium as Coach Weeb Ewbank looks on. (News photo by Jack Clarity)

ODDS ON

Reno, Nevada, August 23—A bookmaker quoted the Green Bay Packers and Los Angeles Rams as 2-1 co-favorites today to win the National Football League championship this year. Green Bay is defending champ.

North Swanson of the Reno Turf Club said the Oakland Raiders are 7-5 favorites to repeat as champ of the American Football League.

Namath at QB as Jets Tackle Falcons in 'Bama

Birmingham, Alabama, August 23 (Special)—Joe Namath exposed his $400,000 arm and his 10 cent knees to the hard knocks of an opposing club for the first time in this exhibition season tonight as the Jets took on the NFL Falcons before a crowd of about 30,000 in sweltering Legion Stadium.

The Jets led, 16-6, at the end of the first half.

Namath missed the Jets' first two pre-season games, complaining of pain in his left knee. He looked physically sound in a 45-minute workout here right after the team's arrival, although coach Weeb Ewbank noted he overthrew several passes and did not appear at peak sharpness.

Ewbank started Namath and planned to go with him for at least a half before relieving with Babe Parilli.

Three Jets starters—tight end Pete Lammons, center John Schmitt and flanker Don Maynard—were on the bench with injuries when the game got under way in 90 degree weather. Maynard was expected to be used briefly during the course of the game.

Bob Talamini, the All-AFL guard acquired in a deal with Houston, also was on the sidelines. Talamini pulled a leg muscle overextending himself in one of the earliest drills with the Jets on Tuesday.

Although the Jets had drawn crowds of more than 50,000 in previous visits here to the land where Namath played his college football, the crowd was considerably smaller tonight, due primarily to the humidity and the uncertainty about the star QB's physical condition.

Ron Vander Kelen, one-time Rose Bowl hero and No. 2 quarterback for the Falcons, started, with first stringer Randy Johnson ready to step in if the Atlanta offense

Monroe Lerman (l.) drove 1,400 miles from Miami, Florida where he now lives, to see NY Jets star Joe Namath in his first workouts at Hofstra. (News photo)

COLT WATCH COLT WATCH COLT WATCH COLT WATCH

MORRALL DEALT TO COLTS

by Norm Miller
Daily News

August 26, 1968—New Haven, Connecticut—The Giants announced just before today's exhibition against the Cards here that quarterback Earl Morrall has been traded to the Colts for a "high draft choice," but there was some uncertainty whether he would report to his new club.

Morrall, whose departure was foretold when the Giants claimed Gary Wood on waivers from New Orleans more than a week ago, had not signed a '68 contract. His decision on joining the Colts depended on whether he could negotiate a satisfactory contract

Earl Morrall

with coach Don Shula. Morrall, a 34-year-old vet of 12 NFL seasons, spent three spotty years with the Giants. He hauled them back to respectability with a 7-7 record in '65; missed most of '66 with a broken hand, and played very little behind Fran Tarkenton last season.

sputtered. The Falcons lost to the Giants, 17-13, last Saturday night.

The game originally was scheduled for Saturday night but was moved up 24 hours so it would not have to compete with the nationally televised clash between the Packers and Cowboys, last season's NFL division champs.

"How's the knee? It hurts. It hurts worse than I thought it would at this stage," Namath said. "They say rest is the only thing I can do for it..."

Debut: Namath OK, Boozer Out

by Larry Fox
Daily News

The celebrated knees of Joe Namath and Emerson Boozer are hurting. Namath, who has never missed a regular season pro game because of injury, can be expected to be in the lineup opening day September 15 at Kansas City. Boozer is not so sure.

Namath, who missed the Jets' first two exhibitions because of soreness in his left knee, the "good" one that underwent a "minor" operation this winter, probably will play tomorrow's preseason game in Memphis against Cincinnati.

"How's the knee? It hurts. It hurts worse than I thought it would at this stage," Namath said before yesterday's workout at Hofstra. "They say rest is the only thing I can do for it, but that's what they've been telling me for three years and I've been resting it for three off-seasons."

Boozer underwent serious surgery on his mangled right knee midway of last season. His recent six-week Army tour set him back at least that much in conditioning. He'll make the trip to Memphis, but will just be along for the ride.

The same may be true for the final exhibition game against Detroit at Cleveland September 7.

The Jets originally had hoped to have their explosive halfback available for at least some duty in the last two exhibition games. Weeb Ewbank still talks optimistically about that timetable. "I'd rather not take a chance on Boozer this week and we'll play next week by ear," he says.

However, Boozer was more pessimistic yesterday. "It's coming along slowly," he revealed. "I can't see myself getting in there until the first, second or third season game. I won't even give it a try against Detroit if it doesn't feel just right. I don't want to waste seven-eight months' work for just one test."

Boozer isn't going to take any chances with his knee.

"I'm not too anxious to get in there right now. I'm not going to push it," Boozer said. "I'm concerned with getting the strength back and the soreness out."

Boozer says he can tell by "the pain, flexibility and swelling" that his knee is still not right.

"Pain is your worse enemy," he said softly. "Pain can stop about anything if it's severe enough and it keeps you from doing things your mind wants you to do."

If Boozer is not ready by opening day, Ewbank probably will go with the five running backs now

Joe Namath

on the roster—Bill Mathis, Matt Snell, top rookie Lee White, Mark Smolinski and Billy Joe. Ewbank plans to give White a lot of work against the Bengals now that he's convinced that Snell, injured early last season, "is his old self again."

Joe, who got his biggest shot early before White reported, appears most vulnerable because Ewbank feels he can play only fullback while all the others can run from both spots. Smolinski, who finally may get some work at tight end, is invaluable on special teams and it is this unsung skill that probably will determine Ewbank's final few personnel decisions.

Jets/It Depends on Joe and Emmo

by Larry Fox
Daily News

The Jets were inside the Lion 10. That's touchdown country, where the defensive linemen curse and growl as they scratch to protect their goal line.

Emerson Boozer knows what it's like down there. Ten times last season he squirmed through that mass for running touchdowns until in the eighth game they put him down for good in Kansas City.

Now, in Cleveland's mammoth Municipal Stadium, he was coming back against the NFL Lions, known for years for their vicious defense.

Before the game, Boozer talked with Joe Namath, his quarterback. "Look, if we get inside the 10, you'd better call somebody else. I don't think you can count on me," said Boozer, who was apprehensive about his knee.

The man listening in heard Namath reply, "If you feel that way, why bother to suit up?"

The short answer had its desired effect. Boozer suited up and now the Jets were inside the 10 and Namath called on his halfback and Boozer slashed for six yards to the one. Alex Karras, Detroit's mean-as-mustard defensive tackle, was waiting there. He

threw a shoulder low into Boozer and the Jet halfback somersaulted to the ground.

Maybe Emmo didn't bound up like a spring, but he didn't lay there holding his knee, either. And on the next play, he led the interference for Matt Snell's touchdown run by driving the Detroit safety almost out of the end zone.

The entire Boozer affair, including his confrontation with Namath, is of utmost importance in assessing Jet prospects for the 1968 season, which opens in Kansas City Sunday afternoon.

Without Boozer's outside running threat, the Jets' title bid last year collapsed even faster than his shattered right knee. And, although Namath has emerged as the AFL's premier passer, there has always been a question of whether he could exert championship-caliber leadership.

Of the way Namath pulled Boozer up short, one close observer of Jet affairs noted: "That's the first time I've ever heard him show that kind of leadership. I think it's a good sign."

The Jets are a team that could win a championship...even the Super Bowl...or finish deep among the also rans. A lot de-

pends on Boozer. More depends on Namath. When he's hot—with receivers like Don Maynard and George Sauer—he can beat anybody, even the Packers. He also is capable of throwing six interceptions a game. Fans remember the vicious beating Namath took last year at Oakland in the next-to-last game of the season. The Raiders already had clinched the Western Division championship and they had nothing to lose. But the Jets still were mathematically alive in the East. Oakland's only loss all year had been to the Jets and the Raiders didn't want to chance meeting them again in a championship game.

That day they voted Namath to their all-opponent team. He almost didn't survive.

Joe's famous knees still bother him and he missed the Jets' first two exhibition games this year. But in his past three years as a pro he has yet to miss a game that counted because of injury. None will deny he's a pro.

The Jets have made few personnel changes. They feel new tackle Sam Walton, a rookie, is a blue-chipper on offense and they feel their deep secondary is the best they've ever had. Bob Talamini at guard was a great pickup.

The Jets' main rival in the AFL Eastern Division will be Houston, the team that caught them in the stretch last season. The Oilers did it with defense then and they return a top unit headed by 1967 Rookie-of-the-Year George Webster at linebacker. The personnel on offense hasn't changed much, but coach Wally Lemm expects his attack to be vastly improved with Pete Beathard available from training camp on. Beathard didn't join the Oilers until last mid-season in GM Don Klosterman's daring trade with Kansas City.

Boston and Buffalo both have good defense...and quarterback trouble. The Bills lost Jack Kemp for the season when he was hurt in a freak accident during a "punishment" scrimmage called by head coach Joe Collier. Tom Flores, his backup, also has been hurt and so far it's up to rookie Dan Darragh. Darragh has moved the team, but his inexperience showed in last Sunday's opening loss to Boston.

The Pats have been rebuilding over the last couple of years and appear in better shape for a comeback than Buffalo if ex-Jet Mike Taliaferro can step out as a starter. In Jim Nance, they've got the league's leading rusher the last two seasons. He missed the opener with a bad ankle, but he still should make his 1,000 yards.

If Buffalo and Boston don't pull themselves together, Miami could move ahead of both of them in the standings. The Dolphins did manage to beat out Boston last year and finished in a tie for third with Buffalo. They'll be better this year now that quarterback Bob Griese has had a full season under his hip pads. Rookie Larry Csonka

from Syracuse will be a bull in anybody's backfield.

Out in the West, the league champion Raiders will be favored to repeat, but they'll have a lot of competition in what has been the AFL's stronger division the last several years.

The Raiders are a team without any great weakness. They lost a standout back like Clem Daniels to injury after nine games

Joe Namath

last season and didn't even miss him as Pete Banaszak came through as a replacement.

The Raiders will miss slow-healing Tom Keating, their fine defensive tackle who looked so good in the Super Bowl despite the injury that eventually put him on the operating table, but he's not the only weapon in their gun rack.

Sid Gillman, coach and general manager at San Diego, is more optimistic than usual. He's

still got that explosive offense, which features John Hadl throwing to Lance Alworth, and he thinks he's patched up last year's sieve-like defense. Tackle Russ Washington, their 280-pound No. 1 draft choice, shows signs of filling a couple of holes all by himself.

Kansas City had planned to make this a rebuilding year, but suddenly Hank Stram who, with Gillman, is the only AFL coach still working the same street corner for the ninth year, is talking titles. Two reasons things look a little better is the way fullback Wendell Hayes and cornerback Goldie Sellers, both obtained in trades from impatient Lou Saban at Denver, have moved into regular roles. The big change in Kansas City is the shift of linebacker E. J. Holub, a holler guy with hollow knees, to center.

One thing about Denver, Saban won't get complacent. He took over a loser before last season and can't be accused of standing pat. A serious injury to Steve Tensi has left the quarterbacking up to comebacking John McCormick, who sat out last season, and soph pro Jim Leclair of C. W. Post.

Cincinnati has surprised a lot of people with its fine play during the exhibition season and in a close loss to San Diego in last Friday's opener. Rookie Dewey Warren has come up from the back of the line to be an exciting quarterback and Paul Brown has come out of retirement with his brain still running like IBM. But before anybody gets too excited, wait until that initial enthusiasm wears off—the Bengals were going to war the night they upset the Jets—and a few front liners get hurt and Brown can't find replacements.

Pro football is a game of injuries. Everybody gets people hurt. The winners can replace them.

Joe Namath/ How It Really Is

by Dick Young
Daily News

Q Joe, what is your reaction to your playboy image?

A. I think, in all seriousness, that it's overplayed. I don't fool around nearly as much as what is made out to be. I go out, sure. I live in Manhattan, I'm a bachelor, but…(pause)…it's built up too much, too big.

Q. Do you feel you have just the normal attraction and reaction to the opposite sex? That of any healthy American boy?

A. It has helped me, being a football player, I guess, being in New York. I meet more girls, different girls. Still, it's just a normal thing.

Q. Your reaction isn't any different than it would be, say, for a boy in Beaver Falls (Pennsylvania)?

A. (Smiling) Well, it's different than it would be in Beaver Falls, because you're pretty well limited in Beaver Falls. I should know, I was raised there.

Q. What about the camp-jumping incident last year and all the publicity it received? What happened between you and coach Weeb Ewbank?

A. Well, I've said before I was wrong in leaving the camp,

but I just had to leave. I had some problems. It was something personal. And I was fined. A lot of people don't figure I was fined. I don't think it would have been played up if it had been somebody else. Not so much.

Q. I seem to recall that Sonny Werblin had said that while he did not tell Weeb not to fine you, if he had been Weeb he would not have fined you.

A. Well, look, we have regulations where you just have to treat people the same way about things, and I don't care who'd it have been, I'd have had to fine him myself.

Q. You were aware that you were going to be fined?

A. Yes. Absolutely. We discussed this before I left.

Q. What about the alleged fight that took place in an East Side bar while you were away?

A. That's ridiculous. It didn't take place. I think we're acting now as far as counter-suing the guy for libel and defamation of character.

Q. What about the mink-coat? How do you feel about that?

A. Sometimes I like it and sometimes I don't. The coat that is. I like the coat because it is

beautiful, I mean it really is. And other times I don't like it.

Q. It seems too much?

A. Sometimes it seems that way, but just so you'll understand—the contract I have with them, I can say anything I want about the coat, push it, or wear it anytime, but I never have to do anything. So I told them, all right, we'll take some pictures at the fitting. Well, good Lord, you know, they build it up pretty good. Maybe someday I can have it changed around to fit my mother.

Q. How do you get along with your teammates?

A. Very good. I know some fellows better than others, but I don't have any problems with anyone at all on the team. In the last three years, I've had disagreements. Any player has. But we've always gotten straightened out. Right now, I don't know anyone on the team that has any animosity towards me, nor I towards them.

Q. Do you think some of the guys think you're aloof at times?

A. Sure, I would think you'd have to think that at times. It's human nature to figure that about somebody else who is, like, in a different position both financially and publicity-wise. But most of the fellows know me now.

Q. It took a little while?

A. Oh, God, yes! The first year was ridiculous.

Q. What would they say? Things like, "There's the big star?"

A. "Star," "owner's pet," you know. But that doesn't exist at all now.

Q. Do you think that Sonny Werblin kind of put you on the spot by catering to you, or being in your company?

A. I would like to be put on that spot more often. (Laugh) No, I was put in a set of circumstances that were pretty hard for me to understand at the time, but it worked out.

Q. But it created a condition, a situation…

A. Right—that I certainly wasn't used to.

Q. For example, I've heard it said that Weeb wanted you to take an apartment in Flushing, near the ballpark, to be near the other players, and Sonny said you belong on Park Avenue.

A. When I first went to New York, Weeb wanted me to live close to the stadium. It's better.

Q. To be one of the guys?

A. Sure, Weeb was thinking along these lines, because he was more familiar with a football team than Mr. Werblin was at that time. But I wanted to live in Manhattan.

Q. Why?

A. Being from Pennsylvania, and down South, I always heard about New York. I wanted to live there. You know, learn what it was like.

Q. Your midtown pad has been depicted as a playpen, with nightly orgies on a llama rug. That's the impression many people have. Just how much action is there?

A. Well, you know Ray

Abruzzese, for one (former Jets defensive back, and before that Namath's teammate at Alabama, a bachelor). We live together. Well, we have the fellows up, and occasionally we have parties with some girls up, but they're not as wild as people make them out to be. I wish they were. I think it would be a lot of fun.

Q. What about the apartment itself?

A. It's a little wild, I guess.

This decorator I had was something else, see. I'll tell you. He said he could decorate the apartment for about $13,000, $15,000. Actually, we got up to around $20,000.

Most of the things in the apartment were his idea—like the llama rug, and the Siberian snow leopard and zebra pillows, and cheetah bench and stuff. I never really thought of anything like that.

Joe Namath on the sidelines. (News photo by Dan Farrell)

Jets quarterback Joe Namath relaxes in his penthouse in Manhattan with a good football book and his left knee in a cast. (News photo by Detrick Leonard)

Q. Let's talk a little about the fans. What is your reaction when they get on you?

A. I get angry occasionally. Not during the games, because I can't hear them that often, but the folks down around the sidelines that yell things out, damn! When you stop to consider how much they know about the game, you figure it's their ignorance just yelling out. They don't understand football plays, or techniques and things that we have to do.

You know, you might throw a ball 15 yards over a guy's head. They don't know why you did that. They think it's a bad pass. It could be just that the guy's covered so you're just throwing it away rather than take the loss.

Q. Do the fans shout per-sonal things at you?

A. That's what bugs me more than anything. It's like, why is your hair so long? Why ain't you in the Army? You don't need a mink coat, you fag! They just don't know, but a lot of them sure don't like me.

Q. What about your treat-ment in the press?

A. I think it's been fair the majority of the time. The only time I think it's unfair is when some-body writes about me without even talking to me. Like the guy in Houston who knocked me for wearing a red jacket when every-body else wore green and white. He also said I was signing auto-graphs J. W. Smith.

Q. He didn't know that the quarterbacks wear red for protec-tion during drills?

A. He didn't know.

Q. What's the J. W. Smith thing all about?

A. That's what he had heard, that I was signing autographs J. W. Smith, being smarty.

Q. And that wasn't true?

A. No. I may have one time or so signed J. W. Smith jokingly, and corrected it. If I didn't, it was a bad mistake.

Q. Anything, Joe, that you'd like to say that we haven't touched on?

A. Well, no. I do a lot of wrong things, bad things, like I don't improve myself mentally enough, scholastically, but I'm trying to. What I'm trying to say is people shouldn't really form opinions as quickly as they do about people from just hearsay, or reading about them. I get a lot of letters, a lot of bad letters about things that I've never done or never considered doing, but these people are sure that I do it, and these people dislike me, hate me and everything else because of it.

Q. Do you get propositions?

A. No, very rarely.

Q. Proposals of marriage?

A. No, I don't recall ever getting a proposal of marriage.

Q. What are your plans, romantically.

A. Oh, I want to get married, and have a family, but when, I don't know. I don't have any definite plans. I have a girl, you know, that I see pretty frequently, you know, when I'm in the South. She comes up here and visits, but I don't have any immediate plans.

Q. Is she pushing you?

A. She's starting to, a little bit. (Laughter) No, she hasn't really, not at all. But I would like to get married sometime.

Q. Would you like to have a lot of kids?

A. Well, I'm Catholic, so I'll have to see what happens.

Joe Namath with the Playboy bunnies. (News photo by Jim Garrett)

CARDS CLINCH AGAIN

Yanks Streak to 10th, 3-2; Mets Plunge, 3-0

GIANTS, 34-20; JETS, 20-19

—Stories Pgs 66, 67

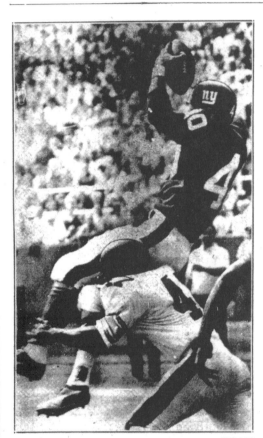

UPI Telephoto

Giants' Joe Morrison leaps to make spectacular catch and score touchdown during second quarter of game in Pittsburgh. Morrison, who took the pass from Fran Tarkenton, was hit hard by Steelers' Marv Woodson but managed to hold on to ball. Official ruled he was over goal line and Steelers' protested vehemently. As usual, the ref's word was law. Giants won opener, 34-20.

The Giants Join the Jet Set

Chiefs' Goldie Sellers [→] reaches out for Jets' Don Maynard as big Don gathers in a 56-yard Joe Namath pass and scampers for the Jets' first touchdown of game at Kansas City yesterday. The Jets edged out the Chiefs, 20-19, before a sellout crowd of 48,871. —Stories p. 66

UPI Telephoto

Bird Bath of Bubbly. Cardinals' Orlando Cepeda pours champagne for Roger Maris in Houston as manager Red Schoendienst joins the fun after Birds won National League pennant. Cards beat Astros, 7-4, to clinch tie; then Cincinnati eliminated Giants to nail it down for Cards.—Story on page 66

Associated Press Wirephoto

SEPTEMBER 15, 1968

New York 20, Kansas City 19

New York	7	10	0	3	—	20
Kansas City	3	0	10	6	—	19

In the season opener in Kansas City, the Jets held on to a narrow lead to upset the Chiefs, 20-19. Newly elected offensive team captain Joe Namath threw two touchdown passes to Don Maynard, while two field goals by Jim Turner sealed the win. Maynard caught eight passes for 203 yards, surpassing the 200-yard mark for the first time in his career. Emerson Boozer led all ball carriers with 18 carries for 75 yards. Off the field, starting fullback Matt Snell remained unsigned, talking after the game of exploring his options.

In the NFL, Colts' star quarterback Johnny Unitas sat out the season opener against San Francisco due to a sore elbow. Newcomer stand-in Earl Morall led Baltimore to a 27-10 win, completing 16-of-34 passes for 198 yards and two touchdowns.

Jets "On Guard" for Chiefs

by Larry Fox
Daily News

Emerson Boozer isn't the only Jet with bitter memories of his last visit to Kansas City. The steady improvements of rookie guard Randy Rasmussen also came to an end after his introduction to the Chiefs' monstrous right tackle, Buck Buchanan.

As the Jets prepare to open their season at Kansas City this Sunday, Boozer is slogging up the comeback road on his post-operative knee and Rasmussen is fighting for his job.

How much Rasmussen plays Sunday will depend on what little tricks Hank Stram, the ultra-intensive Kaycee coach, has planned.

One of Stram's stratagems which worked for four pass deflections at the line of scrimmage in last year's 42-18 victory at KC, is to place both his tackles, the 6-7, 287-pound Buchanan and the 6-9, 313-pound Ernie Ladd, on the right side of the line. The more agile Buchanan plays end.

But this season Weeb Ewbank can do some maneuvering too.

"When Buchanan plays tackle, I'll probably use Bob Talamini at guard," Ewbank explained before yesterday's workout. "Talamini has the experience to handle Buchanan, he's played him ever since he came into the league. But if Buchanan goes to end and Ladd moves over to the right side, I'll probably use Rasmussen more. Ladd is a more straight-ahead guy and Randy is big enough and strong enough to play him."

Drawing Ladd as an opponent is not exactly soft duty. He is the most frightening defensive lineman in pro football. But he can be stopped.

"The trouble with Ladd is he goes all out to punish the man opposite him. He tries to hurt him," one All-AFL guard has pointed out. "And when he's trying to hurt you, he's not doing his job. He can't get to the passer or make tackles while he's beating up on you and you're glad to sacrifice your body to the cause."

Al Atkinson, the still-improving middle linebacker, missed yesterday's workout but he's expected to play Sunday. A year ago he suited up and went all the way despite one of the most painful injuries known to man. This week he just has a bruised leg.

If Atkinson can't go, however, his place probably will be taken by Mike Stromberg, a taxi grad from Brooklyn's Tilden High who was drafted out of Temple last year. "He's a fine tackler and he made his mark on special teams during the exhibition season just the way Atkinson did," points out assistant coach Walt Michaels.

Carl McAdams, a college linebacker, can also play there, but he's getting more work at defensive tackle behind Paul Rochester. "Carl is a lot more active than Rocky and it can really shake up a team if you keep changing off between two different styles like that. They almost have to set up two game plans," Michaels explained.

GORDON READY FOR JET START

by Larry Fox
Daily News

September 14, 1968—Cornell Gordon, who says only half facetiously that it was his injury and not Emerson Boozer's that cost the Jets the AFL East championship last year, is coming back.

With Bill Baird just getting over a slight muscle pull, Gordon has been working with the first unit at free safety and probably will get the start at Kansas City tomorrow.

Gordon, entering his fourth pro season, was a regular cornerback when he hurt his knee in last year's opener at Buffalo.

"We were leading, 17-0, when I got hurt and we ended up losing. Since we missed the championship by only one game, I figure that could have cost us the title," Gordon explained yesterday as the Jets dodged tacklers and little kids on bicycles in their ultra-public workout at Flushing Meadow Park.

The injury to Gordon forced the Jets to give Randy Beverly a chance and the little cornerback from Wildwood, N.J., grabbed a lock on the job. This week, at least, Gordon is a safety and that could be where he remains even though Weeb Ewbank has worked him all around the secondary in practice.

"No, I don't think I've lost any speed because of my injury and I can still play the corner," Gordon maintained. "If anybody gets hurt there, I'm sure they'll move me in. My legs is fine. I worked hard on it and from now on I might not even tape the knee."

Last year, Gordon didn't get back into the lineup until the finals at San Diego when he subbed for the injured Jim Hudson at strong safety.

"Actually, I was ready to play anytime in the last four games, but for some reason they wouldn't put me in. I think Weeb regrets this now," Gordon said ruefully. "I know I could have helped."

As it turned out, the Jets lost all three games in which Gordon says he was available (and with a note from the doctor), but unrostered. His absence was most felt in the next-to-last game against Oakland. The Jets still had a mathematical chance at this point, but lost, 38-29, when Hudson was hurt and Raider tight end Billy Cannon murdered his replacement, Solomon Brannan.

The Jets' lineup for tomorrow remains set on offense with Emerson Boozer scheduled to open at halfback once again. Boozer may feel his injured leg still isn't as strong as he'd like, but he went through a full workout on the rock-hard park turf yesterday. Ewbank says he'd "play it by ear" in deciding when to sub Bill Mathis for Boozer tomorrow.

Al Atkinson, the middle linebacker, missed the regular drill and is still doubtful with Mike Stromberg due to replace him. Carl McAdams and Paul Rochester are still sharing workout duty as defensive tackles.

As for the Chiefs, 6-1/2-point favorites after their opening 26-21 victory over Houston, halfback Mike Garrett (shoulder) probably will play but tight end Fred Arbansas (broken finger) may not.

Tale of Openers: Jints by 5-¹/₂, Jets 6-¹/₂ Under

by Larry Fox
Daily News

Linebacker Larry Grantham, who has been around since the AFL was a gleam in Harry Wismer's eye, said it: "This is the best team I've ever played with."

Weeb Ewbank, who brought his Jets here as 6-1/2-point underdogs against the Chiefs tomorrow afternoon (4 p.m. kickoff to be seen in New York over channel 4), agrees: "This year the boys really believe they can win it."

But, for confirmation of all these high hopes, there's another whisper heard many times daily among the Jet family. It sounds like, "Gee, this would be a great one to win."

Upsetting the favored Chiefs would indeed be a tremendous boost for the Jets. They've lost three in a row to Kansas City, including 42-18 and 21-7 last season. In the 42-18 romp here, the Jets took a terrible physical beating.

In common with everyone else in the AFL, they're in awe of the Chiefs' tremendous natural talent. To beat a team such as this—and on the road too—would turn championship dreams into realistic goals.

The last time the Jets beat Kansas City was in 1965. The score was 13-10 and a rookie quarterback named Joe Namath came off the bench to lead the winning and second-half rally. He has not been on the bench since.

The Jets have a special edge against the Chiefs. Kansas City played its league opener last Monday night. That means almost two full days of preparation and healing were lost to the Chiefs. If the Jets are really as good as they think they are that could be enough of an edge.

The rest of tomorrow's AFL schedule is not too exciting. Oakland, opening defense of its AFL championship, is a 13-1/2-point favorite over the crippled Bills in Buffalo. And expansion Cincinnati, which lost its opener to San Diego after playing the Chargers a tough first half, is a surprising 1-point favorite at home against the bumbling Broncos.

Lou Saban, the Denver coach, served as a linebacker and team captain for Cincy boss Paul Brown with the old Cleveland All-American Conference franchise.

The Jets and the Giants, Atlantic Coast League division, will meet at Mt. Vernon's Memorial Stadium next Saturday night. These, of course, are the farm teams of the two New York pro clubs, the home Westchester Bulls affiliated with the Giants and the Bridgeport Jets represent the, uh, Jets.

The two teams met earlier this year in an exhibition game with the Bulls winning, 28-14, on four touchdown passes by Hank Washington.

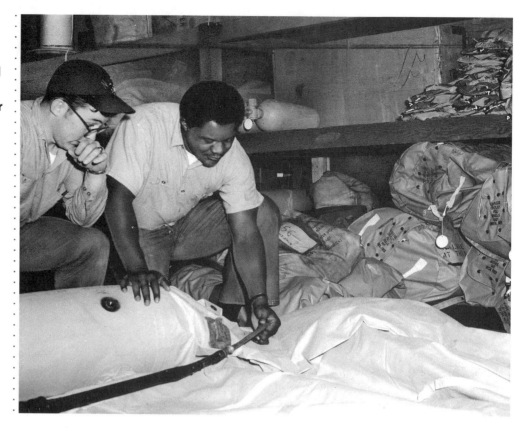

Jets running back Matt Snell (r.) inflates a raft under the watchful eye of his instructor at Floyd Bennett Field. Snell has been a member of the Naval Air Reserve. (Daily News photo)

JETS' SNELL UNSIGNED

by Larry Fox
Daily News

Kansas City, Sept. 15 —The Jets opened the season here today with two players still unsigned, and one of them, fullback Matt Snell, says he will play out his option.

The other unsigned veteran is defensive end Verlon Biggs, who last season didn't agree to terms until after the seventh game.

The Jets went into this weekend with five players unsigned. Ace receivers George Sauer and Don Maynard, who finished one-two in the league last year, agreed to terms on Friday. Veteran cornerback Johnny Sample wasn't brought into the fold until two hours before today's kickoff after threatening he would not play unless he had a contract.

"If I'm not signed, I don't have any choice but to play out my option and go elsewhere," Snell said today. "I took a big chance, playing in five exhibition games without a contract and I don't want to take more chances during the regular season without an opportunity to get something out of it."

Weeb Ewbank, Jet GM, expressed no concern. "We're not far apart. It's just a question of finding time to talk to these men," he said.

Snell said he has talked with Ewbank twice in recent days. "He made me an offer which I thought was ridiculous. Then I went to my tax man and I made an offer which Ewbank probably thought was ridiculous. He knows where to find me, but he hasn't talked to me yet."

Jets "Control," Upset Chiefs, 20-19

by Larry Fox
Daily News

Kansas City—The Jets controlled the ball for almost six full minutes at the end of the game to gasp out a 20-19 victory over the Chiefs in their season opener before a record Kansas City crowd of 48,871 today.

For the Jets, 6$^1/_2$-point underdogs, Joe Namath threw touchdown passes of 57 and 30 yards to Don Maynard and Jim Turner kicked field goals of 22 and 42 yards. For the Chiefs, who had opened their AFL season by beating Houston last Monday night, Noland Smith scored on an 80-yard punt return and Jan Stenerud kicked field goals of 33, 18, 21 and 28 yards, the second game in a row he has made four three-pointers.

But, in the end, it was a sustained drive that didn't produce a point that told the story of the game.

The Jets, who blew a 17-0 lead in their opener last year, jumped off to a 17-3 advantage at the half today. But then Kansas City, ignited by Smith's brilliant run, marched back into contention. The Chiefs recovered a fumble by Emerson Boozer to set up one field goal and intercepted a Namath pass to set up another that brought them to within a point at 17-16 only 45 seconds into the final period.

Turner and Stenerud then matched field goals and, with 5:56 to go, the Jets were on the ropes. They almost knocked themselves out of the ring with the kickoff. Stenerud, a Norwegian-born soccer-style kicker who went to Montana State on a skiing scholarship, had been kicking off through the end zone. But this time he shanked one toward the sideline.

Instead of letting the ball go out of bounds and forcing Stenerud to try again from five yards deeper, Earl Christy fielded the kick at his five—and then stepped out of bounds, himself. The situation smelled of disaster, especially when Boozer, who played most of the game, lost a yard on his first carry.

Namath's next call was a pass to Maynard and cornerback Emmitt Thomas jarred the ball loose for an incompletion. So here it was, third-and-11, the decision hinging and KC in position to win on a field goal with the strong-legged Stenerud on the bench.

Namath, just elected offen- sive team captain of the Jets, met the situation. He called the same pass pattern for Maynard and this time hit his favorite receiver with a 17-yard first down pass. Up the field the Jets marched. Twice Namath threw for a first-and-10 on second down and then, just after the two-minute warning, he hit Maynard for 19 yards on third-and-eight.

For 14 plays, plus a delay-of-game call, the Jets controlled the ball and the frustrated Chiefs couldn't do a thing about it. The game ended with the Jets on KC's 33 and Matt Snell taking a slow-motion crack at the line. It happened to be fourth down for the Jets, but Kansas City never got the ball.

Hank Stram, coach of the losers, summed it up. "The last drive by Namath was fabulous. There was no way in the world I thought they could go from the four-yard line and maintain possession until the end of the game. I thought we could hold them and get into position for a field goal to win."

Namath completed 17 of 29 passes for 302 yards and looked bad only on the play when he was rushed by Buck Buchanan and threw blindly for an interception. The other significant statistics belonged to Maynard and Boozer.

Boozer, looking often like his old self on the field where he was hurt so badly last year, played most of the game on offense, and led all ball carriers with his 18 carries and 75 yards gained.

Maynard, who played only the last exhibition game after recovering from a heel injury, caught eight passes for 203 yards and the two touchdowns. It was the first time in his career that he had gone over 200 yards and he was only seven yards short of Bake Turner's 1963 team record.

The Jet defense continued its outstanding play and for the second straight game, including the exhibition victory over Detroit, could not be charged with a touchdown. Smith's run came against the special teams, which drew some criticism from coach Weeb Ewbank. The play of tackle John Elliott, however, drew nothing but praise from his coach after the Jet defense got to Kaycee QB Len Dawson four times during the game.

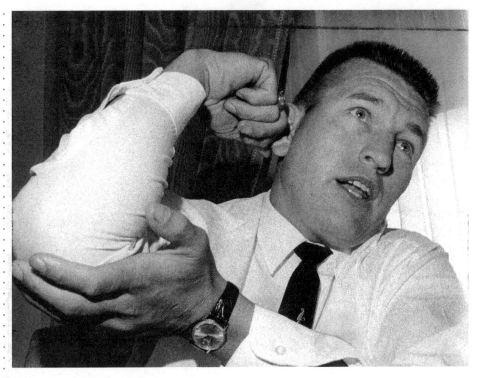

Johnny Unitas crooks his arm to illustrate his problem elbow that hampered his quarterbacking for the Colts. (News photo)

ACHING UNITAS MAY SIT OUT COLT OPENER

Baltimore, September 10, 1968—The premier passing arm of quarterback John Unitas of the Colts is aching worse than ever and the possibility arose today that he would miss Sunday's NFL opener against San Francisco.

"I can't raise it, or straighten it out and it hurts when I try to do something with it, like lifting," said the all-time pro great.

"It's real sore, puffed up, black and blue."

The 35-year-old star said he hurt his arm against Dallas Saturday. Unitas said the pain is in the same spot that has ached for years, inside the right elbow.

But "it hurts more than it ever has," he said. "I couldn't even throw a

pop pass. What next? I really don't know. All I know is that I don't expect to be doing any throwing for awhile."

Coach Don Shula said Unitas would not try to pass before Wednesday.

"It really is nothing new," Shula said. "The same old sore elbow. It's a chronic condition that John lives with and we can just hope it doesn't act up too much too often."

If Unitas does sit out Sunday's game, the Colt quarterbacking will be done by 34-year-old Earl Morrall, who was acquired August 25 from the Giants.

A 12-year veteran, Morrall played with San Francisco, Pittsburgh, and Detroit before going to the Giants three seasons ago. He broke his wrist

in 1966 and played sparingly last year.

Unitas said he felt pain in his arm after throwing a snap pass in the first quarter against Dallas.

"I thought the bottom dropped out of my arm," he said. "I felt something pop."

He said out the second quarter and in the second half he said he "felt it pull again."

Ironically, the news of the injury to Unitas came out the same day he was introducing a book written by him.

The title is *Playing Pro Football to Win* and he held a luncheon to plug it at his restaurant named "The Golden Arm."

DAILY ⬦ NEWS

NEW YORK'S PICTURE NEWSPAPER ®

64   New York, N.Y. 10017, Monday, September 23, 1968

GIANTS, 34-25; JETS, 47-31
VIKINGS JAR PACKERS, 26-13

Stories Pages 52, 53

In the Company Of Eagles...

NEWS photo by Frank Hurley

Ball goes flying as Eagles' Joe Scarpati (21) and a teammate blast into Giants' Aaron Thomas (88) in first period at Philly yesterday. Ref ruled interference on play. Giants copped second straight, 34-25.

Tour De Force

NEWS photo by Walter Kelleher

Boston's Mike Andrews forces Yankees' Bill Robinson at second base on front end of an Andy Kosco double play in fifth inning at Stadium yesterday. Andy bounced to shortstop Luis Alvarado to start play, then Andrews whipped ball to first baseman George Scott to nail Kosco. Boston soxed it to the Yankees again, 5-1, for Bombers' sixth straight loss. —Story p. 53

Standing Pat? Not Anymore...

UPI Telephoto

The Pats' ace fullback and last year's leading rusher, Jim Nance, doesn't awe the Jets' defense, which stops him for no gain on a first quarter rush in Birmingham, Ala., yesterday. Jets soared over Boston, 47-31.

SEPTEMBER 22, 1968

New York 47, Boston 31

New York	14	6	17	10	—	47
Boston	3	7	7	14	—	31

Going into game two of the regular season, the Jets were 12 $\frac{1}{2}$-point favorites over the Patriots. The New Yorkers demonstrated that they were worthy of that spread as they defeated Boston in a convincing 47-31 win. Emerson Boozer scored his first touchdown since being injured, and Don Maynard scored his third of the season. Jim Turner set a club record with four field goals, giving him six straight for the season. Matt Snell remained unsigned, leaving Jets fans uncertain about his future with the team. In an effort to influence Snell's stubbornness, Coach Ewbank benched the holdout fullback in favor of Billy Mathis until Mathis left the game early in the third quarter with a bruised knee.

As for the Colts, while quarterback Johnny Unitas remained on the sidelines with an injured arm, all eyes were on Earl Morrall as he led the team to a 28-20 victory over the Atlanta Falcons, passing for three touchdowns.

Jets 12½ Over Pats in 'Bama, Giants 8 in Philly

by Larry Fox
Daily News

Mike Taliaferro, the former Jet, is looking forward to playing his old teammates for keeps today, but the Patriot QB has one reservation.

"It's supposed to be our home game and here we are playing Birmingham and there'll be more people cheering for them than us," he said with a perplexed shrug and a grimace.

The Boston home game was shifted to Birmingham by mutual consent because the Pats couldn't get into Fenway Park. If the game draws well, it could provide the Pats with a possible future home, should Boston not provide the club with a new stadium soon. And, even if the game draws poorly, the Jets figure to take home a bigger visitors' check than they could have cashed out of Boston.

Meanwhile, the Giants are making it a short road trip to Philadelphia where some commuters may give them a live cheer in their Capitol Division clash.

The Jets scored a one-sided victory over Boston in their exhibition meeting earlier this year

> "It's supposed to be our home game and here we are playing Birmingham and there'll be more people cheering for them than us..."
>
> — Mike Taliaferro

and Taliaferro had a poor game. So, Jet coach Weeb Ewbank has been busy all week trying to convince his players that the Patriots "are tougher than they looked that night."

Ewbank's Boston opposite, Mike Holovak, insists, "Taliaferro has gotten better with every game since we started camp and I think it will continue.

This one will be for the Eastern Division lead, no less, since the Jets and Pats both won their openers. Boston comes off a week's bye, which helped Jim Nance and Art Graham recover from injuries. The Jets are still 12½-point favorites.

Giant coach Allie Sherman should have no trouble psyching up his players, who remember how they were supposed to beat the Eagles easily in an exhibition game and then were humbled, 21-7.

The Eagles have all hands healthy this week but might replace QB King Hill with ex-Jet, ex-Pat, ex-Notre Damer John Huarte, after their opening, 30-13 loss to Green Bay. The Giants, favored by eight, expect to be healthy except, possibly, for tackle Steve Wright.

BEHEMOTHS AT BIRMINGHAM— JETS' WALTON VS. PATRIOTS' BYRD

by Larry Fox
Daily News

September 21, 1968—The red-shirted quarterback hunkered down under the center, sounded the familiar "hut-one, hut-two" and the ball was snapped up into his palms. The linemen growled and collided. Their practice is for real.

On the right side of the line, the defensive left end closed with his man, the right tackle, dipped a shoulder to the left, spun to the right and walked in on the quarterback. A pat on the shoulder pads of Joe Namath and Gerry Philbin had done it again.

As he walked back to the huddle, Sam Walton, the 276-pound rookie tackle, threw his hands in the air. "Oh, Samuel!" he exclaimed. But he didn't feel too badly. He knew teammate Philbin would probably be the toughest defensive end he'd face all season.

Tomorrow afternoon against Boston in Birmingham, Walton drew another rookie, Dennis Byrd, 275-pound No. 1 draft choice from North Carolina State. Byrd, the Jet coaching staff warns, has improved considerably since Walton handled him in the Jets' exhibition victory in Richmond earlier this summer.

But, Walton says, he hasn't been standing still either.

Last week the rookie from East Texas did himself quite a job against Jerry Mays of Kansas City. "All Sherman Plunkett had told me about was 'Mays, Mays, Mays,'" Walton recounted. "It sure helped my confidence to be able to do well against him. Only trouble is, we don't play them again this year. I try to learn from every guy I play against. I take notes on each guy and put 'em in a little book so I'll remember next time."

Needless to say, Walton has made a few notes about Byrd and it will be interesting to see which of the well-regarded rookies has made the most progress in the last few weeks.

Grid Grist: Jets are counting out middle linebacker Al Atkinson against Pats. He'll be dressed and available, but Weeb Ewbank says, "Why take a chance? We put our faith in Mike Stromberg last week and I think it helped him play better. He made errors, but he's not the type to repeat them." Ewbank says he has no more contract meetings planned with Matt Snell and his attorney until next week.

Jets Cruise Over Patriots, 47-31

by Larry Fox
Daily News

Birmingham, Ala.— Boston and Birmingham took a beating here today as the Jets scored a 47-31 victory over the Patriots before only 29,192 Legion Field fans, less than half the number that turned out to see Alabama play VPI in the same stadium last night.

This city has been seeking a pro franchise, but apparently local fans are more interested in seeing Alabama heroes of the present than those of the past, like Joe Namath.

The Jet point total was the second highest in team history— topped only by a 52-13 victory over Houston in 1966. The New Yorkers could have scored more— and held the Pats to less—except that Weeb Ewbank emptied his bench in the final period.

The one-sided triumph gave the Jets undisputed possession of first place in the AFL's Eastern Division over Boston and capped a weekend during which every one of the New Yorkers' division rivals was defeated. The Jets are now 2-0 and will be heavily favored to hand Buffalo its fourth straight defeat next Sunday.

Those fans who did come out to see Namath and fellow Alabama product Paul Crane got their money's worth. Crane blocked a Boston punt that was recovered by Mark Smolinski for a touchdown while Namath passed for two touchdowns, 39 yards to Don Maynard and 27 to Pete Lammons.

The Jets also got TDs from Randy Beverly on a 68-yard interception return and from Emerson Boozer on a one-yard plunge.

It was Boozer's first touchdown since his serious knee injury last year and one of the few times since his return that he's been sent crashing into the line on a straight plunge. Maynard's TD, on the only pass he caught all afternoon, was his third of the season.

The Jets also got a club record of four field goals from Jim Turner of 30, 27, 27, 48 yards, which gives the Tank six straight after missing his first try. He'd

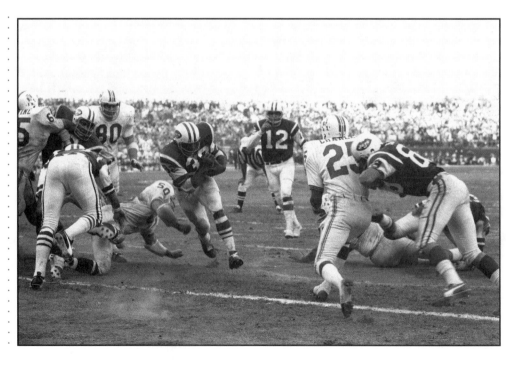

Jets' Emerson Boozer finds a gaping hole in the Boston line and drives through for a TD after taking a handoff from Joe Namath (12). (News photo by Dan Farrell)

never kicked more than three in one game before and the 48-yarder was the second longest of his career. His record is 50. Turner and Curley Johnson, who punted five times for a 53-yard average, were each given a game ball for their parts in the victory.

Namath ended with 13 of 25 completions for 196 yards and two TDs. His lone interception handed Boston an easy score, and for the only time made the one-sided game a contest.

Just before the half, Mike Taliaferro had passed 70 yards to Aaron Marsh for one touchdown and then, at 2:33 of the third period, Namath tried to throw, under heavy pressure, from his end zone. Mel Witt, a 265-pound defensive end, intercepted at the four, and it was an easy matter for the big guy to trundle over for the score that made it 20-17.

However, the Jets struck back quickly on the blocked punt and were leading by 44-17 before the Pats could counter again against the subs.

Taliaferro, the ex-Jet, suffered a tremendous pass rush by the Jet front four and his statistics were better than his performance. He was intercepted four times.

A big factor as the Jets chased down their former teammates four times for 45 yards in losses was the way Weeb Ewbank used Carl McAdams to spell both Verlon Biggs and Paul Rochester in the 84-degree heat. Gerry Philbin and John Elliott went most of the way. Then, when middle linebacker Mike Stromberg was hurt late in the third, McAdams moved back to the second line of defense.

Stromberg suffered a bruised right knee that will be given further examination Tuesday, which means it's not fatal. Since the score was quite one-sided when he was hurt, Ewbank presumably decided to give Al Atkinson another week to recover from his own bruised leg and thus went to McAdams.

Other Jet injuries were to center John Schmitt's neck and a "bumped" knee suffered by Bill Mathis.

Mathis Replaces Snell

by Larry Fox
Daily News

Birmingham, Ala.—Weeb Ewbank today dropped holdout fullback Matt Snell from the starting lineup. The coach announced the switch less than an hour before his Jets took the field against Boston in the battle for first place in the AFL's eastern division.

Ewbank's decision wasn't announced until the players had taken the field for pre-game warmups and thus were unavailable for comment. Ewbank said Snell would play, but that Billy Mathis would start.

A Jet spokesman quoted Ewbank as making the following explanation: "Because of all the uncertainty over Snell's situation at the beginning of the week, I have been working Mathis with the No. 1 unit, therefore he'll start. Snell will play. I hope to sign him Monday."

Jet running back Bill Mathis (right) discussed his new role as general chairman of the Olympic Boxing Gala at the Vanderbilt Club. (News photo by Leonard Detrick)

Before last week's opener at Kansas City, Snell had threatened to play out his option if he wasn't signed by kickoff time. Then, when the No. 2 fullback, top draft choice Lee White, was knocked out for the season with a knee injury in the first quarter at KC, Snell changed his tactics. He said he wouldn't play today if he wasn't signed during the week. Still later, he was reported to have changed his mind again and would play without a contract.

Mathis, who has gained more ground running than any other active AFL player, is a Titan original. He was the club's starting fullback until Snell was signed as No. 1 draft choice in 1964 and made Rookie of the Year. That season Mathis moved over to halfback, a position he held until Emerson Boozer became a starter late in the 1966 season. He took over again when Boozer was hurt last year.

Bill was coaxed out of retirement this season and reported late to training camp where he again served as No. 1 halfback while Boozer worked his way into condition.

Mark Smolinski took over as nominal No. 2 halfback, with Billy Joe and utilityman Curley Johnson in reserve.

The Snell shocker took some of the edge off Joe Namath's return to his college country before a slim crowd in Boston's transplanted "home" game and ex-Jet Mike Taliaferro's first regular-season crack at his old team.

Joe Namath waits on the sidelines as the defense takes the field. (News photo by Dan Farrell)

COLT WATCH COLT WATCH COLT WATCH

MORRALL PITCHES 3 TDS, COLTS RIP FALCONS, 28-20

September 23, 1968, Atlanta—Veteran Earl Morrall, filling in again for injured Johnny Unitas, passed for three first-half touchdowns, then set up another midway through the final period with an 84-yard bomb today to lead the Colts to a tougher-than-expected 28-20 victory over the fire-up Falcons.

GIANTS ROMP; JETS EDGED
BOB GIBSON ANALYZES WS

Stories Pages 52, 53

With One Goal In Mind...

Giant fans cheer the first score of the season—a 32-yard field goal by Pete Gogolak (▼) in the first period at the Yankee Stadium opener yesterday. And that wasn't all the faithful had to cheer about. Two Fran Tarkenton bombs to Homer Jones, another pair of interceptions by Spider Lockhart (one for a TD) and a second Gogo field goal kept the 62,979 fans in ecstasy as the Giant clobbered the Redskins. 48-21.

NEWS photo by Phil Stanziola

PRO GRID

NFL				
Washington	7	7	0	7—21
GIANTS	3	21	17	7—48
Dallas	7	7	14	17—45
Philadelphia	3	10	0	0—13
Baltimore	3	21	3	14—41
Pittsburgh	0	0	0	7— 7
Detroit	0	7	10	6—23
Green Bay	10	0	0	7—17
St. Louis	0	0	0	21—21
New Orleans	3	7	7	3—20
Chicago	14	6	0	7—27
Minnesota	0	3	0	14—17
Los Angeles	10	0	0	14—24
Cleveland	0	6	0	0— 6
Atlanta	0	10	3	—
San Fran	7	7	7	—

AFL				
JETS	7	14	0	14—35
Buffalo	10	10	3	14—37
San Diego	0	17	0	14—31
Cincinnati	3	0	7	0—10
Oaklan	0	10	7	—
Houston	7	2	0	—
Boston	7	3		
Denver	3	7		

NEWS photo by Frank Hurley

Even a strong show of hands by the Washington defense can't stop Gogolak's soccer-style boot from the 32 in the first period.

Fans greet their Giants: Picture story on centerfold

SEPTEMBER 29, 1968

Buffalo 37, New York 35

New York	7	10	0	14	—	35
Buffalo	10	10	3	14	—	37

New York fans had their pick of sports the weekend of Game 3, with the Jets, Giants, Yankees, and Mets playing as well as Columbia and Grambling football games, the Rangers playing Montreal in an exhibition, a heavyweight boxing doubleheader, and the Knicks playing the U.S. Olympic squad. The spotlight was on the Jets, though, as things were looking promising for the team. Matt Snell finally came to terms with the Jets and signed a multi-year contract. With the Jets going into this week's game as 17-point favorites over the 0-3 Buffalo Bills, it was likely that fans may have taken the game in stride, assuming their mighty Jets would prevail easily.

The game turned out to be a nightmare for the Jets, as they left Buffalo for the sixth straight year as the loser after a 37-35 shocker. Joe Namath, always the center of attention, was a key player in the loss. He threw five interceptions, three of which resulted in Buffalo touchdowns. Jim Turner missed a 37-yard field goal—πhis first miss after putting his first six in a row through the uprights. One of the only signs of life in the Jets was newly signed fullback Matt Snell, who carried 12 times for 124 yards.

The Colts, on the other hand, were victorious with a 41-7 pummeling of Pittsburgh. Bob Boyd, Charlie Stukes and Roy Hilton returned three interceptions for touchdowns, setting a new NFL record for returns of pass interceptions.

Snell Signs Multi-Year Pact; Jets Pick by 17 Over Bills

by Larry Fox
Daily News

Twenty-four hours after being dropped from the starting team, fullback Matt Snell has come to contract terms with the Jets. The agreement announced yesterday between Snell's agents, Probus Management, Inc., and the AFL team called for a "multi-year contract" and no other terms were revealed.

Snell's signing leaves only defensive end Verlon Biggs out of the fold. Since Biggs didn't sign last year until mid-season, Jet coach and GM Weeb Ewbank is not concerned. He went down to the wire before the opener two weeks ago with Don Maynard, George Sauer and John Sample and solved the disputes with all of them by offering multi-year contracts too.

Snell was replaced in the starting lineup against Boston by Bill Mathis, but then took over full-time when Mathis limped off early in the third quarter with a banged knee. Mathis is not believed seriously injured but Snell probably signed his way back onto the starting team for Sunday's game at Buffalo in which the Jets opened as 17-point favorites.

Actually the biggest disciplinary move against Snell was not his demotion from the starting lineup but his insertion in the suicide wedge on kickoff returns. The wedge is made up of the four players just in front of the two deep receivers and survival is the prime concern for this unit.

When AFL statistics are released today, they will show that the Jets' two kicking specialists, for whom Ewbank has been seeking replacements the last couple of years, are in the No. 2 tryharder position in their departments.

Curley Johnson, after his 53-yard per kick performance against Boston, is second in the league to San Diego rookie Dennis Partee with a 48.2 average, Jim Turner, 27, is second in both scoring and number of field goals to KC's Jan Stenerud.

Johnson, 33, has been doing his finest kicking since he joined the old Titans from the old Dallas Texans in 1961. Turner, who came to the Jets in 1964, also seems to have found new consistency. He made nine of 10 field goals in exhibition play and shows six in a row after an initial miss in two counting games. His six field goals

and 25 total points are second only to Stenerud's 10 and 37.

Both veterans have adopted new training routines this year. Turner used to work long hours with a weighted boot strengthening his kicking leg in the off-season. He also kicked hundreds of practice shots. This past winter he eliminated the boot, cut down on his kicking and rode a stationary "bike" in front of his TV set every morning.

Johnson, unmindful of the damage it might do to his image as the playboy of the southwestern world, worked out at a Houston health club all off-season and, the opposite of Turner, for the first time spent hours with the weighted shoe.

Since the two veterans reported to training camp, they've also cut down on their actual kicking work. They both used to kick every day; now, they alternate.

Actually, both get plenty of general conditioning since they also play real positions. Johnson is a spare tight end and running back and Turner is No. 3 QB and also can be a receiver or a runner.

Turner's early field goal

accuracy is especially noteworthy because, ever since they broke camp at Hofstra two weeks ago, the Jets have been working out under sandlot conditions at Flushing Meadow Park. Among other drawbacks, there are no goal posts and the club hasn't bothered to bring its portable uprights over from Shea.

"How do I practice? I kick at a tree," says Turner. "Doesn't everybody?"

Despite his early season contract dispute, Matt Snell's powerful running led the Jets in their march to the Super Bowl. (News photo by Dan Farrell)

JETS LOSE STROMBERG FOR FIVE WEEKS

September 25, 1968—Linebacker Mike Stromberg was placed on the inactive list for five weeks by the Jets yesterday because of stretched ligaments he suffered in Sunday's game against Boston.

Stromberg, who had moved into the starting linebacker post for injured Al Atkinson, will have to wear a cast for three weeks. Atkinson has recovered from contusions of the legs and will be back in the lineup for the Jets this week.

Jets Have Spot for McAdams But They're Not Sure Where

by Larry Fox
Daily News

The "nightmare" is over for Carl McAdams. At last he's a football player earning his money, making a contribution to team victories. It's a good feeling. It almost makes up for the pain.

On the plane back from Birmingham last week, McAdams clenched his fists in eye-searing pain. "It's the ankle," said Jet assistant coach Walt Michaels. "It's something he's got to live with, but he will. He's a pro."

Yesterday, as he dressed for practice, McAdams revealed it was more than the famous ankle that has undergone three separate operations. There was a blister on his big toe that had burst and filled his sock with blood during the game, and a head cold and heat cramps, too.

But there was also the satisfaction of putting in more time in a league game than he had since he left Oklahoma as an All-America linebacker many claimed was superior to Tommy Nobis.

Against the Patriots, McAdams filled in on defense for left tackle Paul Rochester, right end Verlon Biggs, right tackle John Elliott (for two plays), then finished the game at middle linebacker when Mike Stromberg was hurt in the third period.

It was quite a workout and it also might have helped silence any critics who thought McAdams, who signed a four-year $325,000

> ## "I used to wake up thinking about that. It gave me nightmares every night. When I first came up here, I figured people would be afraid that's how I was, but I hope they realize now I'd rather play football than almost anything."
>
> ## —Carl McAdams

contract in 1966 and then broke his ankle, was just another one of those spoiled bonus boys.

"I used to wake up thinking about that. It gave me nightmares every night," McAdams admitted. "When I first came up here, I figured people would be afraid that's how I was, but I hope they realize now I'd rather play football than almost anything.

"If anybody ever said anything to my face about it, it was in a joking manner," he added in his southwestern drawl. "They've got a real good bunch of guys on this club. I don't guess I could have stood the last two years if they weren't."

McAdams figures he's actually still a rookie and so is lucky to play anywhere. "If I stay healthy, I'd like to get a position to play, linebacker or tackle even," he said. "But right now it's great just making a contribution and I just hope I can make a few more . . . including the Super Bowl."

McAdams should play another major role at Buffalo this week with Stromberg out and regular Al Atkinson just coming off a leg injury that apparently was more serious than originally announced. It's a bone bruise and even though Al suited up for the opener two weeks ago, he admits now, "I'd have been out for the season if I tried to play then."

He was ready to go in for Stromberg at Birmingham, but the Jets had a lead and they had McAdams. If Al's leg isn't ready for 100% effort this week, they've still got McAdams.

PRO GRID LINE

Tomorrow Night

Favorite	Pts	Underdog
KANSAS CITY	17	Miami

Sunday

Favorite	Pts	Underdog
GREEN BAY	8	Detroit
Baltimore	14	PITTSBURGH
Dallas	14	PHILADELPHIA
Los Angeles	9	CLEVELAND
GIANTS	5	Washington
MINNESOTA	8-1/2	Chicago
St. Louis	4	NEW ORLEANS
SAN FRANCISCO	14	Atlanta
Jets	19	BUFFALO
San Diego	9	CINCINNATI
Boston	3	DENVER
Oakland	7-1/2	HOUSTON

Home team in CAPS

AFL Standings

Eastern Division	W.	L.	T.	PF	PA
Jets	2	0	0	67	50
Boston	1	1	0	47	54
Houston	1	2	0	59	66
Miami	0	2	0	31	71
Buffalo	0	3	0	36	98

Western Division	W.	L.	T.	PF	PA
San Diego	2	0	0	59	27
Oakland	2	0	0	95	27
Cincinnati	2	1	0	71	62
Kansas City	2	1	0	79	43
Denver	0	2	0	12	58

BILLS MAY LOSE NO. 2 QB DARRAGH

September 27, 1968—The chances of the Jets moving out to a 3-0 record atop the eastern division of the AFL on Sunday were further enhanced yesterday by news of the Bills' quarterback status. Not only is Jackie Kemp out for the season, but the No. 2 man, Dan Darragh, has such a sore finger on his pitching hand the starting assignment may go to No. 3, Kay Stephenson.

The Jets (2-0) are at Buffalo (0-3) tomorrow.

COLT WATCH COLT WATCH

St. Louis, which has lost two in a row, is expected to give Army officer Charlie Johnson a start at New Orleans, while Baltimore, 2-0 with Earl Morrall in control, again may have to go without premier passer John Unitas at Pittsburgh. So far, the schedule has allowed the Colts to survive Johnny U's absence.

SPORTS OF ALL SORTS

New York sports fans will be men for all seasons this weekend.

In baseball, the Mets finish at home with a weekend series against the Phillies, while the Yankees play at Boston. In pro football, the Giants open their home season against the Redskins on Sunday, while the Jets are at Buffalo. In college football Saturday, Columbia opens at home against Lafayette, while Grambling plays Morgan State at Yankee Stadium for charity.

The Garden has a full schedule. Thursday it's a heavyweight boxing doubleheader, Friday the Rangers play Montreal in an NHL exhibition and Saturday there's a pro-basketball doubleheader involving Baltimore against Detroit and then the Knicks against the U.S. Olympic squad.

Oh, yes, Belmont and Yonkers will still be going strong.

Nightmare in Buffalo: Bills Intercept (5) Jets, 37-35

by Larry Fox
Daily News

The Jets' nightmares are on re-runs and it isn't even summer. For the sixth straight year, they've left this town a loser, bowing today in a shocking upset to the Bills, 37-35. It was the Jets' first loss after two victories and Buffalo's first winning effort after three straight losses.

As is almost always the case in Jets victory or defeat, the principal figure was Joe Namath. On this overcast afternoon before 38,044 fans, Namath threw a total of seven touchdown passes. Four of them were to his teammates and three went into the arms of Bills defenders.

All told, Joe was intercepted five times and the three TDs came on returns of 100 yards by Tommy Janik, 53 by George Byrd and 45 by Booker Edgerson. The latter two were within a span of 62 seconds in the final period and gave Buffalo a 37-21 lead.

The Jets managed to get close only with 1:04 remaining when Paul Crane's second punt block in as many games set up an easy score.

Two field goals, one missed and another not tried, played an important part in the game. In the second quarter, the Jets' Jim Turner, who had kicked six in a row, was short from the 37 and that, as it turned out, would have been enough to win. Last year, as the Jets blew a 17-0 lead for a 20-17 loss in their opener, Turner missed one from the 15.

On the series before Turner's miss, with Buffalo leading 10-7, the Bills had fourth and goal on the Jet 3. Disdaining the sure three-pointer, new Buffalo coach Harvey Johnson had his team go for the touchdown and the Bills didn't make it. The fact that the Jets could have won with a field goal made this a big play.

However, as Namath was the first to admit, he was the whole story in the defeat of the 19-point favorites.

"Of course I blame myself, I was the one who threw the damn ball. It's all the dumb guy sitting right here," Joe said, his face flushed and red from exertion and a pounding by the always-tough Buffalo defense.

"Weeb (Ewbank) told us we took this team too lightly but that wasn't the case to me. These guys are professionals and they're always tough. You can't take them lightly. I just wasn't throwing good. What was it? Five interceptions, three for touchdowns. That's the whole story," Namath added.

Ewbank kept the dressing room closed for several minutes longer than usual after the game and could be heard through the door delivering a tongue-lashing to his players. This was a game the Jets should have won and you need to win this kind to be a true title contender.

The course of the game resembled last year's Jet tie with Houston, in which Namath was intercepted a club-record six times and the Oilers set a league record of 245 yards in returns.

Today the Bills returned Namath's passes 235 yards and Janik's 100-yard dash tied the AFL record of San Diego's Speedy Duncan.

Ewbank said he considered at one time using backup QB Babe Parilli, but then decided to stick with Namath. "The other guy's the one who gets you there and he did come back for two touchdowns," Ewbank said.

Namath pointed out, "I've had days like this before and I'll have 'em again. Even good pitchers get knocked out." He said it never occurred to him that Parilli might come out of the bullpen.

Namath, who also lost the ball on a fumble, labeled the Janik interception as critical and the most reprehensible. The Jets trailed by only 10-7 and, after Turner's missed field goal, had just regained possession on the Buffalo 10 when Ralph Baker recovered a Dan Darragh fumble.

Two passes misfired and on

the third, Janik picked off a pass intended for Curly Johnson and went goalline to goalline without being interfered with. Johnson, incidentally, was in the game at tight end because Pete Lamons had suffered a pulled groin muscle that could be serious.

Namath's TD passes went to George Sauer for four and 10 yards, to Don Maynard for 55 and to Matt Snell for three. Snell was one of the Jets' few bright lights as he carried 12 times for 124 yards and set up two touchdowns with runs of 60 and 36 yards.

Emerson Boozer, who went out for a brief period late in the game with leg cramps, matched Janik's TD with a short second-effort plunge and the Jets were behind by only 23-21 going into the final period. But in the opening minutes of the last quarter, Byrd and Edgerson pulled their steals to assure Johnson of his first victory in his second game as head coach.

Although Buffalo scored 37 points, the Jet defense could not be faulted. They actually only gave up one touchdown, Buffalo's first. The other three came on the interception returns. There were also three field goals by newly signed Bruce Alford, the Redskin and Bear reject. Today Alford got on the scoreboard for the first time as a major league pro on fielders of 35, 41 and 37 yards.

It all had a familiar ring to it, almost as if the game had been played before.

Majorettes show the pageantry of a professional football game. (News photo by Dan Farrell)

COLT WATCH COLT WATCH COLT WATCH COLT WATCH

COLT DEFENSE SETS MARK IN BEATING PITT, 41-7

Bubba Smith and Billy Ray Smith applied the pressure that led to three scoring interceptions, tying an NFL record, as unbeaten Baltimore defeated hapless Pittsburgh, 41-7 today.

Bob Boyd, Charlie Stukes and Roy Hilton returned pass interceptions for touchdowns, the fourth time in NFL history a team has run back three thefts for scores in a game.

Earl Morrall passed to Tom Mitchell for one Colt touchdown and set up a scoring plunge by Timmy Brown with another long completion.

GRID GRIST . . . Jets' Paul Crane named AP defensive player of the week in AFL for a key punt block against the Pats.

Jets only 2-3 against Buffalo over last five years, including five straight losses in antiquated War Memorial Stadium.

★★★★
FINAL

SUNDAY NEWS
NEW YORK'S PICTURE NEWSPAPER ®

MORE THAN TWICE
THE CIRCULATION
OF ANY OTHER
PAPER IN AMERICA

160   New York, N.Y. 10017, Sunday, October 6, 1968   4 Sections | MAIN, SECTION TWO MAGAZINE, COMICS

CARDS SWAT TIGERS
M'Carver, Cepeda HR in 7-3 Win

UPI Telephoto

Even his sideburns seem to be flaming as Cardinal Tim McCarver gives third base ump Bill Haller el Bird. Ump's view was that McCarver was out trying to steal third in fourth inning. McCarver has a dim view of Haller's view. Card coach Joe Schultz, who can't see having Tim bounced, intervenes.

Winning Ways?

Larcenous Lou Brock (→) kicks up a cloud of dust as he swipes second in the third inning. Ball skitters away from Tiger shortstop Mickey Stanley. It was the second of Brock's three steals yesterday. At game's end—he had stolen six bases in this Series.

Story p. 146; other pics. centerfold

Associated Press Wirephoto

Jets Charge, 23-20, Before 63,786

Story on Page 146

OCTOBER 5, 1968

New York 23, San Diego 20

San Diego	0	7	6	7	—	20
New York	3	6	7	7	—	23

The Jets went into Game Four against the Chargers as 5 $\frac{1}{2}$- point favorites. Veteran player Curley Johnson was set to step up at tight end for the Jets, and rookie Sam Walton was ready to put his previous week's performance out of the picture with a solid showing this week. The Jets fans were just as ready, jamming Shea Stadium with an AFL-record 63,786 on hand for the game. The Jets did not disappoint them, beating the Chargers in a down-to-the-wire win, 23-20. Emerson Boozer scored on a fourth- down dive from the one-yard line and Jim Turner hit the extra point to put the Jets up by three with 1:43 left to play in the game. San Diego surged down the field in the ensuing minutes, but was unsuccessful in the end as the Jets pulled out the thrilling win.

Meanwhile, the Colts ran over the Chicago Bears in the NFL. Morrall threw four long-range passes for touchdowns in the 28-7 win, putting the Colts at 4-0 for the regular season.

Game 4 Jets vs. Chargers

Walton Eager to Make Amends

by Larry Fox
Daily News

Weeb Ewbank gave rookie tackle Sam Walton failing grades in pass protection in Sunday's 37-35 upset loss to Buffalo, the Jet coach revealed yesterday.

Ewbank had been lauding Walton continuously ever since he opened up a spot for the rookie by releasing veterans Sherman Plunkett and Jim Harris. But Sunday, as one Buffalo fan put out a sign "Bring back Shermy P.," Walton played his worst game against Bill veteran Ron McDole. Ewbank maintains this contributed to Joe Namath's five interceptions, plus three more passes that were knocked down at the line of scrimmage.

They certainly contributed to Namath's bumps and bruises and forced the Jets to delay their offensive work from Tuesday until yesterday. Namath, naturally, was still stiff-legged yesterday, but he did work out.

To Ewbank, Walton's most flagrant failure came in the second period when he actually "tackled" McDole from behind. It was an obvious case of holding, and right in front of an official, who failed to call it! Coming as it did, deep in the backfield, it could have

> "We don't condone that kind of play. Tackling a man like that is a confession that you can't handle him and I told Sam if he can't do the job, we'll get somebody else.
> — Weeb Ewbank

amounted to a 30-yard penalty from the line of scrimmage.

"We don't condone that kind of play," Ewbank said. "Tackling a man like that is a confession that you can't handle him and I told Sam if he can't do the job, we'll get somebody else.

"Maybe he's started to believe his own press clippings," Ewbank continued. "I know he took movies of McDole home with him and maybe somebody's been 'coaching' him. Anyway, we took the projector away from him this week."

Walton Saturday night meets third-year pro Houston Ridge of the Chargers and promises he won't let last week's experience get him down. "I know I didn't have a good game, but I consider it an education, not a shock," he said. "That guy was a lot smarter than I was and I got rattled when I realized I was being out-smarted."

Walton said his home movie session fouled him up because McDole came up with some moves that weren't on those films.

Winston Hill, the other Jet tackle, is Walton's closest advisor among players. "I told him not to let that game get him down, that it wouldn't be fair to us (veterans) if he didn't have a bad day now and then," Hill said.

"Actually, he's progressed faster as a rookie than any rookie since I've been here, including myself. He's been playing good ball, but he came up against a good man."

5¹⁄₂ Pick Jets May Use Johnson at Tight End

by Larry Fox
Daily News

" Fair and cool." That's the forecast for tonight at Shea from *The News* weather bureau. It's good news for Jet fans, who'll show up in SRO numbers to see their 5-1/2-point favorites play the undefeated Chargers, but it's even better news for Curley Johnson.

Curley Johnson is 33 years old. His hair is thinning, he fights a paunch and it's been a long time since he did anything but punt for a living. Starting at 8 tomorrow night, as he did on another cool day in Buffalo last week, he may have to play a lot of tight end for the Jets.

"Curley's all right. He caught a couple of big passes last week and, because he was originally a running back, he's a pretty good blocker," Weeb Ewbank says bravely.

Weeb leaves unsaid his realization that Curley Johnson, tough old cookie that he is, will need relief, maybe lots of it. "I just Pete Lammons tore a groin muscle against the Bills. Lammons would like to play this week. "That's what I get paid for," says the rugged Texan, but Weeb and those who know about those injuries aren't counting on him. Another little tear and Lammons is out for six weeks.

In support of Johnson, the Jets will have fullback Mark Smolinski.

The Chargers also have some tight end problems. A couple of weeks back, Willie Frazier hurt his knee and on the next play sub Jacques MacKinnon, the old Colgater from Dover, N.J., pulled both groin muscles. MacKinnon couldn't even walk, so Frazier went back in and limped through the rest of the game.

That gung-ho effort knocked Frazier out for a few more weeks and tonight it will be up to MacKinnon, with Jim Allison, a running back, in reserve. A 185-pound rookie end named Ken Dyer also is supposed to be able to fill in there, which should make George Sauer happy. George would probably get the call after Smolinski and he feels bad because he's only 195.

> "Curley's all right. He caught a couple of big passes last week and, because he was originally a running back, he's a pretty good blocker."
> —Weeb Ewbank

COLT WATCH COLT WATCH COLT WATCH COLT WATCH

Colts Rip Bears, 28-7; Morrall Pitches 4 TDs

Baltimore, October 7, 1968—Earl Morrall uncorked four long-range touchdown passes, three of them in the second quarter, in carrying the unbeaten Colts today to their fourth NFL victory, 28-7 over the injury-handicapped Bears.

Record 63,786 as Jets Win, 23-20, With 1:43 Left

by Larry Fox
Daily News

D own to their last offensive thrust, the Jets sent Emerson Boozer hurtling into the line from a yard out to score the winning touchdown in a 23-20 victory over San Diego last night as a record AFL crowd of 63,786 at Shea Stadium screamed their excitement at the thrilling finish.

Boozer scored on fourth down with only 1:43 left to play, but Jim Turner's conversion put the Jets only three points on top and a field goal still could tie.

The crowd, exhausted by its outpouring over the touchdown, sat virtually limp as the Jets kicked off and then set their defense to fight off the Charger counterattack.

The Jets went into what is known as a "prevent" defense, meaning the alignment of three linemen and five deep backs prevents long touchdown passes but allows the opposition to nibble you to death. After an incomplete pass and a holding penalty set the Chargers back to their 8, the visitors began nibbling. And the

crescendo of emotion began mounting.

It was John Hadl, San Diego's veteran quarterback who had passed for all three Charger touchdowns, all the way. He hit

Joe Namath is pulled to the ground after hitting his receiver. (News photo by Dan Farrell)

Gary Garrison, who had caught two TDs, for 23 yards to the 31. Then he went to rookie Ken Dyer for 22 and into Jet territory at the 47.

Then it was Garrison again for 15 to the Jet 32, in range for field-goal kicker Dennis Partee, whose miss on the middle TD conversion had put the Chargers out of reach of a field-goal victory.

On the next play, with 55 seconds remaining. Hadl was incomplete to Garrison, but the Chargers were offside. This close to a field goal, the Jets needed distance, not downs. They took the penalty. Again Hadl faded. Gerry Philbin, who played an outstanding defensive game, put on a fierce rush. He appeared to hit Hadl just as he released the ball to Dyer at the goal line.

Whatever the cause, the pass was a little off. John Sample, the Jets' veteran cornerback who had drawn a critical personal foul penalty by whacking Lance Alworth out of bounds to help set up San Diego's first TD, swooped in for the interception. He grabbed the ball at the 4 and skittered upfield to the 44 while attempting to stay in bounds and keep the clock running. He eventually was thrown out and the Jets were called for clipping, but that was the game and the game ball went to Sample after the Jets ran the clock.

Jets split end George Sauer breaks away from the defense. (News photo by Frank Hurley)

DAILY NEWS
NEW YORK'S PICTURE NEWSPAPER ®

84   New York, N.Y. 10017, Monday, October 14, 1968

JETS, GIANTS FALL SHORT
Black Hawks Clip Rangers, 5-2
KENYAN WINS 1ST MEDAL

— Stories Pages 70, 71

NEWS photo by Frank Hurley

Denver's Charlie Greer grabs Joe Namath pass intended for Don Maynard in 4th quarter.

NEWS photo by Dan Farrell

Jets' Joe Namath, who has delivered some fine passes in his day, is hit by Denver's Richie Jackson but manages to get the ball away in second quarter at Shea yesterday. It was intercepted. The Broncos, who hadn't stolen a pass all season, picked off five of Namath's aerials and walked off with a 21-13 victory. See photo top left. —Story on page 70

Jets and Giants Are Ambushed at the Pass

← Falcons' Lee Calland intercepts a Fran Tarkenton pass intended for Giants' Aaron Thomas (88), who's being given a rough time by Nick Rassas in fourth quarter at Atlanta. Calland made the swipe on the Atlanta three-yard line with 1 minute, 16 seconds remaining in game. The Falcons held on to the ball for a 24-21 win. —Story on page 70

Associated Press Wirephoto

OCTOBER 13, 1968

Denver 21, New York 13

Denver	7	7	7	0	—	21
New York	7	3	0	3	—	13

The Jets were encountering a few off-the-field problems that needed solving going into the fifth game of the season. Emerson Boozer had taken a beating the previous week against San Diego, and he was sore throughout the week's workouts. Coach Ewbank was looking to Billy Mathis to replace Boozer at halfback against the Broncos this week. Ewbank also fitted guard Dave Herman with a new pair of contact lenses to combat his severe near-sightedness and to help him with his vision during the game.

The Jets, at 3-1, were 19-point favorites going into the game against the 1-3 Broncos. Unfortunately, this wasn't enough. In a 21-13 loss, Broadway Joe Namath was intercepted five times in front of a stunned Shea Stadium crowd. The game was almost a mirror image of the Jets' loss against Buffalo two weeks earlier when the Jets were picked as 20-point favorites and Namath threw away five interceptions as well. After only five games this season, superstar Joe Namath has given up 13 interceptions—almost halfway to his season high of 28 with nine games to go.

Jets "Contact" Herman; Played 5 Yrs. From Memory

Finding that old needle in a haystack isn't easy. But it's not half as difficult as expecting the Jets' Dave (Haystack) Herman to find a needle…or even pick out a matching pair of socks.

Herman's a five-year veteran at guard, is near-sighted with uncorrected vision that measures between 20-200 and 20-300. He's color blind, too, and he also has unusually shaped eyeballs. Sunday against Denver at Shea, the Jets hope to have Herman fitted with a $200 set of contact lenses.

It won't do a thing for his color-blindness, but says Jet coach Weeb Ewbank, "Maybe now he'll be able to see what he's doing instead of just feeling his way."

Herman says he used to wear contacts at Michigan State, because he played both ways and had to be able to see the ball carrier. (Sometimes this was difficult, even with the glasses,

Blood streaming down his nose did not hamper New York's Dave Herman from performing his duties as offensive guard. (Daily News photo)

because his color blind condition made every play a hidden ball trick when the other team wore dark jerseys.)

But when he came to the Jets, he was assigned strictly for offense. "I've never missed a pass block or a block on a straight-ahead running play, but last year a blitzer ran right by me because I just didn't see him," Herman admitted.

He says his vision problem—he wears glasses off the field—hampers him most on end sweeps.

On those plays, when he pulls to lead the interference, he goes inside or outside depending on which way tight end Pete Lammons turns the linebacker. Sometimes he has found himself helping Lammons double team a man who has already been blocked.

Ewbank yesterday revealed he didn't notice Herman's vision problem until just before this season when reviewing last year's movies. "I wondered why Dave kept shaking his head from side to

side," Weeb said.

Herman tried standard contacts two years ago but they hurt his eyes. This time Ewbank's eye man in Baltimore recommended a New York specialist who made a mold of Herman's eyeballs and will grind the customized glasses to Dave's prescription. "Weeb seems to think those little contacts will make me into a superstar," Herman grinned.

Ewbank says, "Dave hasn't been playing badly but this could make a big difference."

BOOZER STIFF, MATHIS MAY START

by Larry Fox
Daily News

October 12, 1968—It probably won't happen, but Weeb Ewbank yesterday warned Jet fans not to be too surprised if Billy Mathis starts ahead of Emerson Boozer at halfback against the Broncos tomorrow.

Boozer carried the ball for a season-high 24 times against San Diego last week and, for the first time since his knee operation, ran quite often up the middle for tough yardage. He also bobbled three pitchouts, which set him up for unexpected rackings by enemy tacklers.

With Mathis, who has been secretly nursing a sore knee for several weeks, unavailable for more than occasional duty, Booz also had to carry a full blocking load for teammate Matt Snell.

The Jets ran a total of 40 ground plays, including their first 10 from scrimmage, and Boozer took a beating.

When the Jets resumed workouts earlier this week, Boozer was stiff and sore. As late as Thursday, Ewbank thought he would have to give Mathis the starting assignment. Boozer looked a little looser in yesterday's drill, but the Mathis ploy is still an outside possibility.

"It will depend on how Boozer looks in our pre-game warmup tomorrow," Ewbank hedged.

He added that the same test would apply in the punting department. Curley Johnson kicked for the first time yesterday and did well, but the pre-game workout will determine whether he or Bake Turner gets the game assignment.

Pete Lammons has been declared "go" at tight end, which means Mark Smolinski can return to the running back department.

Smo and Johnson, another spare running back, were tied up at tight end last week and thus unable to give Boozer a hand. With Mathis not 100%, the only extra was Billy Joe, who can only play fullback and in whom Ewbank still does not seem to have blocking confidence.

GIANTS + 14; JETS + 19

October 13, 1968—The local pro football powers are heavy favorites to sock it to the opposition again as the NFL and AFL stage another large-scale operation this afternoon. The Giants, who haven't won their first five since 1941, are 14-point picks to equal that feat against the Falcons in Atlanta. They can be seen on Channel 2 at 1:30 p.m.

The Jets, who have a score to settle with the Broncos, are expected to settle it 19 points in their favor when they joust with Denver before the usual sardine-can crowd at Shea Stadium. It was the Broncos who KOd the Jets' title hopes with a 33-24 win here last season.

AFL STANDINGS
Eastern Division

	W.	L.	T.
Jets	3	2	0
Boston	2	3	0
Houston	2	4	0
Buffalo	1	4	1
Miami	1	3	1

Western Division

	W.	L.	T.
Oakland	4	0	0
Kansas City	4	1	0
San Diego	3	1	0
Cincinnati	2	3	0
Denver	1	3	0

NFL STANDINGS
Eastern Conference
(Capitol Division)

	W.	L.	T.
Dallas	5	0	0
Giants	4	1	0
Washington	3	2	0
Philadelphia	0	3	0

(Century Division)

	W.	L.	T.
St. Louis	2	3	0
Cleveland	2	3	0
New Orleans	2	3	0
Pittsburgh	0	5	0

Western Conference
(Central Division)

	W.	L.	T.
Minnesota	3	2	0
Detroit	3	2	0
Green Bay	2	3	0
Chicago	1	4	0

(Coastal Division)

	W.	L.	T.
Los Angeles	5	0	0
Baltimore	4	0	0
San Francisco	2	2	0
Atlanta	1	4	0

Jets Lose, 21-13; Namath Intercepted 5 Times

by Larry Fox
Daily News

Interception, the play that drags Joe Namath from Broadway to the Bowery, did in Joe and his Jets once again yesterday. The Broncos, who hadn't stolen a pass all season, picked off five of Namath's aerials and walked off with a stunning 21-13 victory as 62,052 fans rocked Shea Stadium with derisive boos.

The Jets went into the game as 20-point favorites, almost the same spread by which they were picked to defeat Buffalo two weeks ago. That afternoon Namath also was intercepted five times as the Jets threw away a victory they should have packaged in tissue paper.

The victory was Denver's second straight after three opening losses while the Jets now are 3-2. Next week they play the Oilers in Houston and an Eastern Division race that should have been a walkover has become a battle for survival.

So far it looks like 1967 all over again. Last year too, the Jets jumped off winning in the East and the final disaster came in this same stadium against this same team and it was just as unbelievable an upset. Last year, the Broncos also intercepted five Jet passes, four of them off Namath in a 33-24 shocker.

Now, after only five games, Namath has given up 13 interceptions and, while he hasn't equaled his one-game record of six, achieved against Houston last year, he is almost halfway to his season high of 28 with nine games to go.

As a rookie in 1965, Joe was intercepted only 15 times. The following year that figure jumped to 27 and it increased by one again in '67.

Weeb Ewbank, a man who will protect his No. 1 quarterback to the end, again pointed up excuses for Namath.

"That was a coked up football team that beat us, they rocked us back on our heels," he said. "The interceptions were not Joe's fault. They were really rushing in there and we couldn't stop that Jackson (defensive end Richie Jackson) all day. Joe was moving us in there at the end but we had several holding penalties and they were rushing him and hooking his arm and not giving time."

Against Buffalo, Ewbank said he had considered using sub Babe Parilli but decided against it. Yesterday he went so far as to have the Babe warm up briefly in the third period, but then sat him down.

"I just felt you go with your No. 1, the same as I've always believed," Ewbank explained.

Namath, as always, rejected any alibis. "I just stink," he said, and those booing fans in Shea, at least, agreed with him even though they were screaming with excitement as Namath brought the Jets back within striking distance of a possible tie (on a two-point conversion) in the final seconds.

The Broncos did, indeed, put on a ferocious rush. Dave Costa, the veteran tackle from Yonkers, N.Y., was one culprit, but the main guy was Jackson, a 6-2, 255-pounder who had played linebacker until he was obtained in a deal with Oakland before last season. Jackson has been terrorizing quarterbacks all year and he ran the man trying to block him, rookie Sam Walton, right off the field.

Joe Namath lobbing one of his famous passes. (Daily News photo)

"The interceptions were not Joe's fault. They were really rushing in there and we couldn't stop that Jackson (defensive end Richie Jackson) all day. Joe was moving us in there at the end but we had several holding penalties and they were rushing him and hooking his arm and not giving time."

—Weeb Ewbank

Namath was intercepted five times by the Broncos at Shea Stadium. (News photos by Dan Farrell)

DAILY NEWS

NEW YORK'S PICTURE NEWSPAPER ®

88   New York, N.Y. 10017, Monday, October 21, 1968

U.S. JUMPS 1-2; KEINO 1ST
JETS, 20-14; GIANTS BOW

— Stories Pages 72, 73

NEWS photo by Walter Kelleher

Doing His Thing.

Dick Fosbury of Medford, Ore., goes over the bar backward with his unique "Fosbury Flip" during Olympic high jump yesterday in Mexico City. He won a gold medal with a leap of 7 feet, 4¼ inches, setting a new Olympic record. It was one of four track gold medals for U.S. yesterday. —Story on page 72

UPI Telephoto

Hat in The Rink

Rangers' Phil Goyette skates away from LA Kings goalie Gerry Desjardins after beating him in second period of NHL game at Garden last night. Goyette also scored in the first and third periods to net him a hat trick. Rangers had their first superb game of year, winning 7-0. *Story on page 75*

He Doesn't Lack Go-Go

San Francisco 49ers' Johnny Fuller [→] attempts to stop ball as Giants' Pete Gogolak kicks for a 24-yard field goal during second period at Yankee Stadium yesterday. Fran Tarkenton's sore shoulder and a feeble Giant defense accounted for a 26-10 victory by the 49ers.

Stories on page 73
NEWS photo by Frank Hurley

OCTOBER 20, 1968

New York 20, Houston 14

New York	2	8	0	10	—	20
Houston	0	0	0	14	—	14

With nobody on the injured list, Coach Weeb Ewbank proclaimed the Jets to be in much better shape for Game Six than they were the previous week. Don Maynard had bruised both hands in the Jets' loss to Denver, and halfback Emerson Boozer was recovering from some aches and pains, but both were expected to play in Houston. Ex-Oiler Bob Talamini was looking to beat his old team from which he "retired" after developing a bitterness for management. Things were looking up for the Jets, but in the nine years of the existence of the AFL, the team had never won a game in Houston.

That history was swept aside as the Jets held on for a 20-14 win over the Oilers, but it wasn't easy. After jumping out to a 12-0 lead, the Jets gave up two fourth-quarter touchdowns to fall behind the Oilers, 14-12. At that point, however, Joe Namath returned to his old superman form and drove the Jets 80 yards in the final four minutes, ending with a Matt Snell touchdown with only 46 seconds remaining.

Meanwhile, in the NFL, Johnny Unitas returned for the Colts at the start of the second half, but threw three interceptions and was only one of 12 as the Colts suffered their first loss of the season, a 30-20 defeat to the Cleveland Browns.

Jet Seeks Revenge

by Larry Fox
Daily News

Even if he had been really hurt against the Broncos Sunday, Jet guard Bob Talamini would be well enough to play against the Oilers down in Houston this week.

Talamini had been an Oiler all his pro career and all of the Houston team's existence until this year. After making all-pro last season, he announced his retirement amid considerable bitterness toward his old bosses. The Jets un-retired him with a new contract last summer.

"This week is crucial for us and they'll be ready, too, after beating Boston. Personally, I want to beat 'em bad," Talamini said at yesterday's Jet luncheon at Gallagher's 33. (The Jets are favored by six points.)

At the luncheon, Talamini was asked about his "injury" that stopped the clock in the closing seconds of the fourth quarter with the Jets lacking any further time outs.

"I'm not saying anything," Talamini announced with a broad grin. "But after the game there was a message to call operator 36,

Cecil B. DeMille in Hollywood."

Weeb Ewbank had been a little more candid after the game. "Bob will be all right," he admitted with as much of a grin as the upset loss allowed. "Guard is one position where we have three players of equal ability, so we had it all set up."

Apprised of Weeb's earlier confession, Talamini expanded a little. "Gee, I hate to be known as the guy who takes the gas, but I was all set to fall down in the Buffalo game two weeks ago only we didn't get the ball back.

"Yesterday, they told me what to do when I went in and I did go down on the first play, but I saw George Sauer make it out of bounds and so I got right up again.

"The next play was a complete pass, so I stayed down."

There were some funny bits involving the injury. "Jeff Snedeker, our trainer, came running out and said: 'What hurts?' and I had to tell him, 'Look, don't give me a hard time, just grab something,'" Talamini laughed. Merle Harmon, the broadcaster, noted that Snedeker

was working on one leg while Dr. Jim Nicholas, the team physician, examined the other. Talamini also was observed taking three good steps before he remembered to start limping as he left the field.

Talamini has not been a regular here for the first time in his pro career, but Ewbank has promised him the start against his old club.

"Coming off the bench is tougher psychologically than it is physically, but you just don't walk in and take over from two guys who have been doing all right. I'm a pro and I understand," Talamini said.

Ewbank points out that Talamini gives his team three good guards for the first time. But the 29-year-old Kentuckian adds something else. "I've been with four champions, and I know you can't win by wondering 'what's going to happen now?'" he said. "We've only played five games and we're still in first place. It's ridiculous to give up the ghost now."

GRID GRIST . . . Joe Namath and Matt Snell both had their knees drained after the game.

JETS' MAYNARD OK; ASTROTURF DRILLS SET

October 16, 1968—Don Maynard, the Jets' longball-grabbing flanker, put in a normal workout at Shea yesterday, laying to rest a wild report that he had broken a hand in last Sunday's game against the Broncos.

Coach Weeb Ewbank said Maynard had bruised both hands during the 21-13 loss to the Broncos, possibly explaining why he missed a few tough catches. While the stepped-on right hand was the most painfully hurt, neither was serious enough to require X-rays.

"We're in better condition than we were a week ago," Ewbank said. "We have nobody on the injured list."

The coach added the Jets will hold their practices later this week on the Astroturf at Hofstra to acclimate the players to the conditions at the Astrodome, where they take on the Oilers next Sunday. These sessions, he stressed, would be closed to the public.

In the weekly AFL statistics, George Sauer moved into a first-place tie among pass-catchers with Lance Alworth of the Chargers, while Maynard advanced to No. 3. Sauer caught nine for 191 yards Sunday; Maynard was 7-for-140.

Both Alworth and Sauer have 30 catches, although the San Diego flanker has a 571-486 edge in yardage. Maynard's 555 yards still leaves him with the top average gain, 24.1.

In other categories, Joe Namath remained No. 3 among passers (behind Len Dawson of the Chiefs and Johnny Hadl of the Chargers) and Matt Snell moved up to No. 5 among rushers with 264 yards in 54 carries.

Curley Johnson was the AFL's No. 2 punter with a 46-yard average, Jim Turner the No. 2 scorer with 48 points and Earl Christy third in punt returns and fourth in kickoff inbacks.

The general view of the new Astroturf at Hofstra University. (Daily News photo by Jim Mooney)

GRID GRIST ... Emerson Boozer is getting over his aches and pains. The Jet halfback was able to engage in a Tuesday workout this week for the first time this season...Weeb Ewbank, in extenuation of Sam Walton's poor show against Bronco Rich Jackson last week, said the rookie tackle had an upset stomach and was ill off and on throughout the game. The Jet offensive line is taking a beating over the Denver showing, but blockers can point out that the Jets have been called for fewer penalties than any team in the league and Joe Namath has been thrown fewer times for less yardage than any QB in the league.

Can Jets Find Home in Dome?

by Larry Fox
Daily News

> "It's supposed to be our home field, but we don't get to practice there any more than the visiting team."
> —Oiler coach Wally Lemm

The Jets, who have never won a game in Houston— indoors or out—since the AFL was founded nine years ago, will have a home-field advantage of sorts when they play the Oilers in the Astrodome Sunday.

A record crowd of near 60,000 is expected to cheer for the home team but that doesn't mean the Jets will be operating on completely hostile ground.

The reason is that the Oilers, who just moved in this season, are virtually outsiders when it comes to Judge Roy Hofheinz' stately pleasure dome.

"It provides an ideal situation to play a football game, but there are other questions," Oiler coach Wally Lemm said of the Dome yesterday by phone at the Jets' weekly press briefing.

"It's supposed to be our home field, but we don't get to practice there any more than the visiting team," Lemm said in partial explanation of why the Oilers are 0-3 at home this year.

The Oilers are allowed only one practice session per week on the Astroturf. They usually take Friday or Saturday unless it's raining one day during the week and then they'll move indoors. Since the Jets also plan a Dome workout Saturday, that would make the teams even, except for one added factor.

The Jets, as announced Tuesday, will work out privately today and tomorrow on Hofstra's brand new Astroturf surface.

The Jets come in with a 3-2 record and the Oilers are 2-4, after a tough opening schedule. Last week they shut out Boston, 16-0.

Jets Gush Over Oilers in Final 46 Seconds, 20-14

by Larry Fox
Daily News

Houston—Weeb Ewbank says he sticks with Joe Namath through thick and thin, because "he's the one who can get you there." And that's what Joe did today. After an abysmal 0-for-10 start, Namath drove the Jets 80 yards in the final four minutes and sent Matt Snell cracking over the left side of the line for the winning touchdown with only 46 seconds left to beat the Oilers, 20-14, before 51,710 in the Astrodome.

It was a "must" victory for the Jets. Boston already had beaten Buffalo, 23-6, and that meant a loss would have dropped the Jets into a first-place tie with the Patriots. More important, the Oilers had been making threatening sounds and the Jets still regarded the defending champions as their major rivals in the Eastern Division.

Now the Jets return to Shea for a three-week home stand against division opponents Boston, Buffalo and Houston and they'll meet the Pats Sunday with a one-game lead in the standings.

Houston and Buffalo now are almost out of it with five losses each. The Jets are 4-2, followed by 3-3 Boston and 2-3-1 Miami.

The game was more difficult than it should have been for the Jets, but that's been the story of this season. They led, 10-0, at the half on the improbable combination of a safety, when Paul Crane blocked a Houston punt out of the end zone, his third blocked punt of the season; a one-yard quarterback sneak by Namath; and a two-point conversion pass off a fake kick from Babe Parilli to Billy Mathis.

Jim Turner, who passed up his kickoff duties because of a bad leg, then added a 12-yard field goal two seconds into the final quarter for a 13-0 lead, and it looked as if the Jets, who had never won a game in Houston in seven tries since the AFL was founded, finally would break the spell.

The situation looked even brighter for the visiting team four plays after the ensuing kickoff. Bob Davis, the Neptune, N.J., Kamikaze kid, had been playing quarterback for the Oilers in place of the ailing Pete Beathard and taking a beating. Finally, Verlon

Biggs sat on him and the second-year pro from Virginia U. had to be led off.

In came Don Trull, who had been traded off by these same Oilers the evening after Houston had tied the Jets at Shea last year. Released by the Patriots this season, he came back home just in time for Beathard to get sick.

Now he was on the spot and he put the Oilers into the lead by passing for two touchdowns within a span of just over eight minutes. The first was a nine-yarder to Alvin Reed, the second a 19-yarder to Beirne. Two key penalties against the Jets helped the Oilers get their go-ahead touchdown.

A holding infraction against Dave Herman had put the Jets into a hole and forced them to kick from way back after the first Oiler score. And then, just when the Jets had Houston stopped at the New York 22, Carl McAdams was called for a critical third-down roughing the passer penalty.

When Beirne cut over the middle away from Randy Beverly, whose earlier interception had started the Jets' first TD drive, and put the Oilers in front by 14-12 with 4:19 to go, Jet coach Weeb Ewbank already was preparing his "we beat ourselves" statement.

However, this time Namath was going to write his own post-mortems. Starting on his 20 with about four minutes to go, he completed three straight passes of 14, 9 and 13 yards to George Sauer for a first down at the Houston 44. On the next play, he went to Emerson Boozer cutting over the middle and Booz picked it off his shoetops for a 17-yard advance to the 27.

Now Namath went to the infantry. He wanted to kill the clock, he didn't want to risk any errors or interceptions and he preferred a touchdown so Houston couldn't come back, and win with a field goal.

He got it all. Boozer ran for two and then, just inside the two-minute warning, he followed Herman down the left side for 16 yards to the 10. A block by center John Schmitt sprung Matt Snell for eight to the two and then Namath again called his fullback's number. The play was a 19-straight; sheer power over the left side between

tackle Winston Hill and guard Randy Rasmussen. Into the end zone he went with only 46 seconds left.

The drama wasn't over, however. Curley Johnson kicked off to Zeke Moore, who was blasting up field when Gerry Philbin racked him up, and Bill Rademacher recovered the ensuing fumble. Only then was the issue assured.

Namath wasn't intercepted at all, but he also didn't spend the day looking 40 yards downfield for Don Maynard and that made everybody's job a lot easier.

COLT WATCH COLT WATCH

BROWNS INTERCEPT UNITAS—BREAK COLTS, 30-20

October 21, 1968—Bill Nelsen threw three touchdown passes and John Unitas hurled three interceptions which were converted into second-half Cleveland scores today as the Browns defeated the Colts, 30-20.

Unitas, sidelined most of the year with an ailing right elbow as the Colts won their first five games behind veteran substitute Earl Morrall, started the second half with the Colts trailing 14-7.

Unitas completed only one of 12 passes and several times held his tendinitis-afflicted elbow in obvious pain.

AFL STANDINGS
Eastern Division

	W.	L.	T.	PF	PA
Jets	4	2	0	150	142
Boston	3	3	0	100	134
Miami	2	3	1	96	162
Houston	2	5	0	111	134
Buffalo	1	5	1	100	188

Western Division

	W.	L.	T.	PF	PA
Kansas City	6	1	0	182	66
San Diego	5	1	0	188	98
Oakland	4	2	0	184	99
Denver	2	5	0	84	153
Cincinnati	2	5	0	113	148

NFL STANDINGS
Eastern Conference
(Capitol Division)

	W.	L.	T.	PF	PA
Dallas	6	0	0	213	64
Giants	4	2	0	185	137
Washington	3	3	0	123	181
Philadelphia	0	6	0	95	190

(Century Division)

	W.	L.	T.	PF	PA
New Orleans	3	3	0	124	129
St. Louis	3	3	0	129	141
Cleveland	3	3	0	119	133
Pittsburgh	0	6	0	86	183

Western Conference
(Central Division)

	W.	L.	T.	PF	PA
Detroit	3	2	1	130	124
Minnesota	3	3	0	138	97
Green Bay	2	3	1	126	99
Chicago	2	4	0	101	169

(Coastal Division)

	W.	L.	T.	PF	PA
Los Angeles	6	0	0	160	67
Baltimore	5	1	0	186	88
San Francisco	3	3	0	123	125
Atlanta	1	5	0	85	189

Throughout the Super Bowl season, the Jets'
offensive line gave quarterback Joe Namath the
time he needed to slice through the league's
defenses. (News photo by Frank Hurley)

DAILY NEWS

NEW YORK'S PICTURE NEWSPAPER ®

76   New York, N.Y. 10017, Monday, October 28, 1968

JETS PITTER PATS, 48-14;
JINTS JUST SKIN BY, 13-10

Stories on Page 62

NEWS photo by Dan Farrell

'It Only Hurts When I Laugh...'

Blithe spirit Joe Namath jokes with his team-mates on the sidelines at Shea Stadium yesterday after being taken out in the fourth quarter with an injured thumb. Joe holds on to the bruised digit. The game vs. Boston was a laugher, too, as Jets won, 48-14. The lines that Em Boozer had to crack, however, weren't as funny. Boozer [◄] is met by total of 750 pounds of defense as he tries, but fails, to score in second.

Associated Press photo

OCTOBER 27, 1968

New York 48, Boston 14

Boston	0	0	0	14	—	14
New York	7	3	10	28	—	48

In Week 7 of the regular season, the Jets defeated the Patriots 48-14. It was their second convincing win over the Boston team. With the victory, the Jets moved to 5-2 on the season. Their 48 points scored were the second-highest point total in club history, and the defense also tied a team record with five interceptions. The Jets also gained a new fan as seven-year-old John F. Kennedy Jr. arrived at Shea Stadium for the game.

Over in the NFL, the Colts defeated the Rams 27-10 to move into a tie for the Coastal Division lead. The Colts were again led by Earl Morrall as Johnny Unitas continued to battle problems with his throwing arm.

Pats' Taliaferro, Nance Could Spell Jet Trouble

"I don't hold any grudges. Many people I talk to seem to think I do, but it's not so. I'm part of the Boston team now. I wanted to be traded and Weeb (Ewbank) acted on my request. I'm happy here. It's a lot better than sitting around."
—Mike Taliaferro

Mike Taliaferro comes back to Shea Sunday, spoiling for trouble. You remember Mike. Used to be Joe Namath's caddy with the Jets, but skipped town for Boston a few months ago 'cause he couldn't find enough action.

Mike comes back as No. 1 quarterback for the Patriots and he'll never get a better chance to raise hell with the old gang. A win by the 11-point underdog Pats will snarl things in the AFL's Eastern Division.

Tolly was asked over the phone what it meant to be playing on the other side at Shea Stadium for the first time in his five pro seasons.

"I don't hold any grudges," he said. "Many people I talk to seem to think I do, but it's not so.

I'm part of the Boston team now. I wanted to be traded and Weeb (Ewbank) acted on my request. I'm happy here. It's a lot better than sitting around.

"I just wish we'd get going better than we have," he added.

Until last Sunday's win over Buffalo, things hadn't been going too good for Tolly. Jim Nance, the All-AFL fullback, was injured and the Pats had no running game. Tolly had to pass often; he wasn't sharp, and his receivers dropped throws.

In the Pats' 47-31 loss to the Jets in Birmingham, Ala., Mike was intercepted four times despite a 276-yard game. Two weeks ago the Boston crowd booed the Pats when they dropped the home opener to the Oilers.

Jets vs. Pats—
No Close Shave

by Larry Fox
Daily News

Stretching a point, it will be the beards against the mustaches for the AFL's Eastern Division lead when the Jets and Patriots play at Shea on Sunday.

The Jets are leading by a game and the Pats, who haven't won in this series since 1965, can tie with a victory.

The Boston mustache belongs to Ed Philpott, a 240-pound second-year linebacker from Miami of Ohio, which happens to be Weeb Ewbank's alma mater. Philpott got the idea from reading all the publicity surrounding Ben Davidson's handlebar.

His teammates even call him "Big Ben," but he denies he has a Ben Davidson mustache. "It's an Ed Philpott mustache," he insists.

The Jets will have Philpott outnumbered in the hirsute department. At last count, three members of the defensive platoon were sporting discreet goatees. They have to be unobtrusive because there's a league rule against beards, instituted after Ernie Ladd showed up with one a few years back.

Ewbank says he doesn't want his players to be "characters," but, when he learned the

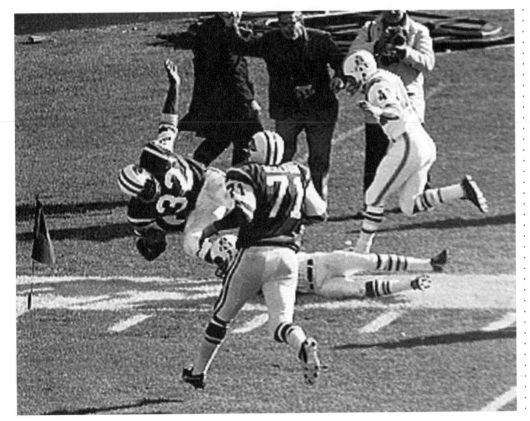

Boston's Leroy Mitchell tackles Emerson Boozer out of bounds at the 2-yard line in the first after nabbing a Joe Namath pass for a 23-yard gain. (News photo by Frank Hurley)

reason for the beards, he commented: "I like the spirit of the thing."

Spirit is the general idea, Jim Hudson, one of the bearded ones, explained. "Actually, Verlon Biggs started it," Hudson said yesterday. "He came in after the Denver game and said he wasn't going to shave it off until we won the Eastern Division championship. Of course, we've got to keep 'em short, but I think it's a good thing for the team."

Biggs, Hudson and tackle John Elliott are the only Jets who've stuck with it. A few others tried and gave up.

Paul Rochester, for instance, quit because the beard made him look like Burl Ives. George Sauer, who's having more fun this week as the AFL's leading pass receiver, is a blond and the beard didn't show up. ("Besides, he only has to shave once a month," Hudson gibed.) And Cornell Gordon says his beard just won't grow.

Most significant angle in the beard project is that it originated with Biggs, until this season the most introverted of all the Jets. "He's come 100% out of his shell," says Hudson, who was a rookie with Biggs four years ago and who worries about such things as how his teammates get along.

"Yes," agreed Ewbank, "he's really opened up. In fact, we've found out he's a pretty interesting fellow. We never knew before, because he never talked to us."

Now if Weeb can only get him to talk about his unsigned '68 contract, everything would be fine.

DON LEAVING 'EM WORDLESS

October 26, 1968—Jet flanker Don Maynard and Patriot cornerback Leroy Mitchell will renew an interrupted conversation at Shea tomorrow.

Last year, in two games against the Boston rookie, Maynard caught 10 passes for 296 yards and one TD. This season, early in the Jets' 47-31 victory at Birmingham, Maynard leaped for a high pass and Mitchell chopped him down just as the ball passed overhead.

"You caught a lot of yards on me last year, but it's not going to be like that this time," Mitchell said.

Minutes later, Maynard got a step on Mitchell and caught a long touchdown pass. "How about that one?" Maynard asked, and then he added some advice: "One thing in the pros, don't ever talk until after the game or the season."

The only last word Mitchell got in was that Maynard didn't catch another pass that afternoon, but Don insists he got the last laugh when he looked at the scoreboard.

COLT WATCH COLT WATCH COLT WATCH COLT WATCH COLT WATCH COLT WATCH COLT WATCH COLT

UNITAS AILING

October 24, 1968, Baltimore—Coach Don Shula pulled Johnny Unitas from the Colts' offensive drills today because his throwing indicated his ailing right arm was hurting badly. It appeared nearly certain that Earl Morrall, who led the Colts to five straight victories while Unitas was sidelined with the arm injury, would start Sunday's test against the Rams. Morrall ran the offensive drills after Unitas was sidelined.

Jets Rout Pats, 48-14; Parilli, Joe Have a Ball

by Larry Fox
Daily News

The Jets smashed Boston's lingering Eastern Division title hopes into the sod and dirt of Shea Stadium yesterday afternoon in a 48-14 rout so complete that even the subs had control in the final stages. In fact, when it came time to award the game ball, the Jets donated two, to Babe Parilli and Billy Joe, who outscored the Patriots, 28-14, in the penalty-filled final period.

The victory, on the second highest point total in club history, gave the Jets a 5-2 record and dropped the Pats, who could have tied for first by winning, to 3-4.

Parilli took over at quarterback after Joe Namath was intercepted on the first play of the last period. Namath suffered a jammed thumb on the play, but said later he has been nursing the wound since the second game of the season and would have stayed in if it had been close.

The Jet QB, who didn't throw a single touchdown pass—but wasn't intercepted, either—also suffered a bruised coccyx when dumped on his pants by Larry Eisenhauer in the first quarter. Stunned, Namath called a time out, but he was able to resume and directed the Jets to a 10-0 halftime lead on the first of two short scoring runs by Matt Snell and the first of two field goals by Jim Turner.

Parilli moved in with the Jets leading, 20-0, three plays after Mitchell's interception when Jim Hudson intercepted in turn on Mike Taliaferro. Hudson's theft, fifth of the game for the Jets as their former teammate, Taliaferro, suffered a demoralizing afternoon, gave the home team possession on Boston's 21.

Three plays later, after an interference call on Mitchell in the end zone, Parilli skirted right end for the score as the crowd of 62,351 cheered in appreciation and his teammates pounded their popular elder statesman on the back.

After that, Billy Joe, another hard-working but seldom-used sub, took care of the offense, tying a Jet one-game record by scoring three touchdowns on runs of 7, 15 and 32 yards. The effort set a record for most TDs in a quarter by a Jet and marked the first time the 1963 Rookie of the Year had ever scored three TD's in one game as a pro.

His 80 yards rushing in 11 carries led both teams and almost doubled the Boston team total of 44.

The Jet defense was superb. It held Boston without a first down for one period and to only eight for the game. It limited fullback Jim Nance to only 14 yards on six carries and smashed Boston quarterbacks seven times for 50 yards in losses.

Gerry Philbin once again was the leader of the bam. Three times his jarring tackles of the Boston quarterback resulted in fumbles that were recovered by the Jets to set up easy touchdowns. The five interceptions tied a Jet club record and a sixth was nullified by a penalty. Johnny Sample picked off two while Al Atkinson, Hudson and Bill Baird, playing in place of the injured Randy Beverly, snatched one apiece.

A couple of near-scuffles involving sub flanker Bill Rademacher and Boston deep back John Charles, who was ejected, and Mitchell, who also intercepted two passes in his duel with Don Maynard, added to the penalty totals in the end. The teams were fined a total of 219 yards and the combined 21 penalties equaled the second highest number ever called in an AFL game. The Jets were called 11 times, the Pats 10.

The Jets' only apparent major injury was to Earl Christy, who hurt his shoulder bumping into Baird while fielding a punt. He's due for X-rays. Pete Lammons bruised a knee.

But the biggest hurt of all had to belong to Taliaferro. The former Jet is now 0-2 against his old teammates and has been intercepted nine times by them in five games. He has to know that the last quarterback Weeb Ewbank traded to Boston was John Huarte.

JOHN'S A JET

Seven-year-old John F. Kennedy Jr. became a Jet fan yesterday.

Young Kennedy, accompanied by a friend, Douglas Woo; his uncle, Stephen Smith; and three Secret Service agents, watched the 48-14 victory over Boston from a seat on the Jet bench. The party had arrived at Shea without tickets, but the AFL club quickly found room.

The youngster said his big thrill was meeting Joe Namath and seeing the Jets play. Joe talked to the boy and worried whether he could see the game, because the sidelines are, actually, the worst spectator spot in the house. However, young Kennedy said everything was fine and surprised Namath by being able to recite all his vital statistics.

He then said that he had been a Green Bay fan, but as of yesterday was switching to the Jets.

COLT WATCH COLT WATCH COLT WATCH COLT WATCH COLT WATCH COLT WATCH COLT

COLTS UPROOT RAMS, 27-10

October 28, 1968, Baltimore—Earl Morrall, his job made easy by a fired-up Baltimore defense, threw two touchdown passes and scored one himself today as the Colts stunned Los Angeles, 27-10, to tie for the Coastal Division lead and snap the Rams' 14-game regular season winning streak.

Morrall connected for TDs on a 44-yard second-period toss to Jimmy Orr and a 42-yard third-quarter pass to Tom Mitchell. The quarterback, who played the entire game in place of the ailing Johnny Unitas, scored on a two-yard run and set up a two-yard plunge by Jerry Hill by combining with Tom Matte on a screen pass that gained 50 yards.

The Jets' Joe Namath hands off to Emerson Boozer for the carry to the Patriots' 1-yard line in the second quarter. (News photo by Frank Hurley)

★★★
LATE

DAILY ⚫ NEWS
NEW YORK'S PICTURE NEWSPAPER ®

MORE THAN TWICE
THE CIRCULATION
OF ANY OTHER
PAPER IN AMERICA

156   New York, N.Y. 10017, Monday, November 4, 1968

COLTS THROW GIANTS, 26-0
JETS CHANGE BILLS, 25-21

— Stories Pgs. 140, 141

PRO GRID

NFL

Baltimore	3	13	0	10—26
GIANTS	0	0	0	0— 0
Pittsburgh	14	7	13	7—41
Atlanta	0	0	7	14—21
St. Louis	7	7	14	17—45
Philadelphia	0	10	7	0—17
Chicago	0	3	7	3—13
Green Bay	0	0	7	3—10
Dallas	0	10	0	7—17
New Orleans	0	0	3	0— 3
Washington	0	0	0	14—14
Minnesota	3	17	0	7—27

Detroit	7	0	0	0— 7
Los Angeles	7	3	0	0—10
Cleveland	3	13	10	7—33
San Francisco	7	7	0	7—21

AFL

Buffalo	7	0	0	14—21
JETS	3	13	3	6—25
Denver	14	7	7	7—35
Boston	0	0	7	7—14
Houston	10	7	7	3—27
Cincinnati	0	3	7	7—17
Kansas City	7	0	7	7—21
Oakland	7	24	7	0—38
Miami	7	7	7	7—28
San Diego	7	10	7	10—34

NEWS photo by Charles Payne

Jets' Bake Turner uses his toes to score three points for the home team at Shea against Buffalo. Turner's kicks made the difference and Jets won a soggy 25-21 victory. Turner tied AFL record with six three pointers for the day. —*Story on page 141*

The Weather
Was Partly
Winning

N.Y. Giants' Fran Tarkenton hangs on to ball for a 1st down in 2d quarter of a wet and gloomy game against Colts at Stadium. Effort wasn't nearly enough and the Colt's riddled the Giants 26-0. *Story on page 140*
NEWS photo by Dan Farrell

NOVEMBER 3, 1968

New York 25, Buffalo 21

New York	3	13	3	6	—	25
Buffalo	7	0	0	14	—	21

Field-goal kicker Jim Turner and the Jets' defense were the stars against Buffalo at Shea Stadium. The Jets were favored by 20 points, despite an earlier upset loss to the Bills, but struggled offensively. The defense scored the team's only touchdown when John Sample picked off a pass at the Bills' 36-yard line and ran it into the end zone. Turner converted the extra point and also kicked six field goals for a club-record 19 points. Namath complained during the week of a jammed right thumb, but the injury was not serious enough to keep him out of the lineup.

Meanwhile, Earl Morrall completed 16-of-24 passes for 201 yards and two touchdowns as he led the Colts past the New York Giants. Less than three months earlier, the Giants had traded Morrall to Baltimore in exchange for tight end Butch Wilson.

Jets Ride On Joe's Thumb

by Larry Fox
Daily News

The injury saga of Joe Namath, who has never missed a regular season game in four years because he was hurt, continues. His knee, as always, hurt and now it's his thumb. He says, "You could call it 'jammed'."

That's what they said a year ago when news leaked that Joe had hurt his throwing thumb the week before an upset loss to Denver. During the off-season, however, Joe confided, "They were afraid it was broken."

As the Jets mopped up Sunday's one-sided victory over Boston, Namath on the sidelines, into a towel-covered ice pack, and that's how it was learned he had suffered a similar injury once again.

"I hurt it in the second game of the season," he said, "and I hurt it again today when I was intercepted."

The Jets took him out at that point, but mainly because of the score—not the injury. There's little question he'll be starting Sunday at Shea in the rematch against Buffalo. (The Jets are favored by 19, which means they're in trouble. They've been favored by that same spread twice before this season…and suffered their only losses to Denver and the Bills.)

The timing of Namath's original injury this year is significant. It came in the 47-31 romp over Boston in Birmingham.

The Jets had opened with a 20-19 victory over Kansas City on a masterful performance by Namath, who was intercepted only once and threw two touchdown passes to Don Maynard and Pete Lammons.

However, the next Sunday, with his new injury, he threw four TD passes (two to Sauer and one each to Maynard and Matt Snell) but also, in a wildly erratic performance, was intercepted five times. Two each of those passes were intended for Maynard and Sauer.

Since that weekend—four games ago—Joe Namath has not thrown a single touchdown pass!

The Jets have won three out of four in that stretch, but the one loss came on a five-interception fiasco against the Broncos. Four of those passes—and both interceptions against the Pats Sunday—were on throws intended for Maynard.

On several occasions through this period, Namath has heaved the long bomb, connecting only once. But can he throw consistently for a distance? Is he learning, by choice or necessity, to discipline his magnificent arm? (Weeb Ewbank points out that the Jets, with Matt Snell and Emerson Boozer, have been able to run the ball into the end zone after Namath passes have brought them close.)

Why all the interceptions on passes for Maynard? Is it because Maynard runs the deepest patterns of any Jet receiver? Most of the interceptions have been underthrows.

And have you noticed that game plans lately seem to have called for the Jets to stay on the ground as long as possible in the beginning?

Ewbank and Namath, of course, know the answers to these riddles, but they can't be blamed for throwing up as much smoke as possible. Buffalo, for one, would like to find the key.

GIANTS DEALT RELUCTANT MORRALL TO COLTS STARDOM

by Norm Miller
Daily News

October 30, 1968—There are two ironic twists to the Earl Morrall Success Story. For one, the Colts had to be "sold" on taking him in the deal with the Giants; for another, Earl had no desire to be traded to the Colts.

From this mutual reluctance began pro football's Comeback-of-the-Year saga, which unfolds a dramatic showdown chapter Sunday in the Giants-Colts game at Yankee Stadium.

Morrall smiles now when he says, "It was the best thing that ever happened to me." In his 13th pro season, he is playing for a serious title contender for the first time.

Yet on the August 24 Saturday when Allie Sherman broke the trade news to Morrall, he was crushed. Even with the limited playing opportunities behind Fran Tarkenton, he did not want to leave the Giants.

It meant moving his wife and four children to a new city. The future with the Colts was dubious. Maybe some fill-in work until Johnny Unitas' arm healed, then back to being a bullpen quarterback, the tag that grated on him most of his NFL career.

For a day or so, Earl considered packing it in.

"I wasn't at all enthusiastic about the deal," he said Monday night at a promotion party here thrown by the synthetic carpeting fabric manufacturer whose product Morrall endorses.

"Your emotions are clouded in a situation like this," he said. "I didn't like the thought of moving my family around. I felt if I stayed here I'd get a chance to play. I felt the way Fran runs around, he was not going to play a full season.

"I told Don Shula (Colts coach) I wasn't sure I wanted to go down there," he continued. "My wife and I talked it over. We thought about the chance of getting to the Super Bowl. I figured maybe it wouldn't be so bad as a sub quarterback with a winning team."

If Morrall had his misgivings about the Colts, the Colts also had theirs about Earl.

The Giants have been criticized for giving up Morrall so cheaply. The deal originally was for

Johnny Unitas, Baltimore Colts quarterback, on the sidelines during yesterday's game against the Giants at Yankee Stadium. Unitas did not play. (Daily News photo)

a future draft choice, which subsequently was converted to Butch Wilson, who has not played much tight end for the Giants this season.

The truth, it is known, is that the Colts, despite their need for QB insurance, did not want to give up even that value. Unaware at that time of the seriousness of Unitas' condition, Shula felt he could deal for another experienced QB just as cheaply. He had to be sold on Morrall.

Morrall bombed in his first few plays for Baltimore. The second pass he tried against the 49ers was tipped by a lineman and deflected to Stan Hindman for a Frisco touchdown.

"I wanted to hide," Morrall confessed. "But no one else on the club seemed concerned about it. The next time we got the ball, we scored. That erased some of my doubts right away.

"That's the difference in playing for the Colts," he stressed. "Things like that upset teams without that confidence in themselves. The Colts have the winning habit. They expect to win every game."

Someone asked Morrall if he felt his tremendous comeback with the Colts was personal vindication for his rejection by the Giants.

"It is a great feeling of

GIANTS (-11-1/2), JETS (+19) IN HOME GAMES

by Norm Miller
Daily News

November 3, 1968—The Giants and Jets both play in their home parks seven miles apart today and aside from the significance of their ballgames, it means 125,000 football buffs get an afternoon of fresh air, there'll be a late-afternoon traffic snarl around the Triborough Bridge, and the home folk will have to wait until 4 p.m. for their TV fare.

At Yankee Stadium, the Giants entertain the Colts for the first time since their famed sudden-death championship playoff of 1958. At Shea, the Jets resume their quest for a Super Bowl berth against the Bills.

While both local clubs start the day with 5-2 records, oddsmen have forecast somewhat varying fortunes for each. The Jets are favored by 19 points; the Giants are underdogs by 11-1/2.

The Jets are healthy and hearty, back on the winning track, and itching for the opportunity to reverse a 37-35 upset by the Bills four weeks ago.

Joe Namath complained of a jammed thumb in last Sunday's win over Boston, but he insists the injury is not serious. All other Jets regulars are sound.

personal satisfaction to be playing and winning," he replied, "but I don't look at it as vindication.

"Naturally, every athlete likes to come back and beat the team that traded him," he added. "He'd like to prove they made a mistake.

"Let's say I'm looking forward very much to Sunday," he added with a grin.

Sunday is Toys for Tots Day at Shea . . . The Jets urged their fans to bring toys, which will be collected by U.S. Marines at the turnstiles and given to underprivileged children.

Jets' Defense Stars, 25-21; Turner: 6 FGs

by Larry Fox
Daily News

The Jet offense was shut out, but the defensive platoon and the record-setting toe of field-goal kicker Jim Turner put enough points on the board for a tingling 25-21 victory over Buffalo before 61,452 slickered fans at rainy Shea Stadium yesterday.

Turner, booed by some after missing his first attempt from the 26 and then having his second try blocked, came back to tie the AFL record with six three-pointers, including two in the last 3-1/2 minutes as the Jets had to rally for the victory.

The Jets' only touchdown came when John Sample, who picked off two for the day, intercepted a Kay Stephenson pass in the second quarter and ran it all the way in from the Bill 36. Turner converted after this and with his six field goals, ended up with a club-record 19 points.

He broke his club field goal record of five, set earlier this year

Joe Namath, who led the Jets to their only Super Bowl championship in 1969, cranks up to pass in a game against the Buffalo Bills. (Daily News photo)

Winston Hill of the Jets rests on the bench during a hard-fought game. Hill, an All-Pro tackle, helped protect Namath during the quarterback's glory years with the Jets. (Daily News photo)

question. "If I told you I didn't I'd be lying."

The Jets had been favored by 20, but they had to struggle, as is their wont when heavily supported by the odds. In fact, their only losses have been in two games they were expected to win by 19, including an earlier meeting with the Bills.

Buffalo scored first on a 55-yard pass from Stephenson to Haven Moses when he slipped into what Weeb Ewbank calls the "seam" in a zone defense between Jim Hudson and Cornell Gordon.

However, four turned field goals and Sample's TD return gave the Jets a 19-7 lead going into the final period and all seemed well for the home forces.

But then the Bills turned the game around. Curly Johnson, back to punt from his 26, saw the Bills pouring in and elected to run for the four yards and a first down. "I figured if I tried to kick, they'd block it and maybe recover for six points. I decided to try and run and maybe we'd hold them to three," said the veteran punter, who pulled a muscle behind his right knee on the run.

Curly didn't make the first down and, as it turned out, he didn't save the six points either. Four plays later, Stephenson passed 10 yards to Paul Costa for the TD and Bruce Alford's conversion brought the Bills to within 19-14.

The Jets were held for downs after the kickoff and again a Johnson punt turned into disaster, this time even less his fault. Despite his hurting leg, he kicked one 42 yards that Hagood Clarke fielded on a bounce at the Buffalo 18. Escaping two tacklers at the start (Bill Rademacker and Mike D'Amato) he headed down the sidelines and, when John Pitts

against Boston, and he tied the AFL mark of six established by the Pats' Gino Cappelletti against Denver in 1964. His eight attempts broke the league record by one.

Turner's field goals came on kicks of 32, 27, 35 and 27 yards. "That's the most I've ever kicked in a game since we played an

intrasquad game at Jersey City and I kicked for both teams," Turner recalled.

He added that this is the first league game he can remember coming out on the field in the final minutes when his kick meant win or lose. "You're darn right I felt the pressure," he said, anticipating the levelled Johnson with a fine block at the Jet 30, he was home for the score on an 82-yard run.

The TD gave Buffalo a one-point lead at 20-19 and Harvey Johnson elected to pass up the two-point conversion gamble for a kick that made it 21-19. If he had gone for two, and made it, the Jets could not have won with a field goal. ("Boy, am I dumb. I was so excited I didn't even think of it," Johnson confessed later). Now, with the aid of a pass interference call on Marty Schottenheimer (against Pete Lammons), the Jets drove into range for Turner to put them back on top with a 35-yarder. Three and a half minutes remained after Turner's kick and the Bills still had time to rally.

But Al Atkinson, who, with Turner, received a game ball, intercepted Stephenson at the 20 and set up Turner's final clincher with 52 seconds to go.

The time remaining was enough to throw another fright into the Jets as the Bills drove back with the kickoff to the Jet 20. However, with one second to go, John Elliott deflected Stephenson's last-play pass and that was it.

For the fifth game in a row, Jet quarterback Joe Namath failed to complete a touchdown pass, but he reminded, "This will be a win in the standings, no matter how we did it."

AFL STANDINGS
Eastern Division

	W.	L.	T.	PF	PA
Jets	6	2	0	231	177
Houston	4	5	0	168	158
Boston	3	5	0	128	217
Miami	2	5	1	138	217
Buffalo	1	7	1	128	243

Western Division

	W.	L.	T.	PF	PA
Kansas City	7	2	0	230	124
San Diego	6	2	0	242	153
Oakland	6	2	0	253	130
Denver	4	5	0	140	181
Cincinnati	2	7	0	140	198

NFL STANDINGS
Eastern Conference
(Capitol Division)

	W.	L.	T.	PF	PA
Dallas	7	1	0	247	95
Giants	5	3	0	198	173
Washington	3	5	0	147	221
Philadelphia	0	8	0	111	240

(Century Division)

	W.	L.	T.	PF	PA
St. Louis	5	3	0	205	175
Cleveland	5	3	0	182	161
New Orleans	3	5	0	144	177
Pittsburgh	2	6	0	133	207

Western Conference
(Central Division)

	W.	L.	T.	PF	PA
Chicago	4	4	0	140	203
Minnesota	4	4	0	189	137
Detroit	3	4	1	144	148
Green Bay	3	4	1	166	129

(Coastal Division)

	W.	L.	T.	PF	PA
Baltimore	7	1	0	239	98
Los Angeles	7	1	0	186	101
San Francisco	4	4	0	158	173
Atlanta	1	7	0	113	260

MORRALL (16-FOR-24) SOCKS IT TO GIANTS, 26-0

by Norm Miller
Daily News

November 4, 1968—Earl Morrall got hunk with the Giants yesterday. He sat there with a big grin after having engineered the Colts' 26-0 rout and he said a lot of nice, polite things about the club that had dumped him three months ago, but this was a win Earl Morrall would not swap for any of his 13 pro seasons.

"It is very gratifying to come back and win like this," he said. What Earl referred to, of course, was his 16-for-24 passing and brainy play-calling that gained 201 yards, produced two touchdowns, and sent the Giants to their first shutout in 76 games.

Quarterback Earl Morrall (l.) #11, and defensive back Dick Lynch (r.) #22, receive the CYO Most Popular Giant Award from Kevin Bruno Rehill (center). (News photo Jack Clarity)

"It is very gratifying to come back and win like this."

—Quarterback Earl Morrall

"You're darn right I felt the pressure.
If I told you I didn't I'd be lying."
    —Jets kicker
    Jim Turner

Kicker Jim Turner was the offensive hero of the Jets' second game against the Bills. (News photo by Dan Farrell)

GIANTS TOP DALLAS, 27-21
JETS SWAMP OILERS, 26-7

Stories Pages 26, 27

PRO GRID

NFL

GIANTS	7	7	7	6—27
Dallas	0	14	7	0—21
Pittsburgh	14	7	7	0—28
St. Louis	0	0	21	7—28
New Orleans	3	0	7	7—17
Cleveland	0	14	14	7—35
Washington	3	6	7	0—16
Philadelphia	0	3	0	7—10
Baltimore	7	3	10	7—27
Detroit	3	0	0	7—10
Los Angeles	0	7	3	7—17
Atlanta	3	0	7	0—10
Green Bay	3	0	7	0—10
Minnesota	7	7	0	0—14
San Francisco	0	6	13	0—19
Chicago	7	17	3	0—27

AFL

Houston	7	0	0	0— 7
JETS	13	3	7	3—26
Kansas City	3	3	0	10—16
Cincinnati	0	3	6	0— 9
Miami	0	0	7	14—21
Buffalo	0	17	0	0—17
San Diego	7	10	10	0—27
Boston	3	0	0	14—17
Oakland	12	14	7	10—43
Denver	7	0	0	0— 7

NEWS photos by Dan Farrell

It Proves That Water And Oilers Don't Mix

Under the cover of umbrellas, hats and plastic rain gear, fans watch the Jets take on the Houston Oilers in a driving rain storm at a soggy Shea Stadium yesterday. Because of the rain, only 36,501 fans showed up as the Jets clobbered Houston, 26-7, for their fourth straight win. The victory virtually clinched the AFL's Eastern Division championship for the Jets. —Story on page 26

Oilers' George Webster nails Jets' Bill Mathis, who toppled across goal line for TD in first quarter.   Joe Namath watches from soggy sidelines.

NOVEMBER 10, 1968

New York 26, Houston 7

Houston	7	0	0	0	—	7
New York	13	3	7	3	—	26

Against the Oilers at Shea Stadium, the Jets tied a club record by gaining their fourth straight victory. The win took them to 7-2 on the season, and virtually clinched the AFL Eastern Division title. Jim Turner kicked four more field goals and Bill Mathis ran for two touchdowns as Joe Namath failed to throw a touchdown pass for the sixth week in a row.

Off the field, news circulated about plans for a television special focusing on Namath's football achievements as well as his fledgling singing career. George Scheck, Namath's manager, also promised that numerous other entertainment ventures were on the way for the football star.

Oilers' Trull is Jets' "Target"

by Larry Fox
Daily News

Don Trull, who is doing more for the Oilers as a freebie pickup than he ever did as a $90,000 college hotshot, is the latest target for the Jets' Bam Squad, which this week leads the AFL in both total and rushing defense.

The Jets Sunday wind up a three-game home stand against their closest pursuers, Houston, and, although they are 7-point favorites and have already beaten the Texans, 20-14, they are wary.

"I think it will be our toughest game of the year. I really do, and the team knows it, too. Why, we even started talking about it in the dressing room after we beat Buffalo," Gerry Philbin, the Jets' standout defensive end, revealed yesterday. "They feel they have to win this one…and we do, too."

Although Pete Beathard, who led Houston to the Eastern title last year, played briefly against the Bengals Sunday, Trull is the No. 1 quarterback. He won the job three weeks ago against the Jets, coming on in the last period to complete two TD passes that forced the visitors to rally for their victory.

Since then, he has led the Oilers to decisions over Buffalo (30-7) and Cincinnati (27-17). In the 2-1/4 games, he has thrown six touchdown passes while completing 28 of 50 attempts for 468 yards. He has been intercepted only once, and that in an earlier game off a fake field goal.

Trull started his pro career with these same Oilers as an All-American out of Baylor. However, he never cut it in Houston and last season was shipped to Boston for a ninth-round draft choice. The trade was announced minutes after Beathard had made his debut in the 28-28 tie with the Jets.

Boston subsequently cut Trull just before the season opened. He telephoned several AFL clubs, including Denver, Cincinnati and Buffalo—the Bills didn't even return his call—then returned home to Houston where he contacted the Oilers. After spending several weeks on the taxi squad, Trull was activated to face Oakland September 29, mainly to hold for place kicks.

But that night Beathard came down with appendicitis and, after Bob Davis got three starts, Trull was called in against the Jets.

Philbin says that although neither Trull nor Beathard is a drop-back passer, each posed a different defensive problem.

"A healthy Beathard is the more dangerous of the two, but I think our best chance is to get Trull out of there, because I don't think Beathard's stomach is ready to take any kind of pounding…and we know it," Philbin said of the measured violence that is pro football.

"Beathard is a better passer and he is the fastest quarterback I've ever chased. What he does is sprint out to throw, not to run for yardage. They put three men—the tackle and both backs—to block the end in the direction he's sprinting, so the burden is on the off end to catch him from the back side.

"Trull's a scrambler like Tarkenton. He looks for a hole. Give him an inch and he'll take a yard. You can't let him get any momentum, you've got to hit him right away. The burden is on the linebackers to be there when he comes up the middle. But if you hit him a few times, you can stop him," Philbin analyzed.

If the Jets succeed in roping the Oiler quarterbacks, this could be a low-scoring game since Houston is No. 2 in total defense and No. 1 in pass defense. And Joe Namath has a team down in Houston plotting to stop him—which they did until the final two minutes last month.

Operate on Jets' Stromberg Today

by Larry Fox
Daily News

J et coach Weeb Ewbank regularly waits until the last minute to activate new players for a given game. This week he broke his own rule and it cost him. The player in question is linebacker Mike Stromberg, who had injured his left knee in the second game of the season against Boston, September 22.

Surgery was not ordered at that time, and Stromberg was put on the active list on Friday. However, in Saturday's workout, he reported the knee did not feel right and he was held out of Sunday's 25-21 victory over Buffalo. Yesterday it was decided to operate on the knee for torn ligaments and removal of cartilage. Surgery will be done today at Lenox Hill Hospital by Dr. Jim Nicholas and Stromberg is through for the season.

The Jets hope to reactivate rookie Steve Thompson, who hurt a knee in the rookie game against Baltimore, July 30. Thompson is a defensive end and that means defensive tackle (and end) Carl McAdams probably will have to work out as a middle linebacker this week as a backup for Al Atkinson.

Jets quarterback Joe Namath (l.) laughs it up as running back Bill Mathis models sport clothes during Joe's show. (News photo by Jim Garrett)

DELAY KNIFE

November 6, 1968—Dr. James A. Nicholas, Jets' team physician, decided yesterday to delay a knee operation on sub linebacker Mike Stromberg for another day or so, pending further examination.

Other than Stromberg, the Jets had no injuries to announce for the AFL's weekly bulletin on player availability for Sunday's game against the Oilers at Shea. Steve Thompson, 6-5, 245-pound rookie defensive end who has recovered from a July knee operation, is expected to be activated to fill Stromberg's roster spot.

NEWS AROUND THE DIALS PLAN SPECIAL ABOUT JOE NAMATH

by Matt Messina
Daily News

November 6, 1968—A television special focusing on the Jets' star quarterback, Joe Namath, is on the drawing boards. It is going to take a look at Namath's budding singing career as well as his exploits on the football field.

The program is one of the show biz projects for Namath outlined by George Scheck, who has become the football celebrity's personal manager. Negotiations aimed at getting a sponsor for the special are under way.

If things go according to plan, Namath will be vocalizing (with the assist of a combo) in night clubs, making personal appearance tours, etc., after the football season. Films, recordings and TV commercials also are on the horizon for Namath, according to Scheck.

AFL STANDINGS
Eastern Division

	W.	L.	T.	PF	PA
Jets	7	2	0	257	184
Houston	4	6	0	175	184
Miami	3	5	1	159	234
Boston	3	6	0	145	244
Buffalo	1	8	1	145	254

Western Division

	W.	L.	T.	PF	PA
Kansas City	8	2	0	246	133
San Diego	7	2	0	269	170
Oakland	7	2	0	196	137
Denver	4	5	0	147	224
Cincinnati	2	8	0	149	214

NFL STANDINGS
Eastern Conference
(Capitol Division)

	W.	L.	T.	PF	PA
Dallas	7	2	0	268	122
Giants	6	3	0	225	194
Washington	4	5	0	163	231
Philadelphia	0	9	0	125	256

(Century Division)

	W.	L.	T.	PF	PA
Cleveland	6	3	0	217	176
St. Louis	5	3	1	233	203
New Orleans	3	6	0	161	212
Pittsburgh	2	6	1	161	235

Western Conference
(Central Division)

	W.	L.	T.	PF	PA
Chicago	5	4	0	167	222
Minnesota	5	4	0	203	147
Detroit	3	5	1	154	175
Green Bay	3	5	1	174	143

(Coastal Division)

	W.	L.	T.	PF	PA
Baltimore	8	1	0	266	108
Los Angeles	8	1	0	297	111
San Francisco	4	5	0	177	200
Atlanta	1	8	0	123	277

Jets Avenge Tie of '67, Muddy Oilers, 26-7

by Larry Fox
Daily News

Inspired by knowledge of this game's importance and by reminders of last year's terrible failure against this same opponent, the Jets virtually clinched the AFL's Eastern Division championship by grinding Houston into the cold, wet sludge of Shea Stadium, 26-7, yesterday.

The Jets tied a club record by winning their fourth in a row for a 7-2 record with five to go. Houston (4-6) and Miami (3-5-1) are each 3-1/2 games back. Boston (3-6) is 4 back. The magic clinching number is two.

The road to a title game in Shea December 29 is clear.

A total of 60,242 tickets were sold for yesterday's game, but only 36,501 showed up in the chilly rainstorm to see Bill Mathis score two touchdowns, Jim Turner kick four more field goals, and the defense limit Oiler quarterbacks Don Trull and Pete Beathard to only 41 yards passing.

However, even the handful that stayed to the finish missed the real drama of this game, which was played out on the Jets' clubhouse bulletin board.

A year ago, the Jets had completed the first half of their schedule with a commanding lead in the Eastern Division. But then

Houston came into Shea and took advantage of six interceptions against Joe Namath to manage a 28-28 tie. A Jet victory would have ended the race, but the tie gave Houston new inspiration. The Oilers won five of their last six and came from behind to win the division title as the Jets lost three of their last four.

The Oilers clinched the championship on a Saturday night in Miami. The next day the Jets played a meaningless game at San Diego and they received the following wire: "Good luck, Sony (sic), on your game with the Chargers. We saved second place for you."

It was signed, "The Houston Oilers." "Sony" of course, referred to Sonny Werblin, then Jet president and the apparently deliberate misspelling of his name was a reference to Werblin's charge a week earlier that Houston was using illegal videotape to scout games. "Anybody hates to be downgraded and that's what they did with that wire," Jet linebacker Larry Grantham said grimly in the victory dressing room.

Also on the bulletin board was a clipping of a newspaper article head, "Will the Jets Blow It Again?" plus an enlarged check for

$25,000 made out to "Every Jet Player" and signed by pro commissioner Pete Rozelle. It was an unsubtle reference to the rewards of winning the Super Bowl, before which, of course, the Jets must take both their division and league titles.

Most of the Jets, however, took the professional road and tried to make light of their coaches' emotional appeals. "We know what this game meant without that," guard Randy Rasmussen said, and Grantham pointed out, "Anybody who doesn't know what this means in terms of a Super Bowl, shouldn't be up here."

However, Turner, who took the AFL scoring lead by one over KC's Jan Stenerud with his 14 points for a total of 97 and broke his own Jet season record of 91 set in 1965, summed it up simply and without humor, "We were ready. We still remember last year's game and we were ready."

Turner's four field goals on kicks of 14, 32, 28 and 21 yards also enabled him to break the club season record of 20 he had tied last week. He had hit six in a row last week and hit on his first two yesterday before holder Babe Parilli bobbled a high snap in the second quarter. "We just kicked it away so they wouldn't run over him," said Turner, who walked the sidelines constantly to keep warm and who still complained later, "I'm froze right through."

For the sixth game in a row, Joe Namath failed to complete a touchdown pass. But the Jets came out throwing yesterday from a new formation that featured three wide receivers and long Namath completions did play a major role. Most of them went to George Sauer, who caught four for 128 yards and received the game ball. "The receiver always has an

Jets cheerleaders do their thing under an umbrella as they try to keep dry on the sidelines during the game between the Jets and Houston. (News photo by Dan Farrell)

advantage on a field like this," he said, before noting that the combination of rain, mud and low 40s temperatures made this "the worst conditions I ever played under, I was wishing it was over from the first play."

Interceptions by Bill Baird and Ralph Baker also set up scores and Johnny Sample's seventh pass theft of the season choked off the Oilers two plays after they had taken over at the Jet nine in the final minutes when Curley Johnson fumbled the snap on a punt.

Don Trull started at quarterback for Houston and was 0-for-5 passing when relieved by Beathard. Emerson Boozer of the Jets played only briefly at the start, held out because doctors feared for his knee on the off track. Weeb Ewbank kept Namath at the controls until almost the very end when Joe had to run on a busted play and gave everybody a start.

But he didn't get hurt, and neither did anybody else as some old hurts were erased.

COLT WATCH COLT WATCH COLT WATCH COLT WATCH COLT WATCH COLT WATCH COLT WATCH COLT

PEARSON GOES 102 YDS.; COLTS VICTORS, 27-10

November 11, 1968—A brilliant 102-yard kickoff return by Preston Pearson following a missed Detroit field goal sparked the Baltimore Colts to a 27-10 NFL victory over the Lions today.

Pearson took the ball two yards deep in his end zone and zig-zagged his way for the first-quarter score.

Earl Morrall's passing game hurt Detroit the most. He hit Jimmy Orr for two long gainers in a first-half drive, one a 54-yard play that took the Colts to the Lions 12 to set up a second-period field goal.

With their victory over the Oilers at Shea, the Jets virtually clinched the Eastern Division title. (News photo by Dan Farrell)

"We were ready. We still remember last year's game and we were ready."
—Jim Turner, after the Jets avenged last year's tie with the Oilers.

JETS, TV BLOW WILD FINISH
RAIDERS WIN; GIANTS COP

— Stories Pages 26, 27

Homer Stays Loose

You can't keep a good man down, and there are some good men, like Homer Jones, who can give you the fits just trying to get them down. Ask Philadelphia Eagle John Mallory, who thought he had Homer nailed after he took 20-yard pass from Fran Tarkenton at Stadium yesterday. Homer twisted away for extra yardage. Giants won, 7-6.

Story on page 26

1—Homer cradles Tarkenton toss as Mallory moves up . . .

NEWS sequence photos by Gene Kappock

2—Eagle defender grabs Homer, who digs in with plans of his own. . . .

3—Mallory seems to have a firm grip on the elusive Giant . . .

4—Eagle suddenly finds he hasn't anything but a fistful of jersey . . .

5—And now, Mallory's out of the picture.

NOVEMBER 17, 1968

Oakland 43, Jets 32

Jets	6	6	7	13	—	32
Oakland	7	7	8	21	—	43

The Jets traveled to Oakland for their tenth game of the season. They were atop the Eastern Division and had a chance to clinch at least a share of the division championship with a victory over the Raiders.

The game was a brutal physical battle, but with just over a minute to play, the Jets went up 32-29 on a Jim Turner field goal. A victory—and a piece of the Eastern Division championship—seemed likely, but the Raiders had other ideas. The Oakland team scored two touchdowns in thirty seconds to snatch victory out of the Jets' hands.

In a turn of events that got even more attention than the Raiders' victory, NBC cut away from the game with a minute to play in order to begin showing the movie *Heidi* at 7 p.m. Unless they happened to be listening on the radio, fans learned about the Jets' abrupt change of fortune on a banner across the bottom of their television screens.

Jets' Grantham Can Smile

by Larry Fox
Daily News

The Jets, surprisingly heavy 7-$^1/_2$-point underdogs against Oakland Sunday, are thinking Super Bowl and to Larry Grantham the dream has a special poignancy. He can still remember the old Titan days when some of his salary checks were no more negotiable than the $25,000 facsimile that decorated the club bulletin board last week.

"In my wildest dreams, I never felt we'd reach a climax like this. This is the ultimate," Grantham said yesterday after the weekly fan feed at Gallagher's 33.

"Oh, I figured that if the AFL survived we'd eventually win something," he added, referring to the fact that the Jets and Broncos are the only charter members never to have won a division title. "But now I don't see any team in pro football that's in as good a position in their race as we are.

"And the fan support! I never thought we'd get 36,000 people to turn out yesterday in that weather. That was really something."

Reminded that in 1963 the Titans drew only 36,161 paid for their entire seasonal descent into bankruptcy while Sunday's actual attendance at Shea was 36,501, Grantham recalled the inflated crowd figures the late Harry Wismer used to hand out. "Boy, I just wish I could count my money the way he counted people," Grantham, a Mississippi banker in the off-season, joked.

"You know, I used to have nightmares about those bouncing (pay) checks all the time, but I don't even dream about it any more," Grantham added.

The perennial all-league linebacker is winding up his ninth pro season. He's 30 years old and still has to push to keep at his listed program weight of 212 pounds. But the brain that makes him one of the most astute defensive signal callers is still sharp. And so is the pride. That's what acceptance of the Jets and the AFL means to him...and Don Maynard...and Bill Mathis...and Curley Johnson, who came here a year later but who can also remember the snide remark and the weekly dash to the bank.

That pride is one reason Grantham isn't considering hanging up his shoulder pads after this season.

"No, I've got to be back to play next year against the Giants in New Haven," he insisted. "Oh, I don't hold any malice or hard feelings against those guys and there aren't many of them left from 1960, but all we've been hearing from folks all these years is how superior they were to us and it's a personal thing with me."

Grantham points to depth in general and a defense that's "come of age" for putting the Jets in a position to wrap up everything this week or the next. "The key to our loss in Oakland last year was when Jim Hudson got hurt. Now we have some depth in the secondary and we've got a defense, which is how great teams of the past, like the Giants and Bears, won championships," he said.

The AFL west is a three-way dogfight with Kansas City at 8-2 followed by Oakland and San Diego tied at 7-2. Although the Jets hold slim victories over the Chiefs and Chargers, Grantham is confident, no matter whom the Jets play for the title.

"We'll have the edge because the game will be played in New York, our home," Grantham said.

Once upon a time, he couldn't have said that.

Namath on Davidson: No Gentle Ben

by Larry Fox
Daily News

Joe Namath finally met Ben Davidson socially at last year's All-Star game. They didn't chat. "I just stayed away from him," Namath recalled yesterday. "I don't like him anyway."

Sunday in Oakland, Namath will meet Davidson once again, this time professionally. He still remembers their first meeting in 1964…and their most recent encounter last season. As a souvenir of that latter occasion, Namath still wears the built-up face mask he had to don the following week to protect his broken cheekbone.

Namath took a frightful beating in Oakland last year, climaxed when Davidson's fist or forearm put him down for the count, but he denies that his blossoming Fu Manchu mustache was instituted as a gamesmanship ploy to counter Davidson's handlebar.

"Oh, I got hit a few times in that game, but there was only one really bad physical thing and actually I hurt worse when I bruised my tailbone against Boston this year," Namath said.

"Look," he added, "they all want to hit the quarterback and they all try to hurt anyone they hit. If you give a guy a good lick, that's okay. But if you knock a guy down and then try to twist his knee or stick a hand through his face mask, that's something else and that's what Davidson tried to do to me three years ago."

Namath added that, since he's turned pro, Davidson is the only opposing player who's tried to damage his knee.

Namath, as a pro, tried to keep his personal feelings out of preparation for Sunday's game in which a victory could clinch at least an Eastern Division title tie for the Jets.

"Every team has a couple of guys who might give you a cheap shot; heck, they even say it about a couple of our guys," he offered. "Just say I think I like Oakland less than any other team in the league, maybe because I've always been frustrated against 'em because we haven't been able to beat them much.

"Do they hate me? Sure, they do, because I'm the opposing quarterback," he declared.

In addition to Davidson's shot last year, Namath also took a few licks from Isaac Lassiter, the other defensive end. As usual,

> "If you give a guy a good lick, that's okay. But if you knock a guy down and then try to twist his knee or stick a hand through his face mask, that's something else and that's what Davidson tried to do to me three years ago."
> —Joe Namath

Winston Hill draws Davidson while rookie Sam Walton gets a major test against Lassiter, whom many consider the better of the two. "There's not much difference whether you're hit by 300 pounds (Lassiter) or 285 (Davidson)," Joe pointed out. He didn't even shudder.

Jets-Raiders: Who's Gonna Hurt?

Oakland, Calif. (Special)—
It's as old as football. Your guys are dirty, our guys are aggressive. The Raiders take pride in their aggressive play and that's just one of the facets of tomorrow's game in which the Jets hope to clinch at least a tie for the Eastern Division championship.

The Raiders this season have moved into brand-new offices near the Coliseum. It is decorated in a silver-black modern Mussolini style. The art work consists of huge football action pictures. At the head of the stairs, leading to the coaches' offices, is that classic from last year's Jet-Raider game featuring Ben Davidson flying

through the air after fracturing a dazed Joe Namath's cheekbone. Namath is on all fours after the blow.

"A helluva thing to be proud of," one member of the Jets family snorted when told of the decoration.

But the Jets and Raiders have always had rugged physical battles here on the Coast and, with the Raiders a half a game off the Western lead and the Jets bidding to clinch a title, this one should be hard fought even without past memories.

The Jets are in top physical condition this weekend and the only change in the starting lineup

is at halfback. Emerson Boozer missed the last two days' work because of Reserve commitments back East and Bill Mathis probably will start.

The Raiders are not so fortunate. Kent McCloughan, their fine cornerback, is definitely out with a bad knee and the uncertainty still lingers concerning Daryle Lamonica. Lamonica hurt a knee, then came up with a back injury and didn't even dress last week. He's supposed to have worked out the last couple of days but Oakland believes in shrouding even simple matters in secrecy. The question of a starting quarterback multiplies the intrigue.

TELEVISION BLEW GAME, TOO

The National Broadcasting Company was deluged with telephone calls last night when the nationally televised AFL game between the Jets and the Raiders was switched to a regular program with one minute to play.

The Jets were leading by three points, 32-29, when the

network made the switch at 7 p.m. (EST) to the special program "Heidi." Oakland went on to score two touchdowns within a nine-second span and viewers were miffed over their missing the final stages of the Raiders' 43-32 victory.

It was impossible to reach

any network spokesman for comment about the incident because the NBC switchboard was flooded with calls for many minutes after play was over. The News switchboard also was deluged with calls for more than an hour after the game ended shortly after 7 p.m.

9-Sec. Disaster: Raiders Blackout Jets, 43-32

by Larry Fox
Daily News

Oakland, Calif.—In nine heartbreaking seconds of the last minute of play, the Jets were denied their bid to clinch at least a tie for the AFL's Eastern Division championship today as they lost a brutal, but brilliant battle to the Raiders, 43-32.

Penalty flags, blood and dazed bodies littered the Oakland Coliseum field from start to finish in a battering replay of last year's brawl in this same stadium between the same two teams.

But the play witnessed by 53,318 fans also was brilliant, and the back-and-forth tide of battle in a game so important to both teams added to the emotional fever.

The Raiders, defending AFL champs, had to win this one, too. They are locked in a three-way battle with Kansas City and San Diego for the Western crown, tied

with the Chargers for second going into today's schedule, half a game behind the Chiefs. Since both rivals won it was up to the Raiders to keep pace. And they did.

The drama of this game hit a crescendo starting with the final period. The Raiders led, 22-19, going into the last 15 minutes, but

the Jets took a 29-22 lead when Joe Namath broke his six-game scoring drought by hitting Don Maynard with a 50-yard TD pass and Jim Turner kicked a 12-yard field goal.

Daryle Lamonica, coming back after missing last week's game with knee and back injuries,

Jets practice on the field. (News photo by Bill Meurer)

then passed 22 yards to Fred Biletnikoff for a TD that brought the Raiders into a tie with 11:10 elapsed.

Now it was the Jets' turn. Maynard, who demoralized rookie cornerback George Atkinson, caught a 42-yarder from Namath and a roughing-the-passer call on Ben Davidson on the same play moved the Jets to the Oakland 18. They couldn't get much closer, though, and Turner kicked a 26-yard field goal, his fourth of the game, for a 32-29 lead with only 65 seconds to play.

That lead, however, lasted only 23 seconds and, after that, in less time than it takes to run the 100-yard dash, the Jets were destroyed.

Oakland started after the kickoff at its 22. Lamonica passed 20 yards to halfback Charley Smith and a face-masking penalty against the Jets put the Raiders at the NY 43. On the next play, Oakland moved in front as Smith beat rookie halfback Mike D'Amato for the go-ahead TD with only 42 seconds to play.

D'Amato was in the game because strong safety Jim Hudson had been thrown out late in the third quarter for protesting another of many similar calls against the Jets. Ironically, in last year's game here, the tide turned when Hudson had to leave the game with an injury and the Raiders also picked on his successor.

The Jets, trailing now by 36-32, still had a chance. Namath has pulled off last-minute miracles before and he had Maynard out

there with the rookie. But they never got a chance.

Mike Eischeid kicked off a hard-to-handle squibber that bounded in and out of Earl Christy's hands at the Jet 15. Instead of falling on the ball, the desperate halfback tried to run against a mob of Raiders. As he twisted and spun, he was flung down and the ball squirted out of his hands toward the goal line. Preston Ridlehuber, a sub fullback, picked it up at the 2, ran it over and flung the ball into the stands in joy.

With 33 seconds left after

Weeb Ewbank. (Daily News Photo)

George Blanda's PAT, the Jets were done and Babe Parilli finished the game.

However, the Jet title hopes are far from over. They still have four games to play—San Diego next week, Miami twice and Cincinnati. Their clinching number is still two over Houston and one over Miami and Boston.

Anything they do, however, will have to be accomplished without Billy Joe, who went out

with probable torn ligaments in his left knee in the third period. He's through for the season and will be operated on in Los Angeles tomorrow. Larry Grantham also missed almost the entire second half with a concussion. He was hospitalized for observation. His sub, Paul Crane, did come up with a TD-saving tackle that led to a fumble and Jet recovery in the third quarter.

This was a game of wild superlatives. Lamonica, who wasn't really expected to play until yesterday by coach Johnny Rauch, completed four touchdown passes, each to a different receiver. He accounted for 311 yards passing to 381 for Namath, who was able to hit Maynard 10 times for 228 yards, a club record. Bake Turner set the old mark of 210 in 1965. Namath, who finally threw for a TD, also ran one across from the one on a bootleg.

And Turner, who now has 111 points for the year, kicked four field goals, giving him 14 three-pointers in the last three games.

But the critical statistics were in the penalty column. The Jets were fined 13 times for 145 yards, a club record, as the flags started flying against them from the opening kickoff to the final extra-point play. The Raiders were called six times for 93 and several of those led to Jet scores, too.

"I guess you could call this a Mexican standoff," said Jet coach Weeb Ewbank, who was fined for criticizing officials after last year's brawl here. At least we all got out alive."

AFL STANDINGS
Eastern Division

	W.	L.	T.	PF	PA
Jets	7	3	0	289	227
Houston	5	6	0	213	201
Miami	3	6	1	180	272
Boston	3	7	0	162	275
Buffalo	1	9	1	151	280

Western Division

	W.	L.	T.	PF	PA
Kansas City	9	2	0	277	150
San Diego	8	2	0	285	176
Oakland	8	2	0	339	169
Denver	4	6	0	164	262
Cincinnati	3	8	0	187	235

NFL STANDINGS
Eastern Conference
(Capitol Division)

	W.	L.	T.	PF	PA
Dallas	8	2	0	312	146
Giants	7	3	0	232	200
Washington	4	5	0	187	275
Philadelphia	0	10	0	131	263

(Century Division)

	W.	L.	T.	PF	PA
Cleveland	7	3	0	262	202
St. Louis	5	4	1	233	230
New Orleans	3	7	0	168	241
Pittsburgh	2	7	1	185	280

Western Conference
(Central Division)

	W.	L.	T.	PF	PA
Minnesota	6	4	0	216	150
Chicago	5	5	0	180	238
Green Bay	4	5	1	203	150
Detroit	3	6	1	157	188

(Coastal Division)

	W.	L.	T.	PF	PA
Baltimore	9	1	0	293	108
Los Angeles	8	1	1	217	131
San Francisco	4	5	1	197	220
Atlanta	2	8	0	139	290

WARD TO THE WISE

**by Gene Ward
Daily News**

November 18, 1968—"Broadway Joe's," the national fast-food franchise system named after Joe Namath, who is on the payroll as board chairman, expects to have 100 restaurants in operation by the end of the next year. But the firm's operators are missing a bet in not blueprinting a restaurant for New York's East Side. Joe never has been seen in any other section of town.

COLT WATCH COLT WATCH COLT WATCH COLT WATCH COLT WATCH COLT WATCH COLT

COLTS, EARL STYMIE CARDS, 27-0

November 18, 1968, Baltimore—The Baltimore defense registered its second shutout of the season today and Earl Morrall pitched three touchdown passes for a 27-0 victory over the Cardinals. It was St. Louis' first blanking in 91 games.

ORANGE PITS PA.ST.-KANSAS

Story on Page 26

Now It Can Be Shown...

Oakland Raider Charley Smith sprints down the sideline for touchdown on 43-yard pass play with 42 seconds left to play at Oakland Sunday. It put Raiders ahead. Jet Mike D'Amato (17) can't catch him any more than TV football fans were able to catch the action. Just a few seconds before, somebody at NBC switched off the game with a minute left to play and Jets leading, 32-29, and treated most of the U.S. to "Heidi," a special featuring Michael Redgrave and Jennifer Edwards (▼). Raiders scored twice in 9 seconds to win, 43-32.

Stories on pages 31 and 27

UPI Telephoto

Associated Press photo

Associated Press Wirephoto

The Champion Hails the Chief

George Foreman, Olympic heavyweight boxing gold medalist, presents plaque to President Johnson during yesterday's visit to the White House. Foreman, 19, a Job Corps graduate, was saluting the Chief Executive "for fathering the Job Corps." Last month, Foreman paraded American flag (◄—) around Mexico City ring after beating Russian boxer Iones Chepulis.

Heidi Aftermath

NBC's decision to cut away from the Jets-Raiders game in order to begin its showing of *Heidi* prompted a massive public outcry. The NBC switchboard received an estimated 10,000 calls protesting the decision, effectively blocking all other callers. Not even network executives could get through to the programming department.

NBC President Julian Goodman explained the move as "a forgivable error committed by humans who were concerned about the children expecting to see *Heidi* at 7 o'clock," and added that he "missed the end of the game as much as anybody else." The sentiment did little to soothe outraged football fans.

Jets 32, Oakland 29, Heidi 14

by Dick Young
Daily News

Television has done it again! Using its customary impeccable judgment, NBC last night cut the Jets-Oakland game off millions of screens at 7 p.m. At that moment, the Jets were leading, 32-29, in a furiously see-sawing battle, but the Raiders were sweeping dangerously down field.

Jim Turner's fourth field goal, with 1:08 to go, had broken the tie. The ensuing kickoff was returned to the Oakland 21. Daryle Lamonica then tossed a screen to big Charles Smith, a crackling rookie who swept to the Raider 42 where he was pulled down, allegedly by the face mask, and the flag-happy officials paced off 15 to the Jet 43.

There were 50 seconds left. Suddenly, the football players disappeared and a commercial came on the screens. When the commercial ended, did Daryle Lamonica reappear? He did not. A little girl named Heidi was being asked by this nice man to please come live with his sick daughter.

Well, if you were fortunate enough to have had on the radio while watching TV, as so many people do, you learned that Oakland scored on the next play, Lamonica to Smith, to take the 36-32 lead. There were 42 seconds left.

The Raiders kicked off. Earl Christy bobbled the ball in the end zone (said Merle Harmon on WABC), picked it up, ran it out, was hit and fumbled. The ball squirted back into the end zone. An Oakland player fell on it for a TD. Oakland led, 43-32—and 33 seconds still remained.

That, as things developed, was the final incredible score. The furious 35 seconds from 1:08 left to 0:33 left, and the two touchdowns therein, were not seen by the NBC-TV audience.

Judging by the spontaneous reaction, most of the millions watching the game must have phoned NBC or The News or the telephone company or the police to ask what was going on here? This is outrageous, was the substance of the calls received at the newspaper and presumably at NBC because people won't call up to say nice of you to have put on *Heidi*.

Not only was the first of the two Oakland TDs important, on the basis of the Jets blowing the game, but the second was just as important to the many Jets backers who had taken their team plus 7 points—and blew that too.

Carl Lindemann, NBC sports director, could not be reached for an explanation. A lesser NBC official contacted at home said he had no idea what had happened, but that the decision to cut off the game was not that of the network sports department; after that it was a high-echelon decision in the programming department.

Later, NBC President Julian Goodman issued a statement: "It was a forgivable error committed by humans who were concerned about the children expecting to see *Heidi* at 7 o'clock. I missed the end of the game as much as anybody else." Mr. Goodman lives in Westchester.

Story lovers, like the unspecified NBC officials who made the decision, may contend that *Heidi* is of the utmost importance to children, but there are those who will tell you that you can miss the first two or three minutes of *Heidi* without tragic consequences because it is not the fastest moving story ever written.

NBC has had some unfortunate luck, or bad estimating, with its programming of major sports events. Two summers ago, the telecast of baseball's All-Star Game from Anaheim was started at 7:15 N.Y. time to reach the prime-period audience. The game went 15 innings; 3 hours and 41 minutes and NBC got more prime time than it had bargained for. With the game running till 10:56, a documentary on Nikita Khrushchev,

NEWS AROUND THE DIALS
NBC PROMISE TO AFL: NO MORE GRID CUTS

by Matt Messina
Daily News

November 19, 1968—It won't happen again. That's what NBC-TV has promised the American Football League in the wake of Sunday's fumble, whereby it cut off the final deciding seconds of play in the exciting Jets-Oakland Raiders game for a children's special, *Heidi*.

Milt Woodard, president of the AFL, said that he had a huddle with NBC sports vice president Carl Lindemann and Lindemann's No. 2 man, Chet Simmons, director of sports, yesterday. "We have been assured that henceforth, if this situation exists again, the game will go to its conclusion," he said.

Woodward said the NBC action in blacking out the game's finale did not violate any clause in the league's contract with the network. However, he added: "I

think they realize now it's a bad practice and bad public relations. I think they've learned a poignant lesson." Woodard added that the assurance that the Jets-Oakland fiasco won't be repeated came from Simmons.

The AFL prexy stated: "We've allowed them to use their own judgment in the past and they have used it with discretion—such as switching last Sunday from the Buffalo-San Diego game to the Jets before the Buffalo contest was over. I think that was proper because there was no doubt about the outcome of the Buffalo game. If you have a 50-0 contest with a half-minute to go, they can use their judgment. I won't be upset if they cut off the game. But any game with any significance whatsoever will go on in its entirety from now on."

Lindemann met with top NBC brass yesterday on the matter. In the afternoon, NBC issued a statement blaming "communications difficulties" for the fiasco.

The statement read: "When it became apparent that the game could not be ended by 7 p.m., specific orders were issued to continue the game to its conclusion, even though it ran past the beginning of *Heidi*. Communications difficulties and operating errors prevented these orders from being carried out."

One spokesman said a jammed switchboard here forced execs to try reaching operating personnel via the lines at NBC headquarters in Burbank, California. Time ran out before orders were executed.

which was to have followed, was scrapped.

Yesterday, three hours was blocked out in the NBC schedule for the Jets game, commencing 4 p.m. N.Y. time. Time was when three hours would be plenty. That was before they interrupted football games for TV commercials. NBC was burned by its own match.

Following the cutoff of the game, I watched NBC intently, waiting for Heidi to tell the final score. She didn't. At 8:22 p.m. almost an hour and a half later against a mountainous snow-capped background and Heidi's grandfather, a taped message rolled across the bottom of the screen:

Final score of the Jets-

Raiders game, it said, was 43-32, Oakland. It said the Raiders scored two TD's in the last minute to overcome a 3-point deficit. "Further details on the 11 o'clock news."

Ward to the Wise

by Gene Ward
Daily News

'␣ve got news for NBC. My kids weren't waiting for Johanna Spyri's 98-year-old story of Heidi to arrive on their video screen at 7 p.m. Sunday night. They were watching the Jets beating the Raiders in a beautiful battle in Oakland. Then, all of a sudden, with 50 seconds left to play, somewhere in the vast communications complex that is NBC someone decided to pull the plug on pro football.

If the score had remained at 32-29, in favor of the Jets, there would have been a rumbling of discontent but no mass outcry. But it didn't. The Raiders scored two touchdowns and stole the victory that would have clinched the Jets a tie for the Eastern Division crown.

Larding the NBC goof with bitter irony was the fact the Raiders tallied their winning points in the first 17-second segment of the blackout—a span in which a promotion for Mel Allen's late sports show and a station break were taking up air time on the network.

In other words, both Raider scores, nine seconds apart, were made before *Heidi* even began.

I had the feeling, as Daryle Lamonica faded from the screen, that NBC couldn't help itself. The communications giant, caught up in its vast technical complexities, couldn't communicate. It was lost in its own electronic maze. Sports director Carl Lindemann's reason for the foul-up was—you guessed it—a communication failure. Lindemann claimed he sent out "countermanding instructions" five minutes before the end of the game, but his all-points bulletin never got through.

However, the full game was carried on the "C" network, west of Denver, where the children presumably have more interest in football than in Heidi.

I also had the strange feeling that NBC was nowhere near as "shook" as its viewers, but there are other precincts yet to be heard from—the sponsors. When sponsors get shook up, particularly sponsors paying around $28,000 a commercial minute, the quake is going to be felt all the way to the top of NBC.

Sponsors do not like unhappy viewers. Unhappy viewers may be unhappy at NBC but they're apt to strike back at the sponsor by boycotting his product. Viewers are a sophisticated lot. They know how to hit where it hurts.

Timex, which bankrolled the $850,000 production of *Heidi*, also has to be unhappy about the turn of events. Instead of building a beautiful cultural image, it has taken the shape of a scapegoat through no fault of its own.

NBC actually cut off two games on Sunday. In that director Lindemann was forced to chop the Chargers vs. the Bills in Buffalo in order to get the Jets vs. the Raiders on the air at 4 p.m. The start in Oakland was late and then the two clubs proceeded to play the longest game of the year, one which consumed three hours, eight minutes, according to NBC, including a 45-minute final quarter.

Over at CBS a spokesman for the purveyor of NFL games stated that the average time per contest the last three years has been 2 hours, 34^1/$_2$ minutes. "We provide 2:45 per game on our double-headers," he said.

Presumably, CBS, with a 3:08 nightcap game on its hands, might well have wound up in the same pickle jar as did NBC.

Last in the hullabaloo was the fact the Jets played a tremendous game. They won the TV version but lost on radio as Lamonica hurled a scoring pass to rookie halfback Charley Smith on the first play after the blackout.

The Jets still had a ghost of a

YOUNG IDEAS

**by Dick Young
Daily News**

"A forgivable error committed by humans who were concerned about the children expecting to see *Heidi* at 7 o'clock. I missed the end of the game as much as anybody else."

—NBC President Julian Goodman

THE POSTMAN ALWAYS KNOCKS AND KNOCKS

November 23, 1968

Dear Dick: Is the rumor about Joe Namath and Heidi true?
—Bob Hickey, Brooklyn

Dear Dick: I know why NBC threw on Heidi when it did. Because "Rebecca of Sunnybrook Farm" is being saved for this week's San Diego game.
—Murray of Brooklyn College

Dick Young: The executive who made the decision on Heidi is 100% correct. He didn't disappoint millions who stood by to see a fine old classic.
—M.B. Hunter, Guttenberg, N.J.

Dear Dick: NBC should change its motto to "the network where more sports are partially seen than any other."
—L.G. Markert, Emporium, Pa.

Dear Dick: NBC should be suspended from showing any games for one year.
—Thomas J. Sheehan, Bronx

Dear Dick: Pay TV would be a joy.
—Sam A. Arena, Elizabeth, N.J.

Dear Dick Young: I can't understand all the excitement. Each Sunday, at 7, I watch Lassie, and I'm the happiest guy in the world!
—Fast Eddie Fay, Cos Cob, Conn.

Dear Mr. Young: I can't wait for the Super Bowl so I can watch it on CBS.
—Joseph Vaccaro, N.Y.C.

Dear People: NBC is sworn never again to abort a sports event. For the gentleman who says the Heidi-watchers of the world had to be considered, it would have been a simple matter to come on with the little brat three minutes or so later and give a quick audio synopsis, much the same as is done when Walt Disney runs a two-parter. And, Mr. Vaccaro, I have bad news for you. NBC is doing the Super Bowl this time.

chance, because Don Maynard had been beating the Raiders' rookie cornerback, George Atkinson, all afternoon and might conceivably do it again.

But Earl Christy failed to field Mike Eischeid's squib kickoff; the ball squirted into the end zone and Preston Ridlehuber plopped on it for the convincer.

It was a game the Jets didn't have to win and a game the Raiders had to have to stay in the tight Western Division race.

Considering the importance of motivation, the Jets covered themselves with glory and came this close to adding the third Western powerhouse, the defending champion Raiders, to a list of victims which already included Kansas City and San Diego.

The Jets used every trick in the book at the end in their attempt to keep the pigskin out of the mitts of the explosive Raider offense. They even took a delayed penalty on Jim Turner's go-ahead

field goal to eat up the seconds.

Television has made much of pro football's frantic finishes and the crowning irony had to be the fact NBC cut off one of the most frantic finishes of all time.

CBS News had the last word. It announced yesterday, in case you missed the ending of *Heidi*, she married the goatkeeper and lived happily ever after.

Oakland Aftermath: Rozelle Fines Jets $2G

by Larry Fox
Daily News

L'affaire Oakland continues to have ramifications—the latest being that the Jets have been fined $2,000 by Pete Rozelle, the czar of pro football, for criticizing game officials and other incidents connected with the November 17 game.

Neither the Jets nor Rozelle's office would confirm the actual amount of the fine levied, but *The News* learned yesterday from an authoritative source that the Eastern Division champs were assessed that amount.

A spokesman for the Jets admitted "we received a letter from the commissioner's office in which certain disciplinary action was taken…and we consider the issue closed."

In addition to the team fine, defensive coach Walt Michaels and safetyman Jim Hudson were fined $150 each, Michaels for berating the game official near the locker room and Hudson for making "obscene gestures" as he was being kicked out of the game.

This ejection also cost Hudson the automatic $50 fine and a similar levy was inflicted on defensive tackle John Elliott, who was banished after decking Oakland pivotman Jim Otto. Elliott later complained that he had been goaded by Otto.

The Jets appeared to have had the game all but wrapped up, 39-29, on a late field goal by Jim Turner, before the Raiders rallied and scored two TDs in nine seconds. Hudson was missed in the defensive setup as quarterback Daryle Lamonica exploited his absence, going over rookie Mike D'Amato with a 43-yard pass play.

Hudson had been ejected for allegedly grabbing the face mask of fullback Hewritt Dixon and arguing the call with field judge Frank Kirkland. Hudson, however, counter-charged that Kirkland used obscene language.

General manager and coach Weeb Ewbank and Michaels were outspoken in their criticism of the officiating and continued to fan the flames the following week in San Diego. The controversial film clip shown to the press, which prolonged the incident and Dr. James A. Nichols' intrusion into the officials' dressing room, doubtlessly provoked Rozelle into lowering the boom on the Jets with one of the largest fines in his tenure as commissioner.

Mark Duncan, the supervisor of officials, investigated the films, taken from the field level, and Hudson was found guilty of holding Dixon's face mask.

Kirkland, who was scheduled to work the Jets-Dolphins game at Shea last Sunday, was reassigned to Patriots-Bengals in Boston. Mel Hein, AFL supervisor of officials, explained the switch by saying, "we had received some threatening letters."

Joe Namath and Greta Thyssen crowd into a dogsled driven by Dick Irwin. (News photo by Dennis Caruso)

DAILY ⬜ NEWS

NEW YORK'S PICTURE NEWSPAPER ®

MORE THAN TWICE
THE CIRCULATION
OF ANY OTHER
PAPER IN AMERICA

100   New York, N.Y. 10017, Monday, November 25, 1968

JETS RIP CHARGERS, 37-15
RAMS EDGE GIANTS, 24-21

Stories Pages 80, 81

UPI Telephoto

Off With His Headgear. Giants' Ken Avery (54) separates Rams' Dick Bass from his helmet as the Los Angeles back picks up three yards in first quarter at LA. The Giants, after tying game at 21-all with 42 seconds left, lost 24-21, when they allowed Rams to get close enough for a 36-yard Bruce Gosset field goal with 4 seconds to go. —Story p. 81

Here's One
For Don...

With the Jets' bench paying close attention, Don Maynard scoots past a diving Bob Howard of the San Diego Chargers on way to 87-yard touchdown with a Joe Namath bomb in first quarter on Coast. Jets clinched at least a tie for Eastern AFL crown with a 37-15 pasting. —Story p. 80

←His Disc
Is Slipping

Oakland's Ted Hampson has Rangers' goalie Ed Giacomin at his mercy and flips the puck into the net for a first-period score at the Garden last night. Harry Howell (3) is too late to help. Blues won, 3-2. —Story p. 80

NEWS photo by Walter Kelleher

NOVEMBER 24, 1968

New York 37, San Diego 15

New York	10	17	3	7	—	37
San Diego	0	7	0	8	—	15

A fter their disappointing loss to the Raiders, the Jets stayed on the West Coast to take on the San Diego Chargers. A variety of problems troubled the team during the week. Namath had re-injured his right thumb against Oakland, and was also nursing a sore left foot. Cornerback John Sample had come down with the flu, and linebacker Larry Grantham was out with a neck injury. Substitute fullback Billy Joe was lost for the rest of the season due to torn knee ligaments suffered against the Raiders. Adding insult to injury, the Jets' road uniforms disappeared en route from Oakland to San Diego.

By game time, however, the team had recovered. The road uniforms were located and arrived in San Diego Sunday morning, and Namath led the way as the Jets defeated the Chargers 37-15. On the East Coast, the Colts continued their quest for a title by beating the Vikings 21-9 to earn their 10th victory of the season.

Jets, Chargers Match Rugged Interior Lines

by Larry Fox
Daily News

Long Beach, California—In San Diego, they call them The Protectors. In New York, they're just a bunch of guys, named John, Dave, Bob, Sam and Winston—Winston?—who get in the paper only when they're caught for holding to blow a touchdown or when somebody breaks through to rub Joe Namath's Fu Manchu mustache in the mud.

But in football nomenclature, they're called the interior offensive line, and two of the best in football at pass-blocking will meet down the road a piece Sunday afternoon.

The Jets' figures on getting the quarterback have been most publicized this season what with the cash pool gimmick and all. There's something catchy about the phrase Fearsome Foursome and the Jet quartet has thrown opposing quarterbacks 33 times, second best in the AFL, for a league high of 317 yards in losses.

However, on the other side of the field, Jet quarterbacks have been dropped only 14 times, second lowest in the AFL, for the least yardage, 99. That's a gold star for center John Schmitt,

A clean-shaven Joe Namath arrives at his east-side oasis with Suzie Storm.
(Daily News photo by Carmine Donofrio)

JETS' SAMPLE ILL

by Larry Fox
November 20, 1968, Long Beach, California—Johnny Sample is down with the flu and the Jet coaching staff is down on their defensive captain, although not irreparably so. Still obsessed with post-mortems of last Sunday's loss to Oakland, they feel Sample's failure to disclose his illness contributed to the defeat.

"He's been around long enough he should have known to tell us he wasn't feeling well. Heck, we could have put (Cornell) Gordon in there," one Jet assistant said.

Coach Weeb Ewbank, who expressed more displeasure just by the look on his face earlier this week, today merely noted, "I don't think John played as good a game as he could. He didn't keep up with the flow at all."

Sample, it now has been revealed, has been playing the last three weeks with a slightly pulled hamstring. He apparently showed up for Sunday's game at Oakland feeling under the weather with the onset of the flu and last night was bedded with a temperature of near 102 degrees.

He probably will be okay for Sunday's game with the Chargers, but at what degree of efficiency it's not known.

Matt Snell, Sample's roommate, was quickly moved out last night but there's a chance Sample might have infected other players. If Sample can't go, Gordon will take his left corner spot with Randy Beverly on the right.

Jet players regrouped here today after a couple of days off and presumably they'll start to talk about next week instead of the past.

---

guards Dave Herman and Bob Talamini and tackles Sam Walton and Winston Hill.

But save another gold star for the San Diego locker room, too. The Chargers' front five of center Sam Gruneisen, guards Walt Sweeney and Larry Little and tackles Ron Mix and Terry Owens have allowed their quarterback to be dropped only 10 times, best in the league, for the second lowest yardage, 104.

"I have the best offensive line in football," says John Hadl of the Chargers, while the mere fact of Namath's survival is tribute enough to his own crew.

Namath is coming off a pretty good beating at the hands of

> ## "I have the best offensive line in football."
> ## —John Hadl

Oakland last week while Hadl escaped from the quagmire up in Buffalo with virtually a clean jersey. In fact, when he was dropped for the one and only time by the Bills on a safety blitz it marked the first time he was dragged down with the ball in three games.

"One reason he gets rid of the ball so fast is that the Chargers run a lot of short 'in' patterns. And if he does call a deep pattern, usually to (Lance) Alworth, he will unload the ball fast to a point in the field. Alworth is so great and they've been together so long that Hadl is confident he will be there.

"You'll notice that on deep patterns Hadl either overthrows his man or it's a completion."

The greatness of Alworth is one reason Ewbank may be less likely to play Johnny Sample at left cornerback if he's still less than 100% from the flu.

JETS REVAMP DRILLS SO JOE'S FOOT CAN HEAL

by Larry Fox
Daily News

November 21, 1968—Long Beach, Calif.—The Jets were forced to change their practice routine today when Joe Namath turned up with a sore left foot that appears to be more annoying than serious.

The Jets usually work on Wednesdays and devote Thursdays to defense. This time they reversed the order "to give Joe some extra time to heal.," Weeb Ewbank explained. Namath missed most of the dispirited workout at the start and finish to undergo treatment. But he did throw a little.

"One of our own players stepped on him last week. I didn't even know that it had happened. He'll be all right," Ewbank said.

Namath declined to discuss this injury but he did reveal that he had jammed his troublesome right thumb late in the Oakland game. This is at least the third time he has hurt it this year.

However, he has yet to miss any time because of this or any other injury, and appeared to be throwing very well during the brief time he practiced today.

"It's nothing. I'll be okay," Namath said of his thumb.

Joe Namath takes a break from playing softball with his Bachelor's 3 team against Your Father's Moustache in a field under the Queensboro Bridge. (News photo by Jim Garrett)

Joe Namath catches a fly ball during a game against Your Father's Moustache. (Daily News photo by Jim Garrett)

Jets Beating Flu

by Larry Fox
Daily News

San Diego, California—The Long Beach area where the Jets are training this week is a smoggy, foggy wasteland that reeks of oil from hundreds of wells and refineries. This city, home of the Chargers, had been wrapped in fog the last few nights, but the days have been sunny and bright.

The Jets, to the accompaniment of knuckles on wood, report nobody as yet seems to have caught Sample's flu. (Sample, incidentally was expected to start working out today. He and Larry Grantham, who will not work until later, are listed as probables for Sunday's game with the Chargers.)

Jet Coach Weeb Ewbank reports his team has been slow shaking the bumps and bruises from last Sunday's punishing game at Oakland and early workouts have shown it. He hopes the team will come strong at the end of the week.

The last couple of days have involved "three" nights for the Jets. They were off from Sunday night until Tuesday noon and several went to Las Vegas during that period. Then, after the squad reported, there was no curfew for the first two nights. Tonight the players must be in at midnight, however, and it's 11 p.m. bedcheck tomorrow and Saturday.

The usual fine for missing curfew is $50, but this trip the players themselves voted a 1,000% increase to five grand. That was the levy before the Oakland game and it will also be the case now.

The players know they are competing for big stakes and they brought that fake oversized $25,000 check along as a reminder. Also transported to their temporary bulletin board in Long Beach is that goading newspaper clipping headed, "Will The Jets Blow It Again?"

YOUNG IDEAS

by Dick Young
Daily News

November 22, 1968— Ike Lassiter ate up Sam Walton in the Oakland game. The Jets' rookie, who took Sherm Plunkett's place, has a few things to learn—and Joe Namath wishes he'd hurry up and learn them before somebody, namely Namath, gets killed.

NBC execs think the Heidi furor will aid, not hurt, their sponsorship sales of football for next season. "It proved how great public interest is in the AFL," says Carl Lindemann, sports director. There were 1,000 protest phone calls in Chicago, a city that doesn't have an AFL franchise.

The Bachelors 3, swinging joint on Lex, is named for its owners—Joe Namath, Ray Abruzzese and Bobby Van. Namath is said to have 25 Gees sunk in it.

Jets Lost Their Shirts in Oakland; Pants, Too

by Larry Fox
Daily News

Long Beach, California—Just one damn thing after another, that's been the story of the Jets' annual West Coast trip so far—insult, injury and aggravation, not to mention defeat.

Latest bother as the Jets try to concentrate on their upcoming game in San Diego, Sunday, has been the disappearance of their road uniforms.

As with all else on this trip, the trouble started in Oakland.

After last week's game, the Jets' road whites were picked up by an Oakland firm to be cleaned. They were then to be shipped down to the Jets' training base, here. As of today, they hadn't arrived.

"The cleaner said he'd drop them off at the express office and now they're gone, but we don't know where they might have ended up," Weeb Ewbank complained.

And so, as soon as he and his staff finished their short yardage strategy session this morning, Weeb had to change from head coach to general manager and get to work on the uniform problem.

First he alerted Bobby Sharp, assistant to equipment manager Bill Hampton, back to Shea to start packing the Jets' home green jerseys for shipment West. And then he had to track down Sid Gillman, head coach and GM of the Chargers to see if his team would mind wearing its road whites for this game.

The teams must wear contrasting jerseys for TV purposes and the home team always wears the dark shirts. The Jets have practice jerseys, but they are not numbered.

> "The cleaner said he'd drop them off at the express office and now they're gone, but we don't know where they might have ended up," Weeb Ewbank complained.

Suggestions that the Jets go topless drew a laugh, but jerseys are important from a safety standpoint, too, since they hold down the sharp edges of players' shoulder pads.

Sample, Grantham Out As Jets Gird for SD

The Jets lead the idle Oilers in the East by two and a half games. A New York victory tomorrow would clinch at least a tie for the championship. However, even if they win, the Jets can't be assured of any title unless Houston obliges by losing to Kansas City on Thanksgiving Day.

San Diego, California (Special)—The game of chess goes on as the Jets, slight underdogs, seek to rebound from their crushing defeat at Oakland against the Chargers here tomorrow.

The Jets are making some expected lineup changes, but at least they'll be recognizable as the visiting team to the crowd of approximately 50,000 (almost capacity) and the TV audience watching in New York over Channel 4 starting at 4 p.m. and continuing hopefully to the conclusion.

The Jets' road uniforms of white finally turned up this morning less than 24 hours after the home greens had been flown out on a rush order from New York. The Chargers had agreed to wear their whites if necessary, but the missing Jet uniforms finally turned up "under a freight platform in Los Angeles," according to Weeb Ewbank.

The uniforms had disappeared en route from an Oakland dry cleaning establishment, where they had been sent after last week's game.

The expected changes for the Jets involved Cornell Gordon at cornerback for Johnny Sample and Paul Crane at linebacker for Larry Grantham. Both regulars will be available for duty, however.

This is a major game for both teams and the Western Division standings could be in a three-way snarl by nightfall.

The Jets lead the idle Oilers in the East by two and a half games. A New York victory tomorrow would clinch at least a tie for the championship. However, even if they win, the Jets can't be assured of any title unless Houston obliges by losing to Kansas City on Thanksgiving Day.

If the Jets should lose today and the Oilers win next Thursday, it's a whole new can of worms. The Jets then would have a one and a half game lead—two in the lost column—with three to play, Cincinnati at home and a pair against Miami.

Jets Clip Chargers, 37-15, to Clinch East Tie

by Larry Fox
Daily News

San Diego, California—While his teammates sat tensely in grim silence an hour before the kickoff, Joe Namath nonchalantly trimmed his Fu Manchu mustache. Then, he went out and trimmed the Chargers, 37-15, to lead the Jets back from the horrors of last week's loss at Oakland and into a position where they can do no worse than tie for the Eastern Division championship they have never won.

The loss, witnessed by an SRO crowd of 51,175, dropped the Chargers a full length off the Western Division pace set by Kansas City and Oakland. The Raiders moved into a tie by beating Cincinnati, 34-0, while the idle Chiefs next play Houston on Thanksgiving Day.

And that's a game that will be watched closely by all the Jets at the annual family Thanksgiving Day dinner sponsored by the club at Shea. If the Oilers lose, the Jets are champions of the East and there'll be champagne to wash down the turkey and fixins.

While Namath was a principal figure in the victory, as always, the entire Jet team played bril-

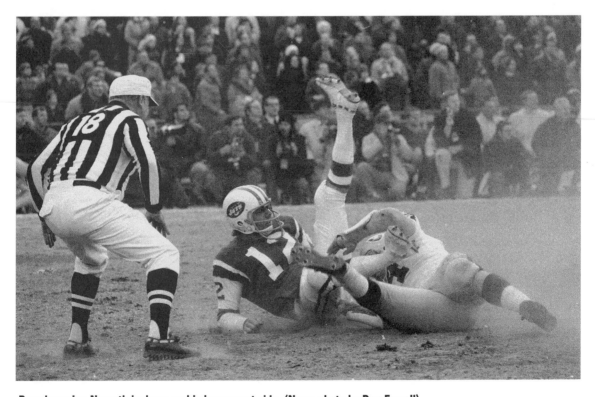

Broadway Joe Namath is down on his lower east side. (News photo by Dan Farrell)

liantly. The offensive line, mauled by the Raiders, provided him with perfect protection. And the defenders, playing without several regulars, intercepted John Hadl four times and didn't allow the Chargers inside the 40 until midway of the third period.

Until that point, the only Charger touchdown had come on a record 95-yard punt return by Speedy Duncan late in the second quarter. On this play, Curly Johnson's kick had bounced over Duncan's head and most of the Jet coverage over-ran the play.

Duncan's burst over the middle broke his own club record of 81 set against Buffalo in 1966 and the AFL record of 93 set by the Jets' own Billy Baird against Houston in 1963.

However, the Jets set some records of their own, too, including a couple by place-kicker Jim Turner and another by the combination of Namath and veteran receiver Don Maynard.

Turner ended up with 13 points for the game on four conversions and three field goals of 13, 20 and 23 yards. For the season he has 124 points, which breaks George Blanda's AFL kicking-only record of 118 established last year. And Jim's 31 field goals breaks him out of a three-way all pro tie at 28 with Pete Gogolak of Buffalo (1965) and

Bruce Gossett of the Rams (1966).

The Namath-Maynard record came early in the first quarter when they combined on an 87-yard scoring pass, longest in the history of the New York AFL

CBS (Ch. 2) won the battle of football viewers with NBC (Ch. 4) yesterday as the Giants (NFL) and the Jets (AFL) vied on the West Coast. The Giants had a 17.8 rating on CBS, while the Jets were 7.7 on NBC. During the half-time ceremonies of the Giants-Rams game from Los Angeles, NBC ran up a 16.5 mark, while CBS slipped to 10—meaning that most fans were switching channels.

A week ago, NBC had a 24.4 rating for the Jets-Raiders from Oakland before Heidi stole the ball.

franchise. The old record of 86 was established by Lee Grosscup and the durable Maynard for the old Titans against Boston in 1962 in the old Polo Grounds.

On that play, Namath credited Pete Lammons and Emerson Boozer with throwing important blocks to hold out the blitzing chargers.

When Namath was relieved by Babe Parilli in the final period,

he had completed 17 of 31 passes for 337 yards and two touchdowns with only one interception. Maynard, enjoying his second straight fine afternoon against an inexperienced cornerback, soph pro Bob Howard, caught six passes for 166 yards.

Snell's yardage was more than double the team total of 46 yards managed by all the Chargers as the Jets' patched-up defense dominated the explosive home team throughout.

Larry Grantham, who had suffered a neck injury last week, didn't play at all and was relieved by Paul Crane, who did better than fine when the Chargers tried to test him early. Verlon Biggs, who suffered a leg injury against the Raiders, didn't start at end and saw only limited service with Carl McAdams going most of the way. And Cornell Gordon started at left corner for flu-weakened Johnny Sample.

When Billy Baird was shaken up early in the third quarter, Gordon moved to his free safety spot and Sample took over at left corner. Before the period was over, Gordon had accomplished the Jets' fourth interception—the others were by Baird, Randy Beverly and Ralph Baker—which enabled the Jets to tie Kansas City for the league lead in this department with 26.

**Jets linebacker Ralph Baker
autographs a football for some of the
Jets' younger fans. (Daily News photo)**

JETS' TITLE AS OILERS BOW
EAGLES FINALLY WIN, 12-0

— Stories on Page 134

The Jets' Sing Hail to the Chiefs

Chiefly, the Jets are a thankful bunch. And they showed their thanks yesterday at their annual Thanksgiving get-together in Shea Stadium by toasting the Kansas City Chiefs' victory over the Houston Oilers. Houston's 24-10 loss assured our heroes of their first Eastern AFL title. The day was for the birds, and the Jets are thankful that Houston was, too.

—Stories pages 134, 135

Oilers' Al Reed drops a pass in 2d quarter.
UPI Telephoto

Joe (Fu Manchu) Namath puts an arm around coach Weeb Ewbank at Shea celebration.

Running Up an Appetite?
An impromptu bit of follow-the-leader spurs the Thanksgiving Day appetite of a group of youthful runners along Raritan Bay beach in Perth Amboy, N.J., as the sun peeks out from behind the clouds for a couple of seconds. Then, it was home to some serious business with a turkey leg or two.

Thanksgiving Day, November 28, 1968

Kansas City Chiefs 24, Houston Oilers 10

KC victory clinches AFL Eastern crown for Jets

On Thanksgiving Day, the Jets players and their families gathered at Shea Stadium for the team's annual Thanksgiving dinner. This year, however, everyone was interested in more than just the food. The Chiefs and the Oilers were playing, and a Kansas City victory would clinch the AFL Eastern Division title for the Jets.

Kansas City triumphed 24-10, prompting celebration and champagne toasts in New York. The coaching staff was especially glad for the chance to let their "walking wounded"—such regulars as Joe Namath, Bill Baird, Emerson Boozer, Verlon Biggs and Larry Grantham—rest and recover before the playoffs.

Jets Clinch Division

T-Day a TV Feast; Title Wishbone for Jets?

by Larry Fox
Daily News

Jet substitutes will be pulling for Kansas City to beat Houston for their Thanksgiving Day dessert today, but the regulars aren't quite so eager.

A Houston loss, of course, would assure the Jets of their first Eastern Division title since the AFL was formed in 1960. Since the Jets have three games to clinch the title on their own, many veterans feel that's just the way they'd like to do it.

"The feeling on the club is that we'd almost like to see Houston win so we can wrap it up on our own Sunday," one of the veterans noted yesterday. "We'd rather do it that way than slip in through the side door."

However, for the rookies and other second-stringers, an early clinching will spell opportunity. The Jets have a lot of wounded who could play if needed to clinch a title.

"A lot depends on what happens tomorrow," Weeb Ewbank said yesterday at the weekly press briefing. "If we've already clinched the title, we'll go on a program of getting people well."

Ewbank said the program would include quarterback Joe Namath, but not completely. "We might rest Namath, but not in a starting way," Weeb promised. "We owe it to our fans of course, and he also must continue to play some to keep his timing."

The Jet walking wounded include such as Verlon Biggs (leg), Larry Grantham (neck), Johnny Sample (flu) and Billy Baird (neck). Biggs tried to play some and Sample had to be thrown in when Baird was injured last week at San Diego. Grantham could have played, but the Jets jumped off to a big lead and Paul Crane was doing well as his sub.

If the Jets have clinched by Sunday, all of the above might be held out another week, and that means the rookies will be able to show what they can do.

Joe (Fu Manchu) Namath, the big gun of the Jets, rests his head on end Pete Lammons' shoulder while watching a game. (News photo by Dan Farrell)

Jets Love That Title Stuffing

by Larry Fox
Daily News

The Jets, who listened to themselves lose a title last year, watched themselves win one yesterday. The occasion was the club's annual Thanksgiving dinner at Shea Stadium, an affair that became a real celebration when Channel 4 flashed the Chiefs' 24-10 victory over the Oilers at Kansas City.

Flanker Don Maynard, a nine-year veteran who will be playing in his first championship game, was thrilled. "It's just wonderful after all this time," said Maynard, one of three players who have been with New York since the AFL's inception in 1960 when they were known as the Titans. The others are linebacker Larry Grantham and runner Bill Mathis.

Weeb Ewbank, whom Sonny Werblin installed as coach and general manager when he bought the bankrupt Titans' franchise in 1963, said it was "a realization that came about after six years."

Ewbank, who won two NFL titles while coaching the Colts, didn't mind "backing in" to the Jets' maiden title. He said it didn't make any difference which Western club the Jets will face for the AFL title, December 29 at Shea, adding the important thing is "to get our club healthy for that game."

His players, many of whom sat in California last December 23 and listened to the Oilers beat Miami to eliminate the Jets from the Eastern Division race, watched TV and reacted to every Kansas City score. "They acted just like real fans," a club official said.

The Jets have three games remaining, two with the Dolphins and one with Cincy, but their future is insured. "Now we can rest some of our injured players, fellows like Em Boozer and Bill Baird," one Jet said.

Having the title wrapped takes the pressure off Joe Namath. He'll continue to play in each game, Ewbank said, but it won't be necessary for him or others like Verlon Biggs and Matt Snell to go all the way.

Ewbank was referring to Baird's strained neck and the tender knees of Boozer, Namath and Biggs.

"We want to win our last three games," Ewbank said, "but

Coach Weeb Ewbank at Shea as new king of the Eastern AFL with fullback Bill Mathis (l.) and Joe Namath (r.). (News photo by Dan Farrell)

Coach Weeb Ewbank at Shea as new king of the Eastern AFL with Joe
Namath. Locals copped the title when Kansas City beat Houston, 24-
10, yesterday. (News photo by Dan Farrell)

YOUNG IDEAS

**by Dick Young
Daily News**

WHAT SOME GUYS WON'T DO FOR $250

November 30, 1968—True to their word, the Jets' hair-faced brigade shaved to celebrate the clinching. Yesterday, Jim Hudson took off the goatee, Cornell Gordon and Bake Turner the mustaches—and they did it for Remington Shavers at $250 apiece. Joe Namath didn't shave. Will Norelco go higher?

They'd Like to Get Hunk for Heidi

Weeb Ewbank has slapped a muzzle on himself and Jet players regarding the question: Would you prefer to play Oakland or Kansas City for the title? Weeb feels the eventual Western winner would use it for hype-fodder. It isn't too tough to figure, though, that the Jets would like to get a return crack at Oakland. They beat Kaycee in the season opener, and would like to get hunk for the Heidi game they blew at Oakland.

Jets owner Phil Iselin (l.) leads the players in christening coach Weeb Ewbank as the new king of the Eastern AFL. (News photo by Dan Farrell)

YOUNG IDEAS . . .

WOULD SONNY SWAP HIS $2 MILLION?

By Dick Young
Daily News

December 1, 1968—The first time Sonny Werblin saw Joe Namath was in the Orange Bowl game. "The moment he came on the field, I knew he was a leader. I knew I had to have him," says Sonny Werblin.

It wasn't the wild cheer of the crowd. It wasn't the distinctive Namath limp. "It was the way he took command," Werblin remembers.

"It was during a timeout. The referee had just whistled time back in. Joe pointed one finger at the Alabama team and the other at the Texas team, to tell them to wait a minute, and then he motioned for the officials and talked to them. I don't know what he said, and I never asked him, but just the way he did it was enough."

That is one fond memory. Sonny Werblin has a lot of them, and a few hurts. One of the hurts is that the Jets are champions of their division for the first time, and Sonny Werblin wasn't there, at the family party in Shea, to drink champagne with his boys.

"Regrets?" said Sonny Werblin when somebody used the word. There was a long pause. This is the time you don't want to say the wrong thing. "No, not really," he said at last. "I made a decision."

"You mean, you couldn't have your cake and eat it." The reference was to $2 million worth of cake.

"I mean I couldn't have peace of mind," said Sonny Werblin, who had to run the Jets his way, without nudging from partners, or get out.

He got out. But first he had something to do.

The Sunday morning papers of May 19 carried the story that Joe Namath had renewed his contract with the Jets for three years, commencing 1969. The Sunday morning papers of May 19 also carried the news, in much bigger type, that Forward Pass (sic) had won the Preakness, and that the Yankees had made a deal for John Wyatt and the Mets had won a ballgame.

It was a strange time to drop in the Namath story. On another day, it would have led the papers. On May 19 it was buried. That didn't seem like Sonny Werblin. He's a better showman that that.

"I had just decided to sell out," says Sonny Werblin. "The whole thing would be wrapped up in a few days. I had signed Namath a long time ago. It suddenly dawned on me why should I let them have the pleasure of announcing it?"

Sonny Werblin had been sitting on the Namath re-signing for eight months. It happened the August before, at a troubled time in Joe Namath's merry life. It was the time he decided to take French Leave from the Jets' camp, and take a small stroll down First Ave. in the small hours. There was an argument with a guy in a bar, and a $500 fine when Joe got back to the base.

"He had a lot of personal things on his mind," Werblin remembers, "family things. People don't realize it, but Joe is very close to his mother and his brothers. Anyway, I figured it was the sort of time he could use a lift in morale. He needed something to happen to him. We were playing an exhibition game in Bridgeport, I remember I said to him, let's sign a new contract. He said whatever you say."

Mike Bite flew up the next day from Alabama and they came to terms. Mike Bite is the attorney who negotiated the famous $400,000 original for Joe. The extension, for the next three years, isn't quite so lavish, but Joe Namath should get along, what with the fringe mink and such.

The new contract calls for the same salary he has received in the first four seasons - $25,000. That doesn't seem like much, but in addition he receives another bonus. "This is a little less than the first one," says Sonny Werblin.

The first bonus consisted of payments of $40,000 a year spread over five years, and deferred till 1969. The new bonus is believed to call for $35,000 a year for an additional three years. Thus, Joe Namath now has eight years of delayed bonus payments coming. He can take them, starting in 1969, or he can hold off till he is through playing, or till he takes on a new tax deduction.

It could happen soon. "He seems to be getting pretty serious with that little blonde he has been going with," said Sonny Werblin. "The one from down South. She's a lovely girl."

Tiptoeing to the Title

by Larry Fox
Daily News

Jet place kicker Jim Turner can climb into the list of pro football's top ten scorers if he doesn't come up with an ingrown toenail Sunday against the Dolphins.

Turner, with three games to play, leads the AFL with 124 points on a pro-record 31 field goals and 31 extra points. In a three-way tie for ninth on the all-time list with 128 points, only a field goal and a PAT away are Gino Capelletti of Boston (1962), Doak Walker of Detroit (1950) and Cookie Gilchrist of Buffalo (1962). All used touchdowns as well as kicking for their totals.

With an exceptionally good day, Turner conceivably could move up to fifth. Capelletti and Gale Sayers of Chicago, both in 1965, are tied for seventh at 132. Gene Mingo of Denver scored 137 points in 1962 for sixth place. Don Hudson of Green Bay scored 138 in 1942 for fifth.

The all-time champ appears out of reach of Turner this season. He's Paul Hornung of Green Bay, who scored a record 176 points in 1960 on 15 touchdowns, 41 PATs and 35 field goals...in only 12 games.

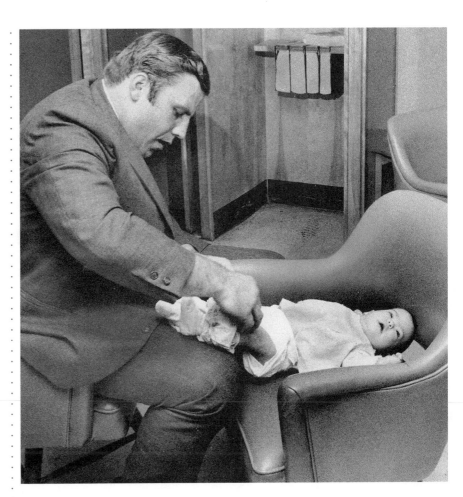

The super guard of the New York Jets, Dave Herman, changes diapers of his six-month-old daughter, Sandra Lynn. (News photo by Dan Farrell)

★ ★ FINAL

DAILY ⚵ NEWS
NEW YORK'S PICTURE NEWSPAPER ®

MORE THAN TWICE
THE CIRCULATION
OF ANY OTHER
PAPER IN AMERICA

84   New York, N.Y. 10017, Monday, December 2, 1968

JETS RIDE DOLPHINS, 35-17
BROWNS CLIP GIANTS, 45-10

—Stories Pages 70, 71

—NEWS photo by Dan Farrell

GRID SCORES

LOCALS

GIANTS	3	0	0	7—10
Cleveland	0	17	21	7—45
Miami	0	10	0	7—17
JETS	0	14	0	21—35

NFL

St. Louis	3	0	0	17—20
Pittsburgh	7	3	0	6—20
Los Angeles	7	10	0	14—31
Minnesota	0	0	0	3—3
Atlanta	0	0	0	0—0
Baltimore	14	14	6	10—44
Chicago	3	13	0	7—23
New Orleans	3	7	0	7—17
Green Bay	7	7	10	0—28
San Fran.	0	7	0	20—27

AFL

Cincinnati	0	0	7	7—14
Boston	3	24	0	6—33
Denver	3	14	6	0—23
San Diego	21	19	0	10—47

Like water running off a duck's back, fullback Larry Csonka of Miami rolls off teammates as he tries to score in second quarter against Jets at Shea. Crowd of 61,766 saw Eastern AFL champ Jets roll to a 35-17 win.

Story on page 70

Nobody's Backing In...

1—In the first quarter, Jets' fullback Matt Snell fumbles a Joe Namath handoff as he's being chased by Dolphins' Manuel Fernandez. Matt grabbed ball, but fumbled before it was recovered by, guess who? Old Fu Manchu, that's who.

2—Matt seems to have recovered, but . . .

3—Joe (12) watches as Fernandez hits and ball pops out . . .

4—And Joe Willie, gimpy legs and all, saves the day.

DECEMBER 1, 1968

New York 35, Miami 17

Miami	0	10	0	7	—	17
New York	0	14	0	21	—	35

Against the Dolphins at Shea Stadium, Jets coach Weeb Ewbank rested several of his regulars. Namath played only the first half before being replaced by Babe Parilli, and Verlon Biggs and Emerson Boozer didn't play at all. The substitutes proved their worth as the Jets scored 21 points in the fourth quarter to come back from a 17-14 deficit and take a 35-17 victory.

Don Maynard caught seven passes in the game for three touchdowns, tying the club record. He also surpassed Raymond Berry to take over first place on the career reception yardage list. His 160 yards in the game gave him a total of 9,332 yards with two regular-season games remaining.

Jets to Rest Biggs, Booz; Namath Starts vs. Dolphs

by Joe O'Day
Daily News

And on the seventh day, coach Weeb Ewbank will rest Verlon Biggs and Emerson Boozer. The student defensive end and equally stickout running back will be grounded tomorrow when the Jets face Miami at Shea stadium in a no-line, non-betting contest.

Verlon Biggs

The pair, of course, have been hurting and now that the Jets have clinched their first Eastern Division title, Ewbank has the luxury of inserting some of his lesser lights. Carl McAdams and Steve Thompson will share Biggs' spot, while Bill Mathis will take over for Boozer.

Joe Namath will start and play at least the first half before giving way to his backup man, Babe Parilli.

Jimmy Hines, a double Gold Medal winner as a sprinter in the recent Olympics at Mexico City, still hasn't been activated by the Dolphins after signing a bonus contract last month. Hines will be on the bench, but not in uniform.

Meanwhile, the Jets announced plans for their first championship game. Season ticket holders will be given the opportunity to purchase their regular locations for the title contest. Authorizing notices will be mailed out next Friday.

Ticket holders will be asked to bring their letters of authorization to Shea Stadium, where the ducats will be placed on sale December 17 through December 22. The ticket windows will be open from 8 a.m. to 7 p.m. daily, with the prices tabbed at $12 for boxes and $10 for reserves.

Under no circumstances will mail orders be accepted.

Standing-room-only tickets will be placed on sale at Shea on December 17. If any tickets are left after the season holders have had their opportunity, the remaining ducats will be available to the public on December 23.

Parilli Prods Jets Over Dolphins in 4th, 35-17

by Larry Fox
Daily News

Just as their pride insisted they do, the Jets did it on their own yesterday setting a team record for victories while beating Miami, 35-17, before 61,766 Shea Stadium fans who awoke with their heroes for a winning fourth-quarter rally.

The Jets had actually clinched their first Eastern Division Championship via Houston's loss to Kansas City on Thanksgiving Day. However, they didn't want to be accused of backing into the long-awaited title, and that was their incentive against the young, hungry Dolphins.

The victory was the Jets' ninth, against only three losses, more than any other New York AFL representative has ever achieved. The previous high was the eight recorded last season

In the first quarter, Jets fullback Matt Snell fumbles a Joe Namath handoff as he's being chased by the Dolphins' Manuel Fernandez. (News photo by Frank Hurley)

and two games remain on the regular schedule.

Joe Namath, as per plan, played only the first half and departed with a 14-10 lead on touchdown passes of 54 yards to Don Maynard and 5 to Pete Lammons.

The Jets then went to sleep in the third quarter and Miami took the lead early in the fourth before Babe Parilli sounded the alarm for the winning rally with three touch-down passes of his own.

Two of the scoring passes—47 and 25 yards—went to Maynard only 42 seconds apart. The third, a 40-yarder, was pulled in by Bake Turner on a dazzling one-handed catch for his first TD since 1965.

Maynard's three touchdowns in one game enabled him to tie the club record held by several players. He pulled in seven passes in all for 160 yards and

Joe Namath's recovery of Matt Snell's first-quarter fumble kept the Jets' drive alive. (News photo by Frank Hurley)

only seven short of the 132 recorded by Cappelletti and Gale Sayers in 1965.

The Jets, as promised, rested several of their aching regulars. Verlon Biggs and Emerson Boozer didn't play and Bill Baird and Namath were given second-half breathers. Larry Grantham started and would have gone most of the way except that he suffered a seven-stitch cut on his finger. A "bumped" knee by tackle Sam Walton was the only other apparent injury.

The crowd appeared to get its biggest kick out of the fine second-half show put on by Parilli, who at 38 and in his 15th pro season, is old enough to have been a teammate of both top Jet assistant coaches, Clive Rish (Green Bay in '58) and Walt Michaels (Cleveland in '58). The Babe, in his most prolonged exposure since he left Boston, completed 10 of 18 for 166 yards and the three TDs.

In contrast, Miami scrambler Bob Griese was a heroic, but battered figure, thrown five times for 46 yards in losses and forced to run with the ball six times for 48 yards.

If the crowd enjoyed Parilli, the feeling was mutual. "Yeah, sure I enjoy playing here with guys who can catch the ball," he glowed, "but these fans are what pick me up. Up there (in Boston) we used to get the opposite, but here they make you feel good."

With two games to go and an upswing finish assured by yesterday's rally, there is no reason for any of the Jets to feel badly. Now they can get themselves healthy and pull for a playoff in the Western Division that would bring their title opponent into Shea Dec. 29, bruised and battered and without benefit of a week's layoff.

that latter figure enabled him to break one of the most prestigious All-Pro records of all time— Raymond Berry's career yardage total on receptions. Berry, who retired last season after playing 13 years, had caught passes for 9,275 yards. Maynard passed him with his second touchdown catch and now has 9,332.

Maynard's total includes 84 yards with the Giants in '58, the rest with New York's AFL franchise. He's 31, in his 11th season and has never been better. Jim

Warren, the man he wiped out Wednesday, is a pretty good corner back and in his fifth pro season.

Maynard wasn't the only Jet to set a record. Jim Turner, who missed field goal attempts from 27 and 51 yards, kicked five extra points that gave him the ninth highest one-year scoring total in pro history.

His 129 total points are one better than Gino Cappelletti (1962), Doak Walker (1950) and Cookie Gilchrist (1962) had posted and, with two games to go, he's

Now Maynard Is Number One

by Phil Pepe
Daily News

There was a time when Don Maynard had trouble holding onto the football when he was running back kickoffs and punts for the Giants.

There was a time when Don Maynard was cut by the Hamilton Tiger Cats because he was an American.

There was a time Don Maynard stood apart from the crowd because he wore No. 13 and long sideburns, but a lot of people wear No. 13 and these days it's the guy without sideburns who stands out in the crowd.

Don Maynard has had this thing about adversity and anonymity, but now Don Maynard stands above the crowd of guys who caught footballs in professional football because of all the guys in all the years the game has been played, nobody has gained more yards catching passes than Don Maynard, No. 13 of the New York Jets. Not Don Hutson and not Bones Taylor and not Elroy Hirsch and not Bill Howton. Nobody.

Yesterday, Maynard wiped out Raymond Berry to stand on top of the heap. He caught seven passes for three touchdowns and 160 yards, giving him 9,332 yards in a career that dates back to 1958.

It began with the Giants a decade ago when Maynard was a jittery kid who heard the boos from the Yankee Stadium crepe hangers. Kyle Rote was there and Frank Gifford, so Maynard caught only five passes all year. Mostly he ran back kicks, until he was tackled, at which time he usually came up without the ball. Don Maynard was not back with the Giants in 1959.

He turned up in Canada, but did not stay there long. "We had a couple of injuries on the club just before the Grey Cup game," Maynard remembers. "They needed a defensive back and an offensive end, so they got one man to play both positions. He was an American. Since they were only allowed a certain number of

Jets Don Maynard settles under a Babe Parilli pass. Maynard's reception gave him 9,332 career yards to break Ray Berry's career mark. (News photo by Frank Hurley)

The Jets' Don Maynard makes a great catch. (News photo by Charles Hoff)

Americans on the squad, they had to drop one. I was the one."

Don Maynard has had a long climb back from adversity. He accepts the knocks philosophically. "I learned a long time ago that you don't measure success by achievements," the Texan drawled. "you measure it by how many times a guy gets knocked down and gets back up. I've been knocked down two or three times."

Down, but not out. If nobody else believed in him, Don Maynard, at least, believed.

"Bobby Layne used to say he was never beat. He just ran out of time."

Time has been Maynard's ally. He was 23 when he joined the New York Titans and in his first year he caught 72 passes for 1,265 yards. And at 31, there are still some good years left to expand his record.

The critics have said that Maynard's success came in a weak league, that he never would have done it in the NFL. At one time, that might have been valid. Now it is not.

"I've played in both leagues and I know the players hit just as hard as they do here."

SWITCH 'HOT' OFFICIAL

Frank Kirkland, the field judge involved in the controversial Jim Hudson ejection at Oakland two weeks ago, yesterday was removed from the team working the Jet-Dolphin game at Shea Stadium, "because we had received some threatening letters," AFL supervisor of officials Mel Hein revealed.

Kirkland was switched to the game in Boston. One other change in officials involved Bob Finley, referee in that Oakland game, subbing for John McDonough, who had the flu. Kirkland was replaced by Bill Summers of Boston's crew. It was Kirkland who called the controversial face-mask penalty against Hudson two weeks ago, then was shown in game movies arguing with the Jet safety before ejecting him.

Hein said any announcement of actions taken on that game "would have to come from the commissioner's office." He said no steps had been taken as far as the officials were concerned. He doubted if anything would, either.

Joe Namath on the field at Shea Stadium. (News photo by Fred Morgan)

"I learned a long time ago that you don't measure success by achievements," the Texan drawled. "You measure it by how many times a guy gets knocked down and gets back up. I've been knocked down two or three times."
—Don Maynard

COLT WATCH COLT WATCH COLT WATCH COLT WATCH

COLTS ROLL, ZIP FALCONS, 44-0

December 2, 1968, Baltimore—Tom Matte scored two touchdowns and John Mackey made a spectacular 41-yard TD run with a swing pass as the Colts defeated the Falcons, 44-0 today.

Earl Morrall completed 17-of-23 for 239 yards and two touchdowns in three quarters. Besides the 41-yard pass to Mackey, he connected on a 34-yard pass to Willie Richardson.

John Unitas, sidelined with a sore elbow almost the entire season, played the whole fourth quarter as coach Don Shula rested the regulars. Unitas directed the Colts on a 56-yard, four-play touchdown drive with rookie Terry Cole going the last six yards around right end. A long pass interference penalty provided the key gain on the drive.

DAILY ☙ NEWS

NEW YORK'S PICTURE NEWSPAPER ®

MORE THAN TWICE
THE CIRCULATION
OF ANY OTHER
PAPER IN AMERICA

80   New York, N.Y. 10017, Monday, December 9, 1968

BROWNS' TITLE; CARDS WIN
5 JETS HURT IN 27-14 WIN

—Stories Pgs. 68, 72

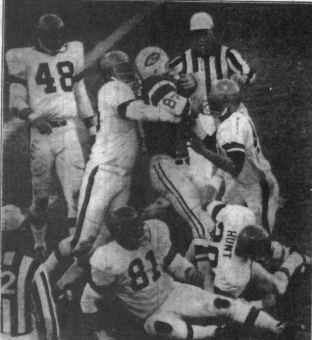

Star-Eyed. Jets' offensive center John Schmitt, named to THE NEWS All-Pro team, greets (l. to r.) linemen Pete Bush, Toms River HS, N.J.; Tom Clarke of Xavier and Jay Cohen, Tilden, at Shea Stadium yesterday. Boys were among 132 NEWS High School All Stars honored in pre-game ceremony. —*Story on page 70*

NEWS photo by Dan Farrell

'Nobody Here but Us Tigers...'

Jets' Pete Lammons catches a Joe Namath pass in the second quarter at Shea Stadium yesterday and then catches it from a pack of man-eating Bengals. Jets beat Cincinnati, 27-14.
Story on page 68

Cooling It At the Garden

Rookie Ranger forward Walt Tkaczuk (18) and Detroit's Pete Stemkowski sprawl behind Ranger net as goalie Ed Giacomin looks over his shoulder at loose disc. Red Wings belted locals, 5-2, as crowd booed. —*Story p. 75*
NEWS photo by Walter Kelleher

Gilbert Ankle Broken; Rangers Beaten, 5-2

Story on Page 75

DECEMBER 8, 1968

New York 27, Cincinnati 14

Cincinnati	0	7	0	7	— 14
New York	14	3	3	7	— 27

Shea Stadium was frozen but the Jets remained hot as they defeated the Cincinnati Bengals 27-14 for their 10th win of the regular season. Namath played the first half of the game before being replaced by Babe Parilli. The switch gave Broadway Joe a chance to rest his famous arm, thumb and knees. The victory did have a darker side, as five Jets—flanker Don Maynard, split end George Sauer, halfback Bill Mathis, and guards Dave Herman and Bob Talamini—sustained injuries during the game. With three weeks remaining before the AFL title game, however, the Jets had time for all their players to recover from all the minor injuries suffered throughout the season.

Not surprisingly, Namath continued to make headlines away from football as he continued to sport his Fu Manchu moustache even after most of his teammates had complied with AFL president Milt Woodard's mandate against facial hair.

Weeb, Paul Still at It 40 Yrs. Later

by Larry Fox
Daily News

Chester Pittser, a spry old gentleman from San Diego, will be looking on Sunday's game between the Jets and Bengals at Shea Stadium with mixed emotions. He's the man who coached the coaches— Paul Brown and Weeb Ewbank—at Miami of Ohio.

While he coached Ewbank a little bit earlier, he might be excused for giving long distance moral support to Brown. After all, the Jets already have their division title clinched while Cincinnati, in its final game of the season, needs a victory to set an all-time expansion club first-year record of four.

And, although both Brown and Ewbank have turned the corner past 60, it's beginning to look as if Mr. Pittser will be faced with the same dilemma next year, too.

In other words, Brown definitely and Ewbank quite possibly will be coaching again in 1969.

Both men, quarterbacks at Miami on the same squad more than 40 years ago, also hold the

Weeb Ewbank. (News photo by Dan Farrell)

title of general manager. However, as the season draws to a close, neither seems anxious to step up to the rocking chair.

Brown, in fact, has told intimates he intends to coach at least another year.

"I'm living again," he says.

Ewbank and Jet president Phil Iselin were braced about the little coach's future yesterday. "Weeb's contract expires February 1 and we have decided to put off all future discussions until after the excitement has died down," Iselin said. "But you can say we feel he's doing an outstanding job."

Ewbank agreed that he owes it to the team to concentrate completely on the rest of the season, hopefully through the Super Bowl January 12.

"But I haven't given any thought to retirement," he said, "and the only man I know who's quit coaching just to be a general manager (Vince Lombardi) is going crazy."

TWO TOPS JETS

December 7, 1968—Defensive end Gerry Philbin and placekicker Jim Turner have been named co-winners of the Jet Parking and Chowder Society's second annual MVP award, club president Don Phelan announced yesterday. Last year's winner was Emerson Boozer.

The club has 525 members, who meet regularly for tailgate parties in the Shea Stadium parking lot before home games. They will cut two big victory cakes in honor of the Jets' Eastern Division championship before tomorrow's game with Cincinnati.

BIGGS' LOSS . . .

December 6, 1968—While the Jets' practice at Shea yesterday was disrupted by a snowfall, Verlon Biggs' contract talk with Weeb Ewbank was kayoed by car thieves. Biggs had to call off his scheduled discussion with his boss over his unsigned '68 pact when he learned his car had been stolen from his home in Flushing.

A snowfall forced the Jets to abandon yesterday's defensive drill after a half hour, an hour less than planned. This delayed their first offensive practice of the week until today.

Jets Land 6 on News All–AFL Team

by Joe O'Day
Daily News

It was a most rewarding year for the Jets, who won their first Eastern Division championship. It was reflected in the balloting for *The News* eighth annual American Football League All-Pro teams, too, as a panel of sportswriters and sportscasters, representing the 10 cities in the league, tabbed six Jets for individual honors.

Quarterback Joe Namath led the Jet set on the offensive unit along with wide receiver Don Maynard and pivotman John Schmitt. End Gerry Philbin paced the defensive vanguard that included tackle John Elliott and Jim Hudson, the strong-side safety.

There were 10 holdovers—four on offense and six on defense. Mix, Sweeney, Alworth and Namath are the repeaters on offense. Philbin, Buchanan, Bell, Webster, Farr and Saimes again were named to the defensive unit.

Schuh, Budde, Maynard, Dixon and Connors—all second-team selectees a year ago—moved up to the first unit, while wide receiver George Sauer of the Jets, center Jim Otto of the Raiders and Jets' guard Dave Herman slipped to the offensive second-team this season. Defensive back Kent McCloughan of the Raiders also fell back to the second squad.

Overall, the Eastern Division outpolled the Western Division, 12-10. A year ago it was the opposite, but the Jets made the difference this season.

Here's how the Jets' All-Pro players shaped up in the AFL's ninth year of operation.

Maynard: One of Namath's favorite targets, this rangy NFL castoff broke Colt Ray Berry's all-

WEEB'S NO. 1

Weeb Ewbank is *The News* AFL Coach of the Year. He beat out a former boss, Paul Brown of the Bengals, for the honor as he coached the Jets to their first divisional title. Ewbank coached Baltimore to two NFL championships in 1958 and '59. He came here and instituted a five-year plan for a title team, but key injuries delayed it till this season—his sixth with the Jets. Ewbank aided in the development of Joe Namath, Matt Snell, Emerson Boozer, Gerry Philbin, George Sauer Jr., John Elliott, Jim Harris, Dave Herman, Winston Hill and Jim Hudson, the nucleus of this year's team.

time yardage total by pass receptions only last Sunday against the Dolphins. Possesses great hands and speed to move with ball. So far this season he has grabbed 52 passes for 1,194 yards and nine TDs.

Schmitt: A taxi-squad man for two years, this five-year veteran from Hofstra has been the regular center for two seasons now. A hard worker, who is excellent on pass protection and cutting down the middle line-backer.

Namath: Joe Willie didn't pass for 4,000 yards this year and was intercepted along the way but he still piloted the Jets to their first title. Has that quick release and has developed into a great play caller. Has completed 168 passes for 2,834 yards and 13 TDs so far this year.

Philbin: Played in shadow of Verlon Biggs but is the acknowledged leader of Jets' rushline. Has good pursuit, speed and is a deadly tackler. Another hard worker who is always trying to improve himself.

Elliott: The hard-nosed type, who played linebacker, defensive end and tackle as rookie last season. Won tackle berth late in season and has that quickness to be solid pro for years to come.

Hudson: Underrated strong-side safety. Is hard hitter and sure tackler with good speed.

Well, that's the AFL team for another year. It's a team composed of some perennials but the new faces are gradually working their way to stardom, which is a testimonial to the league's development and maturity.

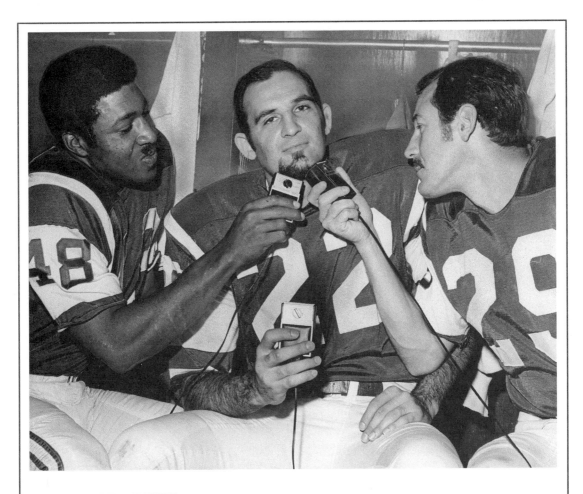

TAKE IT OFF!

December 9, 1968—AFL president Milt Woodard has written the Jets ordering them to cut out the beards, mustaches and long sideburns. Most had already complied and Verlon Biggs, who has a short but full beard, says he'll get out the razor "this weekend."

Joe (Fu Manchu) Namath, however, said "not just yet" to club officials. Biggs, incidentally, is still unsigned and gives no impression that he intends to any time soon.

COLT WATCH COLT WATCH COLT WATCH COLT WATCH COLT WATCH COLT WATCH COLT

COLTS TOTTER PACKERS AT BRINK, 16-3

December 8, 1968, Green Bay, Wisconsin—The Colts' brilliant defense converted three fumbles into 13 points today for a 16-3 victory that virtually ended the Packers' hopes for another NFL Central Division crown. The victory gave Baltimore a full-game lead at least for a day over the Rams in the Coastal Division.

Five Jets Sidelined by Injuries in 27-14 Win Over Bengals

by Larry Fox
Daily News

The Jets maintained their momentum with a 27-14 victory over Cincinnati in frozen Shea Stadium yesterday, but paid the price in injuries to both their wide receivers, both starting guards and halfback Bill Mathis.

The most serious was a pulled left hamstring by flanker Don Maynard on the second play of the last quarter. Three plays later, George Sauer, the split end, went out with a strained right elbow. The injured guards were Dave Herman, who suffered a strained ankle, and Bob Talamini, who hurt his neck. Mathis aggravated a bruised shoulder early in the second quarter.

All, however, have three weeks to recover before the championship game here December 29, and the team physician, Dr. Jim Nicholas, said flatly: "I see nobody who won't be in shape for that one."

Maynard revealed he pulled his right hamstring two weeks ago in San Diego and that this latest injury was "about the same." He didn't miss any games because of the earlier hurt, but probably will

be held out of next week's regular season finale at Miami.

Except for Maynard, all will probably play in Miami.

Joe Namath, as advertised, played only the first half and departed with a 17-7 lead that included touchdown passes of 10 yards to Sauer and 12 to Maynard.

Babe Parilli finished up and threw a 34-yard scoring pass to Bake Turner, who now has caught two TDs in as many weeks after being blanked for three years. At least that should give the country-and-western singer something to talk about when he and Maynard appear on the Johnny Carson show Tuesday night.

The most dramatic moments of the game occurred at the end of the third quarter. Curley Johnson was back to punt from his 48, the kick was blocked by Cincy's Bob Kelly and recovered by Bill Peterson, who ran it 38 yards to the Jet 2.

Here is when Jet pride asserted itself, starting with Matt Snell's extra-point tackle that kept Peterson from going over right there. Four times Cincinnati

smashed into the line from the two and four times they were held in a goal-line stand right out of Joe College.

"They showed what they were made of on that stand," Weeb Ewbank glowed, and it didn't matter a bit that on the very next play Parilli fumbled and defensive end Jim Griffin recovered in the end zone for the easy TD.

The crowd was announced as 61,111, but only a handful remained to the finish. The Jets made only one major adjustment for the cold as equipment manager Bill Hampton had a big pocket sewn onto the front of the jersey of each ballhandler. His wife, Dorothea, was going to do it, but at the last minute he found "a real tailor."

The Jet most bothered by the cold was Jim Turner, who kicked two field goals to expand his pro record to 33, and three conversions for a season total of 138 points. With that figure, he ties Don Hutson of Green Bay (1942) for the fifth highest one-year effort in pro history. A warming thought.

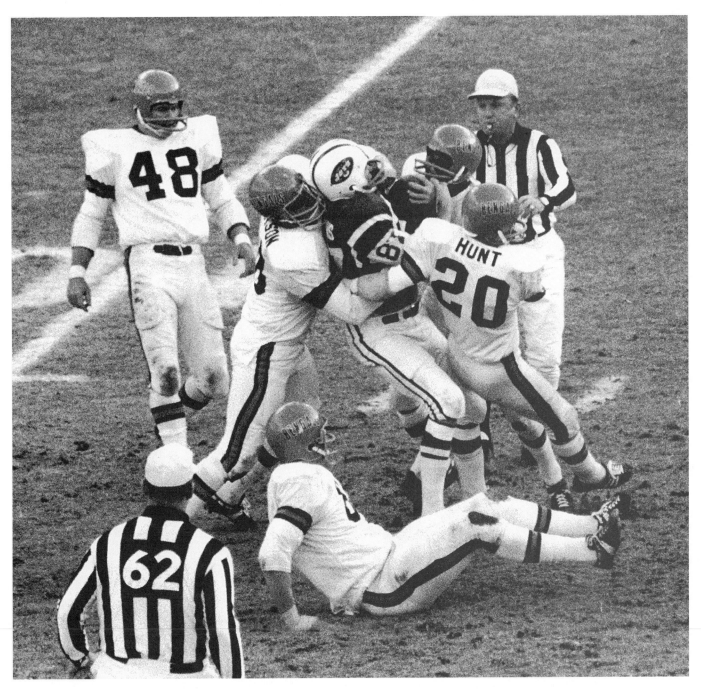

Jets' Pete Lammons catches a Joe Namath pass in the second quarter at Shea Stadium yesterday and then catches it from a pack of man-eating Bengals. (News photo by Dan Farrell)

COLT WATCH COLT WATCH COLT WATCH COLT WATCH COLT WATCH COLT WATCH COLT

COLTS COAST HOME: BEARS KO RAMS, 49ERS FALL

December 9, 1968, Los Angeles—The Bears knocked Los Angeles out of the NFL championship picture, 17-16, today as the Rams were shortchanged one badly needed down in the frantic final minute.

It was discovered that Los Angeles, desperately trying to pull the game out but penalized from the Chicago 32 to its own 47 by a holding penalty, was allowed only three downs on its final series.

The setback gave Baltimore the NFL's Coastal Division crown.

DAILY NEWS
NEW YORK'S PICTURE NEWSPAPER ®

MORE THAN TWICE
THE CIRCULATION
OF ANY OTHER
PAPER IN AMERICA

28   New York, N.Y. 10017, Monday, December 16, 1968

BEARS BOW, VIKINGS CHAMP
JETS ROMP; GIANTS LOSE

Stories Pages 22, 23

Ex-Heavy Champ Jess Willard, 86, Dead

In one of the most controversial bouts in boxing history, Willard stood over a KO-ed Jack Johnson in Havana, Cuba, April 5, 1915.

In prime, "Pottawatomie Giant" was 6'6" and 250 pounds.

Willard on his 85th birthday, Dec. 29, 1967.

'Great White Hope' Loses Last Fight

He was big, he was tough and he was billed as the "Great White Hope" who'd wrest the heavyweight title back from a Negro, Jack Johnson. Yesterday, white-haired and 86, Jess Willard died in Los Angeles of a cerebral hemorrhage. He rose to boxing's heights on a hot day in Cuba, April 5, 1915, when he dethroned Johnson in what is still a questionable fight. Some say Johnson, as he lay on the canvas, shielded his eyes from the sun. The records say Jess fought his last fight at the age of 41. Not so. His last fight, after much illness, was lost yesterday.

Story on page 26

GRID SCORES

NFL

Dallas	0	7	14	7—28
Giants	3	0	0	7—10
Minnesota	0	7	7	10—24
Philadelphia	0	7	3	7—17
Detroit	0	0	3	0— 3
Washington	0	0	0	14—14
San Fran.	0	7	0	7—14
Atlanta	0	0	0	12—12

Pittsburgh	7	0	0	7—14
New Orleans	7	14	0	3—24
Green Bay	7	14	7	0—28
Chicago	10	0	0	17—27
Baltimore	14	0		
Los Angeles	7	0		—

AFL

JETS	10	3	7	7—31
Miami	0	7	0	0— 7
Boston	0	7		
Houston	3	14		
Oakland	3	0		
San Diego	3	10		

DECEMBER 15, 1968

New York 31, Miami 7

New York	10	7	7	7	—	31
Miami	0	7	0	0	—	7

In the last week of the regular season, the Jets' game in Miami took a backseat to the happenings off the field, as an endorsement fee succeeded where AFL president Milt Woodard had failed. Four days before the game, Joe Namath shaved off his trademark Fu Manchu mustache for a electric razor commercial. Namath told the press he liked his mustache, but "knew it had to come off sometime."

Even with many of their recent "walking wounded" watching from the bench, the Jets had no trouble with the Dolphins. Their 31-7 victory was their 11th of the season and their eighth in their last nine games. Jim Turner kicked a field goal and four extra points and ended the regular season with 145 points, making him the AFL scoring champion.

Namath Says Farewell to Fu Manchu

by Larry Fox
Daily News

Joe Namath had better watch out in Miami Sunday—his upper lip could get sun-burned. Yes, Virginia, Fu Manchu Joe has shaved off his mustache.

However, he insists that a recent league edict ordering the Jets to trim their "sideburns, beards and mustaches" had nothing to do with his decision. In fact, the motivation was a lot more basic, like the fee for doing an electric razor commercial yester-day morning.

Namath would not reveal the company, nor the fee, but it was learned that his agent had been asking companies for $10,000 for the privilege of recording Joe's historic shave with their product.

The Jets' beard-and-mus-tache kick started after the upset loss to Denver October 13. Many of the players vowed not to shave them off until the club clinched the Eastern Division champion-ship, which happened on Thanks-giving Day.

Several of the Jets had fallen by the wayside early, like George Sauer, whose blond beard didn't show up, and Paul Rochester, who claimed his beard made him look like Burl Ives. But, the week after Thanksgiving, Bake Turner, Jim Hudson and Cornell Gordon trimmed their facial hair for a publicity still photograph that was widely reprinted.

For their efforts they received $250 each, and the razor. They took their shave for a different

Joe Namath has former teammate John Dockery in a lather. (News photo by Gene Kappock)

company than the one that signed Namath.

About the time of the mass barbering, AFL president Milt Woodard composed his letter to the Jets, suggesting they do what they already had done. Aside from Namath, the only Jet still with extra facial hair was Verlon Biggs, the unsigned end. Verlon shaved off his goatee, but not his mustache, this week.

But he added that he didn't like a lot of what had been said about his mustache and especially "what the league said about it."

"After all," he added, "Who's to say where long sideburns began?"

Namath said he liked his mustache, "but I knew it had to come off sometime." And what better time than when there's a pen and a checkbook handy?

There was no report on whether he had received any inducement to shave and Jet fans wondered whether Ben Davidson, if Oakland wins the Western Division title, will be allowed to play for the championship with his famous handlebars.

Namath said negotiations for his historic shave began soon after the beard stories were printed. "No, the league didn't 'crack down' on me," Namath said before yesterday's workout. "I don't feel it was any of their business. And I feel it's the personal business of any other player.

"I don't understand why hair all of a sudden became bad. Things come in and they go. After all, the most perfect guy in the world had long hair and a beard."

Namath said he took some kidding from his teammates when he showed up with a bare lip. "Yeah, I can scramble a little better now, I'm lighter," he cracked.

AFL STANDINGS
Eastern Division

	W.	L.	T.	PF	PA
Jets	11	3	0	419	280
Houston	7	7	0	303	248
Miami	5	8	1	176	355
Boston	4	10	0	229	406
Buffalo	1	12	1	199	367

Western Division

	W.	L.	T.	PF	PA
Kansas City	12	2	0	371	170
Oakland	12	2	0	453	233
San Diego	9	5	0	382	310
Denver	5	9	0	255	404
Cincinnati	3	11	0	215	329

NFL STANDINGS
Eastern Conference
(Capitol Division)

	W.	L.	T.	PF	PA
Dallas	12	2	0	431	186
Giants	7	7	0	294	327
Washington	5	9	0	249	358
Philadelphia	2	12	0	202	351

(Century Division)

	W.	L.	T.	PF	PA
Cleveland	10	4	0	394	273
St. Louis	9	4	1	325	289
New Orleans	4	9	1	246	327
Pittsburgh	2	11	1	244	397

Western Conference
(Central Division)

	W.	L.	T.	PF	PA
Minnesota	8	6	0	282	242
Chicago	7	7	0	250	343
Green Bay	6	7	1	281	227
Detroit	4	8	2	207	241

(Coastal Division)

	W.	L.	T.	PF	PA
Baltimore	13	1	0	402	144
Los Angeles	10	3	1	312	200
San Francisco	7	6	1	303	310
Atlanta	2	12	0	170	389

SUPER CHARGE

December 10, 1968—Jet players say they have an extra incentive for getting into the Super Bowl—and winning it—this year.

They reveal that next year the $14,000-$7,500 split for winners and losers will be changed to $13,000-$10,000. Narrowing of the spread was reported at the request of the respective player associations.

Ward to the Wise

by Gene Ward
Daily News

NBC has its Super Bowl commercial spots completely sold, with Chrysler, TCA, TWA and Phillips Petroleum as the prime sponsors. The open-rate charge is $135,000 per minute, with discounts to those who have been involved in the overall pro football package.

And don't put the knock on commercials. Under the code, the network could cram from 25 to 30 into the telecast from the Orange Bowl, January 12, but it's holding the line at 18.

Speaking of televised football, there must be some way to blame CBS for the goof that deprived the Rams of that fourth down. As a matter of fact, another clock-stopping completion by Roman Gabriel at that point would have forced the network to pre-empt the start of "Lassie" or give the game the "Heidi" treatment.

As it was, CBS did an abrupt cut from the final gun to "Lassie" and just made it, which reminded me of Bob Cochrane's shaggy dog story. This was a few years back, when Pete Rozelle's lieutenant in charge of TV was working for CBS and had helped put together the $50,000 Sahara Gold Classic. Came the final round and the final green, with Jack Nicklaus putting for first money and time running out on the network.

"Jack stroked the putt beautifully," Bob Cochrane said, "but somebody pulled the network switch and the ball disappeared right into Lassie's mouth."

If I were Weeb Ewbank I'd wrap Don Maynard and George Sauer Jr. in cotton batting next Sunday in Miami and order them to spend the afternoon at the Palm Bay Club pool with the PB's most prominent member, Joe Namath.

Hofstra's John Schmitt, who has hit the top this year as the Jets' all-AFL center, tells this little story on himself:

"Dr. Jim Nichols, who operated on my knee, was congratulating Joe Namath, Don Maynard, Gerry Philbin, John Elliott and Jim Hudson on making *The News* All-Star team. Then he came to me, "I don't know how you made it, John, with no talent and that bad knee!"

COLT WATCH COLT WATCH COLT WATCH COLT WATCH COLT WATCH COLT WATCH COLT

EARL HEADS 5 COLTS ON NEWS ALL-NFL

by Joe O'Day

December 15, 1968—Take portions of Cinderella and the Ugly Duckling and you have Earl Morrall. The veteran 34-year-old quarterback was at the top of his game this season and the modern day rags-to-riches saga just had to be reflected in *The News* 32nd annual All-NFL teams.

The well-traveled Morrall, who did the pots and pans in stints in San Francisco, Pittsburgh, Detroit and even with the Giants, was anything but a surprise choice in the coast-to-coast poll of sportswriters and sportscasters. The aging passer filled in for ailing Johnny Unitas and took the Colts to the Coastal championship to easily outdistance Roman Gabriel of the Rams for signal-calling honors.

The Colts, of course, dominated the balloting with five players being named to the teams, while the Cowboys, the Capitol Division champs, were represented by two players. The San Francisco 49ers, Cleveland Browns, Minnesota Vikings, Los Angeles Rams and Green Bay Packers had two players each on the platoons. The Atlanta Falcons, St. Louis Cardinals and Detroit Lions each had one player on a unit.

Jets End Best Year (11-3); Hose Down Dolphins, 31-7

by Larry Fox
Daily News

Miami—The Jets kept both their momentum and their health today, closing out their most successful regular season with an effortless 31-7 victory over the Dolphins as most of the Eastern Division champ's recent casualties watched from the bench.

Next date for the Jets is the AFL championship game at Shea Stadium December 29 and they should have everyone ready for that one.

One thing is certain, however. The Jets won't be able to practice against pet plays of the Raiders or Chiefs with any degree of certainty for a week. That's because KC and Oakland have gotten themselves involved in a playoff next Sunday for the Western Division title.

Today's victory, achieved before only 32,843 in the wind-blown Orange Bowl, was the Jets'

Weeb Ewbank (l.) and Joe Namath. (News photo by Dan Farrell)

eighth in their last nine games and 11th of the season. Only one other Eastern Division team, Buffalo with 12 in 1964, has won more.

By winning their last four,

the Jets tied their club record for consecutive victories for the second time this season.

Jim Turner, who kicked a 49-yard field goal and four extra points for a total of seven, ended the regular season as the AFL's scoring champion with 145 points. That's the fifth best single-season point effort in pro history and by far the highest by a "pure" kicker.

Sauer, who came in as the AFL's leading pass receiver with 64 catches to 63 by San Diego's Lance Alworth, did not have a big day and pulled in only two for 14 yards.

Snell started today as the AFL's sixth leading rusher with 738 yards, but he went out with only nine more on two first-half carries.

One of today's objects was to get Emerson Boozer sharp and the post-operative halfback, who hadn't played in two weeks with a bad ankle, enjoyed a busy day. He carried the ball 17 times for 83 yards, his highest total of the season, and scored once from the one.

Ewbank had said his game plan also called for the unveiling of another trick play to confound the scouts of his title game opponent. And on the first play from scrimmage he did it—the old flea flicker.

Namath handed off to Snell on an apparent draw, but, after taking a couple of steps toward the line, the fullback lateralled back to Namath, who threw to Bake Turner all alone for a 71-yard gain to the Dolphin nine.

Snell covered the remaining distance on two plunges for his only carries of the day and that was just about the game. Miami didn't score until the last two minutes of the half when the Jets held a 17-0 lead.

Joe Namath and Bake Turner at LaGuardia Airport as the Jets prepare to leave for Miami. (News photo by Charles Payne)

Jets' MVP

Miami, Dec. 15 (Special)—In his fourth year as director of their offense, Joe Namath today was honored as official leader of the Jets when his teammates elected him MVP for the 1968 season. Namath received his "First Down" award from the NEA News Service at half-time in the Orange Bowl after he had led the Eastern Division champ Jets to a 17-7 lead.

COLT WATCH COLT WATCH COLT WATCH COLT WATCH COLT WATCH COLT WATCH COLT

RAMS CLIPPED BY COLTS, 28-24

December 16, 1968—Johnny Unitas, sidelined most of the season with a bad arm, returned to action today and threw one touchdown pass and engineered a 52-yard drive for another score to give the Colts a 28-24 victory over the Rams.

The Colts, who sewed up the NFL Coastal Division title last weekend, finished the regular season with a 13-1 record and now go on to play Minnesota for the Western Conference championship.

Jets Don't Care Who Wins

by Norm Miller
Daily News

Raiders or Chiefs? For which club will the Jets be rooting this weekend as they look beyond tomorrow's game against the Dolphins to the December 29 AFL title playoff? Would they be more charged-up for a grudge battle with the Raiders? Do they feel the Chiefs have more exploitable weaknesses?

The Oakland grudge theory, based on the beating Joe Namath took from the Raiders in '67 and this year's "Heidi" game that was heisted in the final minute, makes for interesting conversation. But it's nonsense, Paul Rochester, the old-pro defensive tackle, insisted yesterday.

And as for any preference of opponent, there is not much to choose between the two rivals, a survey of key Jets disclosed. The Chiefs may have an edge on offense; the Raiders may have certain phases of defensive superiority. But that's about it.

"We don't want to bring up grudges," Rochester said. "As pros, we try to minimize that. The main thing is for the club to be fundamentally sound. If you lose your temper, you just hurt yourself and the ballclub.

Rochester and Larry Grantham, the defensive captain, sized up the Oakland and Kaycee offenses.

"The Chiefs are a power team," Grantham stressed. "They grind it out. They try to beat you with ball-control. Their first down is very important. It's best to put them in a position where you know they have to throw the ball. Stop their first down and leave them with second and long yardage to make."

"The Raiders are a big-play team," Rochester put in. "They have a more diverse offense. They throw longer passes. Usually they don't throw to their backs, but they did against us in the last game, which showed they scouted us pretty well and were pretty smart about it."

Rochester was asked about the offensive lines.

"I don't think Oakland's line is as good as Kansas City's," he replied. "I think we might get to the Oakland passer more. But any difference there would be minute."

Matt Snell was asked to size up the front-line defenses from the standpoint of the running backs.

"The Raiders are quicker in the defensive line," he appraised. "They are more agile. The Chiefs are less mobile but their linebackers are more agile and fluid.

"Bobby Bell and Jim Lynch are outstanding," Snell said. "They are extremely good blitzers and very tough against the run. And

that Willie Lanier in the middle; he's a tough head-hunter.

"You can outrun those outside linebackers on passes," Snell added. "That Bell, he might be faster than Booz (Emerson Boozer) and myself."

Maynard was asked to compare the rival defensive backs. The key man, he pointed out, was Oakland's Kent McCloughan, one of the AFL's top cornerbacks who has been out with an injury.

"If McCloughan is back, that gives the Raiders four men who have been together a long while," Maynard said.

"The Chiefs lost a good man when they let Bobby Hunt go in the expansion draft. I don't think they have the relationship of playing together like the Raiders backs do."

The styles of defense are similar on both clubs, he added. Both stress man-for-man coverage, with very little zone.

Snell minimized the Jets' commonly accepted home field advantage.

"They say the home advantage is worth a touchdown," he said, "but in this case, I don't think so. In a championship game, everybody is so high that anything that might normally be an advantage is nullified."

FINAL

DAILY NEWS
NEW YORK'S PICTURE NEWSPAPER ®

MORE THAN TWICE
THE CIRCULATION
OF ANY OTHER
PAPER IN AMERICA

100   New York, N.Y. 10017, Tuesday, December 17, 1968

JETS RANK 1ST IN DEFENSE

Story on Page 86

Associated Press Wirephoto

Clay Before The Bars of Justice...

Former heavyweight champion Cassius Clay pats the bars of the door to the Dade County (Florida) Jail yesterday as he enters building with attorney Henry Arrington. Clay is serving a 10-day sentence on an old traffic charge. "This will be conditioning for me," he said, alluding to the possibility he might have to serve 5 years for avoiding the draft.

← Two for The Money

Quarterbacks Earl Morrall (left) and Johnny Unitas of the Colts take time out from a practice session in Baltimore, as they look toward Sunday's Western NFL championship game against the Vikings. Game will be played in Baltimore. Morrall, acquired at start of year from Giants as a backup for Unitas, led Colts to 13-1 season after Johnny suffered elbow ailment. —Story p. 89

UPI photo

News photo by Dan Farrell

As the regular season ended and playoff preparation began, eight Jets were voted onto the starting squad for the East in the AFL's annual All-Star game. Joe Namath, Don Maynard, Gerry Philbin, George Sauer, Verlon Biggs, Dave Herman, Winston Hill and Jim Turner were all voted onto the first team by the division's coaches. Matt Snell, Emerson Boozer, Pete Lammons, Bob Talamini, John Elliott, Ralph Baker, Al Atkinson, Larry Grantham, Jim Hudson and Billy Baird were honored as runners-up.

The Jets' defense finished No. 1 in total defense and rushing defense in the AFL, and second in pass defense. The statistics gave the defense something to talk about, as the prominent Jets offensive unit finished only third in the league in total offense.

Oft-Maligned Jets' Defense Is Only the Tops in AFL

by Larry Fox
Daily News

George Sauer

Minutes after the Jets' charter touched down at LaGuardia on the flight from Miami Sunday night, linebacker Larry Grantham rushed to a newsstand. He bought a paper, checked how much yardage Houston had given up against Boston and shook defensive coach Walt Michaels' hand.

"We did it, Walt. We're No. 1," he declared and yesterday the final AFL statistics confirmed that the Jets did it with defense when they won the Eastern Division championship.

Much maligned through the years, many times unjustly, the Jet defensive platoon was superb this season. And, after the Eastern title was clinched with three games to go, pride continued to drive the defenders in their bid to wind up No. 1.

They did it, too—No. 1 in total defense and rushing defense,

plus second in pass defense with a fine last-game effort against the Dolphins that enabled them to move past Buffalo to a spot behind Houston.

Houston was second in total defense by only 12 yards overall while Kansas City was the runner-up in rushing defense by 71 yards over a 14-game season.

While the Jets were only third in total offense, the blockers could claim one major honor— they led the league in protecting the passer.

Jet QBs were dumped only 18 times for 135 yards in losses. Charger QBs were thrown 18 times also, but for 190 yards.

Individually, the top Jet was Jim Turner, who led the league in scoring with 145 points, highest in pro history, just by kicking. His 34 field goals also established a pro record. Curley Johnson tied for second in punting, Johnny Sample tied for third with seven interceptions and Matt Snell was sixth in rushing.

George Sauer, who caught only two of five passes aimed at him Sunday, was beaten out on the last day by Lance Alworth for

the pass receiving title.

Sauer went into the final day leading his Charger rival by one and ended up second by two, 68 to 66. The Jet split end had won the title last year. Don Maynard, who didn't dress Sunday because of an injury, was fifth with 57 catches. However, he was tops in yards-per-catch.

Joe Namath finished third in passing to Len Dawson and Daryle Lamonica, according to the AFL's rating formula but, significantly, saw his interceptions drop from 28 last year to 17. He didn't pass nearly as much this season and all his total figures were down, but so was his interception percentage, from 5.7 to 4.5.

Down the stretch, Namath was the perfectly controlled passer. He was intercepted 12 times in the Jets' first five games, but only five times in the last nine, of which the Jets won eight. In the last five games after his 0-for-6 TD drought, he completed seven touchdown passes and was intercepted only twice.

A quarterback who came of age . . . and a defense that did the same . . . the ingredients of a championship.

by Norm Miller
Daily News

December 18, 1968—Pro football's three league playoffs this weekend will be fought out by basically healthy ballclubs with prospects of seasonally good weather at sold-out ballparks in Cleveland, Baltimore and Oakland, a canvas by *The News* indicated yesterday.

The Jets, while awaiting the outcome at Oakland to determine their December 29 title opponent, reported the first day of their ticket distribution went off smoothly. About 2,500 available standing-room tickets were sold in two hours, and by nightfall, more than 20% of the reserved seats had been claimed by regular-season subscribers.

First in line when the standing-room window opened were six youngsters who had camped there since 9 p.m. Monday night.

WARD TO THE WISE

by Gene Ward
Daily News

December 18, 1968—Speaking at the Long Island Athletic Club smoker Monday night at Hofstra's University Club, Giants' Bob Lurtsema handed the Jets a left-handed pat on the head with the remark: "We're going to start off the 1969 season on the right foot, August 17, by beating the Super Bowl champs." That's the date the Giants take on the Jets in Yale Bowl.

Jim Turner. (Daily News photo)

Eight Jets Voted Starting Jobs For AFL's All-Star Game

by Larry Fox
Daily News

Eight Jets, including Joe Namath, Don Maynard and Gerry Philbin, yesterday were voted East squad starting berths for the AFL's annual All-Star Game against the West at Jacksonville, January 19, by the league coaches.

The five others selected to the coaches' All-Star first team were George Sauer, Verlon Biggs, Dave Herman, Winston Hill, and kicker Jim Turner.

This represented the highest number of Jet players so honored. Last year they had five East starters in the All-Star Game and two others chosen as fill-ins.

Since 10 other of the Jets' 1968 Eastern champs finished second in the coaches' balloting for positions, a few more are expected to be added for the star show at Jacksonville.

The Jet runners-up in the voting were Matt Snell, Emerson Boozer, Pete Lammons and Bob Talamini on offense; and John Elliott, Ralph Baker, Al Atkinson, Larry Grantham, Jim Hudson and Billy Baird on defense.

With a limit of 11 players from any one team for each 33-man squad, not more than three of these Jets can be added as All-Star reserves.

This will be the third All-Star participation for Namath, Maynard, Sauer, Biggs and Hill;

the first for Turner, Herman and Philbin, whose omission last season drew beefs from the Jets.

The starting All-Star squads are voted by the coaches in each division. No coach can vote for a man on his own team.

While the coaches of the All-Star teams have not yet been announced, it was expected that Wally Lemm of the Oilers would direct the East.

Jets with time on their hands are (l. to r.) place kicker Jim Turner, head coach Weeb Ewbank, and flanker Don Maynard. The timepieces were gifts of team management. (News photo by Bill Meurer)

Weeb Has Rooting Interest in Playoffs— NFL

by Larry Fox
Daily News

Weeb Ewbank will be watching three football games on television this weekend and he'll have a sentimental choice in two of them. Saturday, Cleveland, where he served several years as an assistant under Paul Brown, plays Dallas for the NFL's Eastern Conference championship. Sunday, it's Baltimore, where Weeb won two league titles as head man, against Minnesota for Western honors.

The only game in which Weeb insists he has no preference is Kansas City at Oakland for the AFL Western crown also on Sunday.

Ewbank will have tactical reasons as well as personal for looking forward to a possible meeting with the Browns in the Super Bowl. Cleveland has the NFL's leading ground gainer, Leroy Kelly, and Weeb has a pipeline to the one coach who has been able to handle Kelly, Charlie Winner of the Cardinals.

Coaches regularly exchange information, but Winner is Weeb's son-in-law—and former Baltimore assistant—and that should provide some conflict with his NFL loyalties.

Ewbank and his staff will limit their weekend scouting to television, confident that the exchange of movies will tell them more than enough about any future playoff opponents. Rules call for the exchange of several recent films and coaches usually can pick up the others from friendly colleagues for a full season set.

The only eyewitness Jet scouting this weekend will involve the use of a part-time agent at the Kansas City-Oakland game to watch personnel. If a player leaves the game, the Jets want to know if he was limping—and on which leg.

The Jets played Oakland late in the season, but haven't met Kansas City since the opener.

However, the Chiefs have popped up on movies against recent Jet opponents and Ewbank is not concerned over the lag.

"As a matter of fact, Kansas City is playing now the way they did at the beginning," he pointed out. "When we played them they didn't have anybody hurt, and now everybody is well again. The only big difference is that they've uncovered Bob Holmes as a good running back, but, then, we always had a lot of respect for Curtis McClinton."

Incidentally, if the Cowboys, as expected, should knock off the Browns Saturday, the Jets won't exactly be caught short if they go on to the Super Bowl and meet Dallas. "We had a man watching Dallas against the Giants last Sunday…just two bring us up to date," the little coach revealed.

FINAL

DAILY NEWS
NEW YORK'S PICTURE NEWSPAPER ®

MORE THAN TWICE
THE CIRCULATION
OF ANY OTHER
PAPER IN AMERICA

28

New York, N.Y. 10017, Thursday, December 19, 1968

JETS READY FOR TITLE FOE

— Story on Page 23

UPI Telephoto

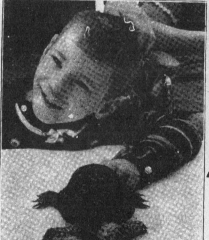

NEWS photo by Joe Petrella

Cold, Calculating

Planning a flurry of punches for Frankie DePaula, Bob Foster shivers as he does roadwork at Spring Valley, N.Y. Foster, the light-heavyweight champ, will have a chance to defend his title against Frankie at Madison Square Garden Jan. 22.

Thinking About Knocking Heads

Onetime bastion of the Giant defense, Dick Modzelewski, presently defensive coach of the Browns, shows members of his platoon a little of what he has in mind for the Cowboys. The Browns tackle the Cowboys for Eastern Division NFL championship in Cleveland Saturday.

← 'Isn't That A Shell of Note?'

Smitty the turtle delights Mark Besterman at the Institute of Rehabilitation Medicine, 400 E. 34th St., where ASPCA put on animal show for handicapped children yesterday. At day's end, kids were talking to the animals.

NEWS photo by Hal Mathewson

December 22, 1968

Oakland Raiders 41, Kansas City Chiefs 6
Baltimore Colts 24, Minnesota Vikings 14
Cleveland Browns 31, Dallas Cowboys 20

On December 22, the Jets were the only division winner to have the day off. The Oakland Raiders and the Kansas City Chiefs had tied for first place in the AFL's Western Division, requiring a one-game playoff for the division title. In New York, the Jets gathered to watch the contest and learn whom they would be facing in the AFL championship game. The Raiders stunned the Chiefs 41-6 to earn the right to face the Jets the following Sunday.

In the NFL, the four division winners met to determine the conference champions. The Cleveland Browns defeated the Dallas Cowboys 31-20 to claim the Eastern Conference championship. In the competition for the Western Conference crown, Earl Morrall and the Colts were victorious over the Vikings, 24-14.

Jets May Alter Offensive Line

by Norm Miller
Daily News

After five months, 14 games and a division championship, Weeb Ewbank yesterday lined up a contest for positions as his Jets regrouped to start practice for the December 29 AFL title game. The contest is in the offensive line, where Weeb feels he cannot stake everything on the inconsistency of rookie tackle Sam Walton.

"In all probability, Walton will start," he added. "But the game is 10 days away. You don't know what can happen."

In the quest for the Super Bowl, there can be no margin for breakdown. The Jets' tackle starter could depend on which Western club wins next Sunday's playoff. Weeb is lining up all possible "savers."

Don Maynard was the only injured Jet for yesterday's practice. The hamstring pull, which kept him out of last Sunday's windup at Miami, was still sore. He did not suit up for the offensive drill, remaining indoors for heat treatment. He did not expect to do any strong running until next Tuesday.

"I hated to stay out last Sunday," Maynard said. "Lance Alworth beat me out for the yardage championship (for receivers) by 15 yards. The coach wanted me to play and so did several of the players.

"But I'd rather sacrifice that (the statistics title) than take a chance on aggravating my leg," he added. "Even if I went in for one catch, it could have been the one that strained the muscle."

In the final AFL standings, Alworth caught 68 passers for 1,312 yards, Maynard 57 for 1,297. Maynard's 22.8 average was best in the AFL.

The coach was asked about his use of hipper-dipper plays in the last two games. Against the Bengals two weeks ago, Matt Snell threw an option pass for the first time. Against the Dolphins, the Jets sprang an oddball Namath-to-Snell-to-Namath exchange, followed by a long toss to flanker Bake Turner.

"Whoever we play, I want them to worry about our pass and run." Ewbank explained. "This should make our draw plays work better."

Ewbank was asked whether it could be assumed that the Jets will have variations off those themes for the title game.

"You can be sure we will," he replied.

SHULA, COACH OF THE YEAR, HOPES HE CAN ENJOY IT

December 20, 1968—Don Shula, described by his players as tough but fair, is the Coach of the Year in the NFL for the third time in five years. This time, Shula hopes he can enjoy it.

"It's a great honor, of course," the Colts' coach said today when informed he finished on top in the AP poll. "But the only way it will be really meaningful is if we win it all."

The first two times he was accorded the honor, Shula came up short.

Chiefs, Raiders, a Study in Psychological Warfare

by Larry Fox
Daily News

Any game involving the Raiders and Oakland is an exercise in psychological warfare that would make the most devious diplomat cringe with envy. Sunday's Western Division playoff between the Chiefs and Raiders is no exception. It might, in fact, be a classic example.

The Chiefs, for instance, are breaking precedent by making their headquarters in the posh Mark Hopkins Hotel across the bay in San Francisco.

Most AFL teams, including the Chiefs as recently as this season, stay at the Edgewater Inn here. It is convenient to the airport and the stadium…and the Raider offices. Al Davis, clever boss of the franchise here, had been known to drop by for a cup of coffee and a paper and if he runs into opposing players in the lobby, of course will chat with them.

("Maybe they finally found out we had the rooms bugged," one member of the Raider family said sarcastically.)

The Chiefs, who usually save their little twists for new formations from the active imagination of coach Hank Stram, take the position that they're in great shape for this game. They've had some flu "but everyone will play."

The Oakland party line—and there always is one for a big game—reads that "We're battered and bruised and lucky to be alive." Meanwhile, the odds favoring the Chiefs continued to rise. The spread is now up to $4^1/_2$ points here and the change proves once again that while coaches may try to hide illness and injury from the public, gamblers have their own sources.

COLT WATCH COLT WATCH COLT WATCH COLT WATCH COLT WATCH COLT WATCH COLT

EVERYTHING POINTS TO COLTS BUT SHULA ISN'T SURE

December 21, 1968—"Jimmy the Greek" makes the Colts an 11-point favorite over the Vikings in the Western Conference title game. A national magazine calls it a mismatch.

The Colts will have going for them the top quarterback in the NFL—Earl Morrall; the most expensive and experienced backup quarterback, John Unitas; their record-tying defense; their home field and highly vocal home fans; and the loyal backing of Vice President-elect Spiro Agnew.

Jets Shocked by Easy Win of Title Rival

by Phil Pepe
Daily News

While the Raiders were having a party at the expense of the Chiefs in Oakland, the Jets were having a party of their own in the Merrick, L.I., home of center John Schmitt. Before the festivities, 25 of the Jets repaired to Schmitt's den to watch with more than passing interest the progress of the Oakland-Kansas City game. The Jets play the winner Sunday in Shea for the AFL title.

The Jets were neither happy nor unhappy, encouraged nor discouraged by the outcome, although they did admit they were surprised by the Raiders' easy victory.

"They were ready," Schmitt said. "They were really up for the game. Kansas City could not do anything against them and I guess we were all disappointed the Chiefs didn't make a better game of it."

To middle linebacker Al Atkinson, the story of the game was quarterback Daryle Lamonica. "He had a great day." Atkinson said. "When a guy is as hot as he was, he's tough to beat. Oakland was a little better prepared than Kansas City."

Both Atkinson and Schmitt said there was no rooting from the Jets during the game. The Jets had no preference for their opponent next week.

"We had to play the winner no matter who it was," Schmitt said. "What's the sense of rooting for one or the other? There was nothing we could do about it." To Schmitt there was a small consolation in the Raiders' victory. "It means I won't have to go against Ernie Ladd and Buck Buchanan," he said.

But both Schmitt and Atkinson hinted they are happy to get another chance at Oakland.

"We owe them something from the game in Oakland," said Schmitt, referring to the Raiders' 43-32 victory in the now-famous *Heidi* game.

"Oakland is the only team we played this year that we didn't beat," Atkinson added. The middle linebacker said he saw nothing new in the Raiders' game against Kansas City. "They just stick to their usual game plan," he said "They figure they're as good as you are and they tell you to try and stop them. Kansas City couldn't. We have to figure we'll see the same Oakland team the Chiefs saw and it's up to us to stop them. They're going to be ready for us...but you can bet we'll be ready for them."

Having to play an extra game will have no effect on Oakland according to Schmitt. "It might have if it had been a close game or if they had a lot of injuries. The layoff helped us a little because we had a few minor injuries. We're healthy now and the guys are in great spirits."

While his players partied, coach Weeb Ewbank watched the game in the quiet of his Westchester home. With typical coachly caution, Ewbank refused to say which team he preferred to meet, but said he was surprised at the ease with which the Raiders handled the Chiefs. Ever the pessimist, Weeb said the easy victory would make the Raiders tougher for the Jets.

Ewbank said he prepared for both teams, watching movies of both teams. "Now, we can throw away the Kansas City films." Ewbank and his coaches will look at the movies closely this week to determine if the Raiders did anything different against the Chiefs. He could really save himself the trouble and consult his chief scout.

"My wife will have plenty to tell me," Weeb said. "She was taking notes."

STRAM TOPS

December 23, 1968—Hank Stram, whose Kansas City Chiefs rebounded from a mediocre 1967 season to reach the playoff for the AFL's Western Division championship, has been named the UPI's AFL coach of the year, it was announced yesterday.

Stram edged Weeb Ewbank, head mentor of the Eastern Division champion Jets, for the honor. Cincinnati's Paul Brown and San Diego's Sid Gillman also won support.

In the balloting, Stram received 14 votes, Ewbank 12, Brown 3 and Gillman 1.

Anxious Jets (l. to r.) John Dockery, Mike D'Amato, John Elliott and Larry Grantham (in front) watch Raiders-Chiefs and are joined by (l. to r.) John Schmitt, Rocky Rochester, Ralph Baker, Carl McAdams, and Dave Herman (rear). (News photo by Jerry Haynes)

COLT WATCH COLT WATCH

COLTS CHAMPS; AWE VIKINGS, 24-14

Norm Miller
Daily News

December 23, 1968—If the Jets and the Browns, and maybe even the Chiefs and the Raiders, were watching on TV today, these Super Bowl hopefuls could not have derived much encouragement from the sight of the Colts dismantling the Vikings 24-14, to win the NFL's Western Division title in muddy Memorial Stadium.

And so now, the Colts meet the Browns next Sunday in a rematch of the 1964 title game won by Cleveland, 27-0. The Browns, incidentally, were the only team to beat the Colts this season.

KC BOWS, 41-6; IT'S RAIDERS VS. JETS

Larry Fox
Daily News

December 23, 1968—The Jets won the wish of their secret hearts today, another crack at the Oakland Raiders. The rematch of last month's bitter, brawling Heidi game—this one for the AFL championship at Shea Stadium on Sunday—was set up when the Raiders humiliated Kansas City, 41-6, in a playoff for the Western Division title as a record 53,605 chilled Oakland Coliseum fans cheered five TD passes by Daryle Lamonica.

For the Raiders, who plan to leave for New York on Thursday, there's a minimum of $6,000, which goes to next week's losers, and a potential Super Bowl share.

Kansas City and Oakland, which finished the regular season at 12-2 after splitting home-and-home series, are the only AFL teams that know what it's like to play in a Super Bowl. Next week in Shea, the Raiders, defending AFL champions, will try to keep the Jets from joining that club.

JETS, COLTS SUPER

| Oak. | 0 10 | 3 10—23 | Colts | 0 17 7 10—34 |
| Jets | 10 3 | 7 7—27 | Clev. | 0 0 0 0— 0 |

—Stories Pages 54, **55**

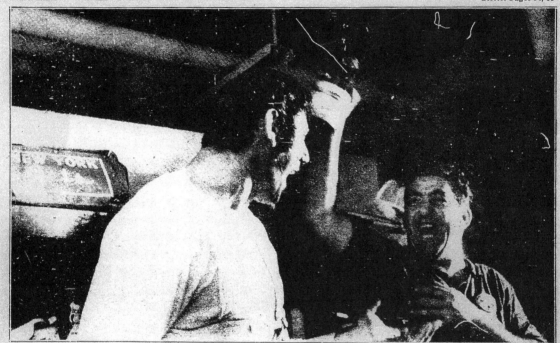

NEWS photo by Dan Farrell

Like Bubbly, Joe Rises To Occasion

Joe Namath is greeted with congratulations and champagne bath by trainer in locker room at Shea Stadium after he led Jets to AFL championship over Oakland Raiders yesterday. The New Yorkers came off the floor, as did Joe, who was several times smothered by Raiders like Ben Davidson (←), to take the 27-23 victory before a record 62,627 crowd. The league title is the first by any New York team since 1964 Yanks. Joe was the sparkplug in win, passing for three touchdowns. And now there's just one more hurdle—the Baltimore Colts in the Super Bowl in Miami on Jan. 12. **—Story p. 54**

UPI photo

DECEMBER 29, 1968

New York 27, Oakland 23

Oakland	0	10	3	10	—	23
New York	10	3	7	7	—	27

S now, sleet, and cold winds were weighing on the minds of Jets players going into the AFL title game against the Raiders at Shea Stadium. After a two-week break in play, however, the $2^1/_2$-point favorite Jets were rested and ready for action. With all eyes on him, newly named MVP Joe Namath proclaimed himself to be in excellent shape for the game.

Before 62,627 screaming fans, the Jets beat the Raiders 27-23 to become the AFL champions. Don Maynard had six catches for 118 yards and two touchdowns, including a six-yarder for the win in the last period. Namath's single interception of the game, which led to an Oakland go-ahead touchdown, was immediately followed by a brilliant winning drive orchestrated by the MVP quarterback. It took just three passes and 31 seconds for Joe Willie to drive the Jets 68 yards for the game-winning scoring pass to Maynard.

The Jets' celebration, however, was tempered by the knowledge that they still had a job to finish. With NFL Player of the Year Earl Morrall leading the way, the Colts destroyed the Browns in a 34-0 victory to gain a spot against the Jets in the Super Bowl.

Jets Dread Shea Winds— Rain and Cold Bad Enough

by Norm Miller
Daily News

A brutally cold wind swept Shea Stadium yesterday when the Jets went out for their noon workout. It was a typical Flushing Bay wind for this time of year, just about what the Jets can expect for Sunday's AFL title game against the Raiders, and yesterday it occupied the thoughts of players and coaches.

The temperature was in the low 30s but the swirling winds made it seem much colder as the Jets ran their plays. The field, covered overnight by a tarpaulin, was firm. Matt Snell pawed at the turf with his foot and observed, "The cleats are digging in. It looks OK."

Yesterday's weather was probably the best the Jets could hope for Sunday's game. There is no avoiding the strong inconsistent winds at Shea. It could even be worse, with snow or sleet, heavens forbid.

That is why plans for offsetting the weather factor have been a part of the Jets' overall preparations this week.

Upon arriving at the Stadium yesterday, Billy Mathis entered Weeb Ewbank's office and dropped a carton with a dozen mechanical hand-warmers on the coach's desk.

How much do I owe you for these? Ewbank asked.

"They're a Christmas present," the old-pro running back smiled, "from the company I work for."

The hand-warmers consist of a charcoal stick wrapped in porous fiberglass, Mathis explained. When fueled, they generate heat for four hours.

"The offensive backs and pass-catchers can use them when they're on the sidelines," Mathis said, "then give them to the defensive backs when the ball changes."

There will be other weather combatants, said Billy Hampton, the Jets' equipment man.

Two torpedo-shaped butane heaters will blow a constant stream of hot air from each end of the Jets' and Raiders' benches. The players will wear thermal underwear and on the sidelines they'll wrap themselves in quilt-lined winter parkas. Some of the linemen will wear gloves to protect their hands from being chewed up by the frozen ground.

"The wind factor is the biggest thing," said Joe Namath. "The rain or cold doesn't bother you nearly as much as the wind."

Someone asked him to what extent the strong wind had bothered him in the win over the Cincy Bengals here nearly three weeks ago.

"I had good flight on the ball that day," Namath replied. "But if you throw it the least bit wobbly, the wind takes the ball and you can forget about it."

Jim Turner, the placekicker, said the winds at Shea and Boston's Fenway Park are "the worst in the league."

"The wind is a factor in every game here," Turner said. Had any of his field goal tries been blown off target this season? "No, not this year," he said, "but in past years I've had several. After kicking five seasons here, I've learned how to handle the wind."

by Norm Miller
Daily News

December 24, 1968—The Jets, their bruises and muscle pulls healed from a week's layoff, yesterday were made 2-point favorites over the Raiders for Sunday's AFL championship game at Shea. The Colts, who came up with a key injured man in offensive tackle Bob Vogel, were tabbed 6-point picks over the Browns for the NFL playoff at Cleveland.

Don Maynard, the only Jet who did not participate in last week's three light workouts, planned to start running all-out on his tender hamstring today when the team resumes practice. Coach Weeb Ewbank said there was no reason why he should not go all the way Sunday.

"Everyone seems anxious to play," Ewbank smiled during a brief break in his day-long strategy meetings with his assistants.

Ewbank was asked if he felt the Jets might be affected by the two-week gap between games, while the Raiders were maintaining a competitive edge with their 41-6 Sunday win over the Chiefs.

"No, I don't expect it to affect us," he replied. "We have worked at keeping the club at a certain level for the last three games, even though we had already clinched."

There was pride involved. The defense tried to sustain its No. 1 rating in the league, even though those games didn't mean much." The last 600 available tickets for the title game were snapped up quickly yesterday. These were made available by season subscribers who had passed up their option to buy playoff seats. Many fans had lined up the night before for these tickets.

NAMATH MVP

December 25, 1968—To the surprise of no one, Joe Namath was named the AFL's Most Valuable Player yesterday by an AP panel of sports writers and sportscasters. The Jets' quarterback received 15 votes while eight other players shared the other 15. Broadway Joe passed for 3,147 yards and 15 touchdowns in leading the Jets to their first Eastern Division title.

COLT WATCH COLT WATCH COLT WATCH COLT WATCH

COLTS' MORRALL PLAYER OF YEAR

December 26, 1968—Baltimore quarterback Earl Morrall, benchwarmer and castoff with four other NFL teams, added another honor to his Cinderella season yesterday when he was named the NFL's Player of the Year by United Press International.

Morrall, who led the Colts to the Western title, was only the second Baltimore player to receive the award, the other being Johnny Unitas, the man he replaced at quarterback, who had been honored three times.

Namath A-1 for Big One

by Norm Miller
Daily News

The Big Man is ready. Joe Namath insisted yesterday he is approaching Sunday's AFL championship playoff against the Raiders "feeling as good or better than I ever have." This applies, he added, both physically and mentally.

To those who have watched the Jets at practice this week, Namath has appeared uncharacteristically serious. The wisecracks are scarcer. Much less kidding with the guys.

From "Bachelors III," the East Side pub in which Namath is a part-owner, the regulars report Joe hasn't been around as much for the past week. A quick early-evening dinner, then home to study game-films, swears Ray Abruzzese, the ex-Jet who is also a partner in the spot.

"This game," Joe Willie remarked yesterday before the workout at frigid Shea, "has been on my mind at this stage more than any I have ever played. This is the biggest game of our lives—for all of us."

Namath's reaction to a personal incident on Christmas Day bears out his mood.

He had planned to leave immediately after Wednesday's workout to spend Christmas with his family in Beaver Falls, Pennsylvania. The practice lasted later than expected, however, and Namath blew his plane connection. He could not make the trip.

Ordinarily, this would have teed him off. In this case, Namath shrugged off his disappointment. This week, the game's the thing.

A newsman asked Joe yesterday if he felt the extra week off prior to the playoff had benefited him.

"Yes, I feel better," he replied.

Do you feel at your peak?

"As good or better than ever," he said.

How do your knees feel?

"I'd rather not talk about that," he said. "They really have nothing to do with the way I play."

How about the thumb which gave him trouble during the season?

"It (the soreness) comes back every now and then," he revealed. "I just bump something and it gets messed up somehow. But it's nothing serious."

Namath was asked to appraise his last few games against the Raiders.

"We lost two of three,"
Namath pointed out.

But he threw for 370-plus yards in the two losing games, the reporter stressed.

"If we scored 35 points and got beat by four, then we should have scored 40," Namath replied, reemphasizing his credo that the only thing that matters is victory.

COLT WATCH COLT WATCH

MORRALL TO GO "ALL THE WAY" AS COLTS' QB

December 27, 1968—The QB job is Earl Morrall's, with no fear of a takeover by Johnny Unitas. Coach Don Shula of the Colts has assured Morrall the job is his, all the way, in Sunday's NFL title playoff against the Browns, and all the way in the Super Bowl if he can get the Colts there.

Jets the Ones! Nip Raiders, 27-23

by Larry Fox
Daily News

Defense, guts of the ground defense, and the sudden-death passing of Joe Namath turned the Jets into AFL champions yesterday with a 27-23 victory over Oakland before 62,627 delirious Shea Stadium fans, the most ever to see this league's title playoff.

They used to say the Jets had no defense, but this season they led the league and yesterday, again, it won for them. They used to say the Jets faded with the cold weather, but now they've won their last five and nine of the last 10. And they used to say the Jets couldn't hold a lead, but yesterday they led most of the way, fell behind, then came on again like thorough-breds against the defending league champs.

And now the Jets take their new championship into the Super Bowl January 12 against the team Weeb Ewbank used to coach to championships, Baltimore. The Jets will be the third AFL team to try its luck against the NFL, but the first with a sundown passer like Namath. For the first time, the AFL entry has the edge at quarter-back.

Don Maynard, leading pass receiver, Coach Weeb Ewbank, George Sauer, another important Jet receiver, and Joe Namath, quarterback, before the AFL championship game. (News photo by Frank Hurley)

Daryle Lamonica, Oakland's quarterback, who had engineered the 43-32 Heidi victory over the Jets on the West Coast November 17, passed for 401 yards on this windblown afternoon but Namath outgunned him on touchdowns, three to one, and that's where they pay off.

Two of Joe Willie's TD tosses went to Don Maynard, the elusive flanker who had another big day at the expense of rookie Atkinson. Maynard made six catches for 118 yards and two TDs, including a six-yarder for the winning score in the final period.

That winning drive followed Namath's only interception of the day, which had set up the touchdown that put Oakland in the lead for the first time all day. After the kickoff, Namath required only three passes and 31 seconds to cover the distance. He hit George Sauer for 10 yards, Maynard for 52

and then drilled a six-yard scoring pass to Maynard again as Atkinson looked on helplessly.

It had been Atkinson who had pulled off the critical interception. The Jets were at their 22 when Namath aimed a sideline pass at Maynard to his left. The ball was underthrown and Atkinson stepped in front of the receiver at the 37. He loped down the sideline to the five, at which point Namath himself drove him out. In the first play, Pete Banaszak slashed over for the score and George Blanda converted for a 23-20 Oakland lead.

Two defensive series earlier in the half for the Jets had proved just as critical as Namath's explosive burst for the winning touchdown. Both were goal line stands and both times the Raiders had to settle for field goals.

The first came midway of the third quarter. After Lamonica had completed a 37-yarder to Fred Biletnikoff, and a 40-yarder to Warren Wells, the Raiders had a first down on the Jet six. Charlie

Smith cracked for three and the tackle. And then Al Atkinson and Hudson combined to stop Hewritt Dixon at the one. Rather than test the Jet line again, the Raiders settled for a nine-yard field goal by Blanda and a 13-13 tie.

The Jets drove 80 yards in 14 plays after this Oakland score to go out front at 20-13 on a 20-yard Namath-to-Lammons pass and, after an exchange of punts, the Raiders again threatened. This time a 57-yard completion from Lamonica to Biletnikoff, who drove both John Sample and Cornell Gordon to the bench with his antics, set the Raiders up at the Jet 11.

This was as close as the Raiders got. Smith was thrown for a yard loss on a fine play by linebacker Ralph Baker and then Randy Beverly and Hudson broke up Lamonica passes. This time Blanda kicked his three-pointer from the 20. The play was significant because it left the Raiders four points behind and beyond field goal reach of a tie and a

chance at sudden death.

This was still the situation after the exchange of touchdowns put the Jets in front at 27-23 with 7:47 to go. Once again the Raiders fought back and now they had a first down at the Jet 26. Three plays, a run and two passes produced no yardage. This was easy field goal range for Blanda, but a field goal meant nothing at this point with $5^1/_2$ minutes to play.

So Lamonica called another pass. As he looked toward the end zone, defensive end Verlon Biggs, who had been giving tackle Bob Svihus a straight outside rush all afternoon, faked inside and then spun around. Lamonica didn't know what hit him as Biggs felled him for a six-yard loss. Verlon still hasn't signed his 1968 contract, and that big play presumably added several dollars to his bargaining position.

The Jets couldn't kill the clock, however, and again needed a clutch defensive play, this time by Baker. A 24-yard pass from

Lamonica to Biletnikoff moved the Raiders from the 15 to their 39 and then Lamonica passed for 37 more to Warren Wells, at which point Hudson was called for piling on and the Raiders were in command at the Jet 12.

Lamonica, under a big rush from Biggs, looped a little swing pass to Smith that went behind the fleet halfback and Baker recovered what was ruled as a free lateral.

Baker actually ran the ball 70 yards to the Oakland end zone but rules say a recovered lateral cannot be advanced. Ironically, officials had goofed to allow a Boston touchdown on a similar play against the Jets in Birmingham early this year. The score in the game was so one-sided, few noticed.

Once again the Jets were unable to run the clock, but, when Oakland took over for a last shot with 45 seconds to go, the Raiders could loose no bombs and the clock died with the visitors still on their side of the 50.

Joe Namath hands off to Emerson Boozer during the AFL Championship game against the Raiders. (Daily News photo)

Image of Colts Limits Jets' Joy

by Phil Pepe and Joe Trimble
Daily News

There was an air of controlled joy in the Jets' dressing room following their big victory over the Raiders yesterday. Part of it was because of the crush of humanity and machinery, those inevitable one-eyed monsters beseeching players to look happy for the world.

But there seemed to be a sobering thought permeating the room, cutting into the joy...the thought that their job was not yet complete.

"I'll be out here tomorrow," said Joe Namath, when asked if he was planning to take a few days off. "We've got some important work to do."

Namath refused to be lured into expressing a preference for Colts or Browns, but seemed resigned that it would be the Colts.

"What's the score now?" he asked.

"17-0," somebody said.

"I haven't seen enough of Baltimore to say anything about them," Joe said. "I don't know anything about them other than their tight end is real great...that Mackey."

Namath sipped from a bottle of champagne and cringed when flash bulbs popped in his face.

"Hey, don't do that," he said, hiding the jug behind his back.

"Those parents hate me enough as it is."

He took another deep swallow, then back to football.

"The wind was bad," he allowed, "but it didn't affect the game. I can't praise our offense enough for what they did."

"Did you think you could come back after they went ahead?" Joe was asked.

"If you don't feel you can come back," he replied, "you don't belong on that field."

Now he had drained the bottle dry . . . after most of it was dumped over his head . . . and went in search of another one. There was Weeb Ewbank, talking to reporters.

"Hey, Weeb," Namath said, "Where's the champagne?"

"We've got a whole case of it back there, Joe," the roly-poly coach said, grateful to suspend training regulations for just this once.

"Everybody from the Giants get out this clubhouse," Namath shouted.

There was Larry Grantham, one of the three original New York Titans along with Bill Mathis and Don Maynard. He remembers how it was and he could savor how it is now.

"Today is probably the greatest day I've ever lived," Grantham said. "Even though we gave up points on defense, when we got behind our offense came back and picked us up."

Johnny Sample, the outspoken defensive back (an offensive defensive back, the Raiders might say) and a former Colt has a special reason for wanting to go against Baltimore in the Super Bowl. Never one to shrink from controversy or predictions, he flatly said, "The way this ball club is playing now, we will win the Super Bowl."

To Joe Namath, this was also the biggest game of his life and they wanted to know if it was his biggest thrill as well.

"Yeah...yeah, I guess so," he said, but there was a note of hesitation in his voice as if he really wanted to say:

"Not yet, baby, not yet."

Broadway Joe Helped Jets Make a Hollywood Finish

You know when I knew this was a great ball game? It was afterwards, in the elevator, when the tall, thin gent with the graying hair said, "This was one of the most spectacular sports events of all-time." It was Don Grant, who said it; Don let football into Shea during the baseball season. If he says it, then you just know yesterday's AFL title spectacular, the Jets over Oakland, by 27-23, had to be something special.

This was the kind of day the Jets could beat anybody; Oakland, Heidi, the NBC network, any network, anybody. They couldn't give it away. They tried a few times but Somebody Up There wouldn't let them. Somebody down there on the field, too. Joe Namath wouldn't let them.

"I'll tell you the biggest thing we have going for us," said Gerry Philbin. "We have so much confidence in Joe, and in our offense. We make mistakes on defense. We make a lot of them today. But Namath is unbelievable. He comes right back."

Gerry Philbin was sitting there in a corner, in front of his locker, in his long drawers. They were pink, because somebody had poured pink champagne all over him.

Across the room, Joe Namath stood on a stool, also in his long drawers, also wet and pink. He looked down on his people, the newspapermen. The bright newsreel floodlights hit him in the eyes and he squinted.

"Hey Joe," somebody called out. "Tell us about that protection you got."

"It was sensational," he said, "The way it has been all year.

They know they give me time, there's a gonna be points on the scoreboard. It's as simple as that."

"He's unbelievable," Gerry Philbin had said. "He came to the side after the interception, and he said 'We'll get it back...We'll get it back.' And he did."

The interception had come well into the fourth period. All day long, the Jets had been leading. At first by 10 points, then by only three at the half, and 20-13 into the fourth. Then the Old Man, George Blanda, kicked one from 20

Namath threw for three touchdowns in the AFL championship game. (Daily News photo)

out and it was down to 20-16.

Earl Christy ran the kickoff from the 1 to the 22, and on first down Joe Namath skipped back, set up and whipped to the left side. He was going for Don Maynard, and they were playing George Atkinson, the pigeon. George Atkinson is great on running back kickoffs, and punts, but as a cornerman he is a pigeon. There are certain men you chip at, third-and-long men who give you a certain sense of security. George Atkinson is one of them.

This once, the pigeon was an eagle. He flapped in front of Maynard, picked off the ball and dashed to the 5 before Joe Namath, frantic, ran him out. On one play, Pete Banaszak ate up the five yards, with a cutback over right tackle, and for the first time, Oakland led.

It was the right time to lead, with only 8:20 left. A stunned silence came over Shea Stadium, as if it were empty instead of filled with more than 62,000 Wheed-up people. The bottom had fallen out of things. By their silence, they had given up.

Not Namath.

It took him three plays, 68 yards and 31 seconds. Earl Christy's battling runback had butted from three behind the goal to the 32. Then Namath hit Sauer on the 42 . . . and a 52-yard bomb to Maynard, against the pigeon, except that it was a great catch, if it was a catch, more than anything the pigeon didn't do...and finally a flat one into the end zone from the 6, again the Maynard, against the pigeon. The big one, the 52-yarder, could have been called either way. As Maynard took the ball over his shoulder, in true Willie Mays style, George Atkinson hit him at the 10. Out of bounds they flew, down in a heap, and the ball squirted free. Maybe he had it; maybe he didn't.

The official said he did.

That was the big break the Jets needed; that and one other. They needed the intended forward pass that was a lateral. The Raiders were sweeping downfield in big chunks. Lamonica hit Biletnikoff. He hit Wells, and now they were on the Jet 26, and when Jim Hudson piled on Wells the ref stepped it off to the 13. There was 2:20 left; plenty of time. A man can go 113 yards in 2:20. Hadn't the Raiders scored two TDs against the Jets in 9 seconds in the Swiss Alps?

Lamonica faded. Biggs charged. Biggs had landed smack on Lamonica a bit earlier. Lamonica got rid of it quicker this time—flat to Charley Smith. Too flat. It was a lateral, and it flew over Charley Smith's head near the sidelines.

Ralph Baker scooped it up and ran the whole field with it—70 yards—but they called him back and said the Jets would have to settle for the ball on their 30 because the rule says you can't run with a picked-up lateral. You can run with a fumble, but not with a lateral. Football has some funny rules.

There was to be one Oakland thrust left, and Jim Hudson was to break it up with the last jolting tackle on Hewritt Dickson, Hudson, Biggs, Snell, and Rochester were all tremendous, in a tremendous ball game...but there is one guy:

"I'll tell you something," one of the Jets said. "During the second quarter, when those two big bucks fell on Joe, he dislocated the middle finger. Doc had to set it, and shoot Novocain into him. It was the left hand, so it didn't hurt passing, but you can bet he was in pain."

That explains why Joe Namath had so much trouble popping the cork on that champagne bottle.

MATTE, COLTS DESTROY BROWNS, 34-0

by Norm Miller
Daily News

December 30, 1968—The Colts, with their colorless but methodically destructive efficiency, clobbered the Browns, 34-0, today to win the NFL championship and set up a beaut of a Super Bowl matchup with the Jets at Miami on January 12.

It will be a matchup of the brainy experience of ex-Giant Earl Morrall against the glamour-tossing of Joe Namath, and it will pit Weeb Ewbank, in his year of comeback triumph, against Don Shula, whom he once coached, plus at least 10 of the Colts who played for Weeb at Baltimore before he left there in 1962.

Today, before a crowd of 80,628 in chilly, drab Municipal Stadium, the Colts clinched their first NFL championship since the two they won under Ewbank in 1958 and '59, in playoffs with the Giants. They also earned the $10,000-per-man jackpot that goes with the NFL title and they qualified for a shot at the $15,000 prize in the Super Bowl.

"It was sensational. The way it has been all year. They know they give me time, there's a gonna be points on the scoreboard. It's as simple as that."

—Joe Namath, when asked about the protection he received from his offensive line during the AFL championship game against Oakland.

1968 New York Jets

COLTS SUPER 16 OVER JETS

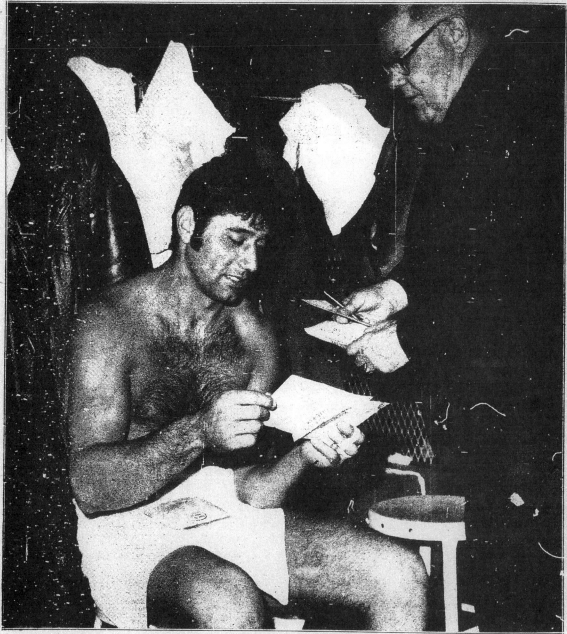

NEWS photo by Tom Gallagher

Couple of Live Wires

Hero Joe Namath of the Jets and his coach, Weeb Ewbank, read some of the telegrams that poured into Shea Stadium yesterday as aftermath of Sunday's title victory over Oakland. Joe was at Shea for treatment of dislocated ring finger on left hand, and some aches and pains. He'll be ready when AFL champs meet Colts in Super Bowl at Miami on Jan. 12.—*Story on page 51*

THE GUARANTEE

'I've Got News For You...'

Daily News

Commissioner Pete Rozelle officially validated the term "Super Bowl" for what was previously known as the World Professional Football Championship game. Along with the game's new name came another new phenomenon—Super Bowl hype. It would be MVP against MVP in the Super Bowl, as Jets' quarterback Joe Namath was set to lead his team against Colts' quarterback Earl Morrall. The Colts were the 18-point favorites, but the underdog Jets weren't paying any attention to the odds. Indeed, Namath's place in sport's folklore was permanently etched when he boldly and very publicly issued his famous "guarantee" of victory.

As usual, the spotlight also shone brightly on Namath's private life. Speculation on his late-night whereabouts ran rampant when he and teammates Emerson Boozer and Matt Snell were fined for sleeping in and standing up 20 photographers for the team's Super Bowl photo date. Meanwhile, Weeb Ewbank's game plan for his players was composed of 40 pages of plays along with one simple message: to remain poised throughout the game. With the trophy arriving safely in Miami, the stage was set for Super Bowl III.

Celebrating Jets Vow They'll Capture Title

The odds may be against them, but last night, in the full flush of celebrating their AFL title victory, the Jets were saying they can be Super Bowl champs, too.

Some 200 Jet players and coaches and their wives, along with some sports writers, had gathered in Shea Stadium's Diamond Club to make Sunday's win official. Club president Phil Iselin was master of ceremonies.

"We know we're underdogs," Iselin said of the coming January 12 encounter with the Colts. "We've been underdogs before. But Weeb's got the playbook and knows every play they can run," Iselin jested, referring to the fact that Jet mentor Weeb Ewbank formerly coached the Colts.

Weeb, happy as a defensive tackle who's jut put an opposing quarterback in the hospital, had words of praise for the New York fans. "When you can fill two ballparks in one city on a Sunday, nothing can beat that," he enthused.

Weeb also thanked the wives of the Jets for standing behind their husbands through the thick and thin of the season.

He was followed to the dais by the man for this season, Joe Namath, who said, "Coach has thanked all the wives, I want to thank all the broads in New York."

COLT WATCH COLT WATCH COLT WATCH COLT WATCH

COLTS 16-POINT CHOICE OVER JETS IN SUPER BOWL

December 31, 1968—The Colts were a surprisingly big 16-point favorite over Joe Namath and the Jets yesterday in the opening betting line for the Super Bowl at Miami, January 12.

Oddly, while the Jets are considered the strongest offensive team to represent the AFL in the world championship game, this spread is bigger than for two earlier super-clashes, won by the Packers.

In the first Super Bowl, the Packers closed $13^1/_2$-point picks; they beat the Chiefs, 33-14. In last year's game, the Packers were the choice by 13; they beat the Raiders, 35-10.

> "I've got news for you, we're going to win the game. I guarantee it."
>
> —Joe Namath boldly proclaimed to the Miami Touchdown Club three days before the Jets' Super Bowl upset of the Baltimore Colts.

Jets off to Florida; Not Impressed by Odds

by Norm Miller
Daily News

Freezing winds swirled, feet slipped on icy pavements and bodies shuddered yesterday as the Jets piled happily on the plane for Florida. Weeb Ewbank, with visions of warm weather and the Super Bowl dancing in his head, was in a joking mood. "We didn't show them any movies (of the Colts)," Weeb gagged. "I'm afraid I'd have trouble getting them on the airplane."

This was Ewbank's manner of scoffing at the odds that have made the NFL champ Colts 17-point favorites over his Jets for the January 12 super game at Miami.

"They must be going on past Super Bowl games," Ewbank said, when asked if he were surprised at the one-sidedness of the oddsmen's appraisal. "Heck, I never pay any attention to that stuff. That's for the gamblers."

"I hope they (the Colts) show up," kidded Gerry Philbin, the all-AFL defensive end. "We need the money."

Earlier, the Jets had reassembled briefly at Shea from a three-day layoff following their 27-23 AFL title win over Oakland.

They took a look at the movies of that game, then immediately boarded a bus for JFK airport.

With the temperature not much above zero, players and coaches were delighted to be headed for the Super Bowl training camp at Ft. Lauderdale, Florida, to start working out this morning in pleasanter weather for the $15,000-per-man challenge against the Colts.

Ewbank said in all probability he would stick to the starting lineup of last Sunday's game against Oakland. That meant Dave Herman at offensive right tackle with Randy Rasmussen at guard and Sam Walton on the sidelines. It also meant Johnny Sample at the left defensive corner, although he was yanked at one stage of the Raider game.

"We were successful with that lineup," Weeb stressed. "We'll probably stay with it. I don't see any changes, as of right now."

Ewbank explained why he was taking his champs to Florida a few days earlier than the past two years' Super Bowl contenders have gone.

The Colts will not leave Baltimore until Saturday night or Sunday.

"We need the practice," Ewbank said. "We haven't had a real good practice session here for two weeks.

"Down there, I want to make it like a regular week's work," he added. "I want them to have grass drills and make it like training camp. I want to work them hard down there."

COLT WATCH COLT WATCH

COLTS BY 18

January 4, 1969—Odds against the Jets in the Super Bowl are reaching super proportions. Latest figures quote the Colts as 18-point favorites with a week to go. The Colts opened as 16-point favorites in New York (17 in Las Vegas). Now the price is 18 points in both places and expected to go as high as 20 by game time.

A Trophy Arrives Safely

by Phil Pepe
Daily News

Among the passengers aboard National Airlines' flight 91 from La Guardia to Miami Friday night was A Trophy. Not Arthur Trophy and not Agnes Trophy. Simply A Trophy, four feet tall, solid gold, said to have been eight months in the making and symbolic of world supremacy in pro football.

This is the Super Bowl trophy and you know it has to be worth money because a cheap trophy couldn't afford to go to Florida in the cold winter months.

Like any self-respecting trophy, this one flew first class. Fare: $165.90 round trip. Menu: hors d'oeuvres, lobster, filet mignon, salad and coffee, tea or gold polish. There was no movie on board. The trophy didn't seem to mind.

The trophy did not fly alone. Its companion was Chris Vecsey, a young man who works in Commissioner Rozelle's office and whose title is vice president in charge of accompanying the championship trophy to the Super Bowl in Miami. It is very difficult work. Sometimes the pressure of the job gets overwhelming.

"I kept worrying that the plane would be hijacked to Cuba," young Vecsey said, "and when we got there, they'd leave everyone alone, but they'd take the trophy and melt it down like Cromwell did when he took over England. He melted down all the gold and silver and turned it into coins. How would I ever explain that?"

Happily, the journey was completed without incident, although Chris Vecsey admits to some disappointment.

"I kept hoping the stewardess would ask me what was in the box," Chris said. "Last year, the fellow who took the trophy to Miami was asked the question and he said, 'They are the ashes of my dead wife and I'm going to Florida to deposit them in the ocean.' I wanted to use that line, but I never got the chance."

The trip started when Chris was picked up by limousine at the NFL offices. From there he was taken to Tiffany's to pick up the trophy.

From Tiffany's, Chris and the trophy (not listed in order of importance) were taken by limousine to La Guardia, where the young man sought out an airlines official who arranged for two seats.

"The trophy got the window seat," Chris said with a note of disappointment. "I had to sit on the aisle."

In Florida, Chris and the trophy were met by someone from the commissioner's office and taken to a hotel with strict instructions not to let the trophy out of sight.

"They told me to sleep with it," Chris said, "but I think they were kidding. They said the same thing to the fellow who took it down last year and he took them seriously."

The trophy will spend 10 days in Florida before returning north on the night of January 12. But travel arrangements are still indefinite. The trophy's return ticket is blank in the space marked "destination." It is not yet certain if the trophy will return to New York or go to Baltimore instead.

COLT WATCH COLT WATCH

COLTS DEPART

January 5, 1969—Tom Matte and Bubba Smith missed practice for the third straight day, then left late today with the rest of the Colt squad for Florida, where they will resume workouts Monday for the Super Bowl game with the Jets.

Matte, recovering from the flu, in addition to back and head injuries suffered in last Sunday's 34-0 NFL title win over the Browns, attended the Colts' offensive meeting but did not get into uniform for the outdoor drill. His halfback job was handled by Tim Brown. Smith, still hobbled by a sprained left ankle, watched from the sidelines in a sweat suit while Roy Hilton filled his defensive end spot in practice.

Joe, Three Sleepy Jets Fined

by Larry Fox
Daily News

Fort Lauderdale—Joe Namath, Emerson Boozer and Matt Snell—the Jets' starting backfield—slept in this morning and stood up about 20 photographers for the AFL team's Super Bowl picture date at the local Yankee Stadium. The extra four hours' sleep was believed to have cost each player a $50 fine, which is the club's standard levy for missing a meeting.

"I always sleep in the morning; it's the thing to do. You've got to get your rest," Namath said when he appeared at poolside in the afternoon.

Namath rooms with Jim Hudson, who did heed the 9 a.m. wake-up call and made the bus to the stadium. However, Hudson said he couldn't rouse his roomie. "I've never seen anyone like Joe for getting his 12 hours sleep." Hudson said. (Incidentally, while Hudson was at the stadium he didn't get in any pictures, either, since he was taking treatment for a charley horse.)

Boozer and Snell room together. "We heard the phone ring, but we figured it was just another one of those calls we've been getting all the time since we've been here and we didn't answer it. If anybody wanted to take my picture this morning they would have had to get me between the sheets," Boozer said.

Weeb Ewbank said he talked to all three players and accepted their explanations. He also will accept their money. "Appropriate action will be taken," he said, adding that it is club policy never to announce the amount of fines.

There's a chance, however, of additional penalties. As soon as he heard of the incident, Jim Kensil, pro commissioner Pete Rozelle's chief assistant, was on the phone to Ewbank for an explanation and he insisted that all three players be made available for photographers before tomorrow afternoon's workout.

"All we care about now is that they be made available," Kensil said. "The commissioner is in New York now and any further action would have to wait until he came back down here later in the week and got all the facts."

Perhaps coincidentally, Ewbank said his team would be put under curfew starting tonight with a $5,000 fine for latecomers. Earlier, he had said he might wait until tomorrow to start a bed-check.

The Jets did their share of horsing around for the photographers and Paul Rochester, the burly defensive tackle, put on a No. 12 jersey and mussed up his hair to oblige any photographers who insisted on having a Joe Namath for pictures. However, nobody took him up on it.

The Colts were able to sleep a little later. They had their picture session in the afternoon. Tomorrow, both teams get down to serious work for Sunday's confrontation and from then on it will cost everybody a lot more than $50 to make an appearance.

Shula Raps, Praises Joe

by Larry Fox
Daily News

Fort Lauderdale—Baltimore's Don Shula doesn't like anyone knocking his quarterback, and that includes Joe Namath.

Namath has been quoted as saying that Oakland's Daryle Lamonica is a better passer than the Colts' Earl Morrall and that Baltimore hasn't played against teams with quarterbacks as good as several in the AFL, like Lamonica, John Hadl and Bob Griese.

This has been interpreted as a further derogation of Morrall, who, in many quarters, has been given credit not so much for leading the Colts to a championship as for not fouling them up.

"I don't know how Namath can rap Earl," Shula said today with a slight edge in his voice. "After all, Earl's number one in the NFL, he's thrown all those touch-down passes (26), he's thrown for a great percentage (57.4) without using those dinky flare passes to build up his average and he's been voted Player of the Year.

"But, I guess, Namath can say whatever the hell he wants."

Shula was high in his praise of Namath.

"He's a helluva thrower and a fine quarterback," Shula said, "and he's moved their offense well ever since he came there. He has a quick release and he sets up with good depth. Namath backpedals more than most quarterbacks in our league and that helps give him such good vision for spotting his second and third receivers.

"He doesn't get caught with the ball very often and the big problem against Namath is just trying to get to the guy."

Shula noted that Namath, because of his knees, doesn't have real speed. "But he has what we call fast feet," the former defensive halfback pointed out. "He has the ability to move back from the center quickly and once he's in the pocket he can move from side to side to get out of the rushing lanes."

He credited Namath with the ability to spot a blitz quickly and with being able to adjust to changes in pass defense from zone to man-to-man coverage. "He knows where to go with the football," Shula said.

Shula declined to compare Namath and Morrall. "They didn't throw against the same defenses," he hedged. As for whom Namath might resemble in technique, Shula pointed to Sonny Jurgenson or Norm Van Brocklin. "Van Brocklin also backpedaled and it was very hard to get to him, too."

> "But, I guess, Namath can say whatever the hell he wants."
> —Don Shula

Jets Get Game Plan and Advice to Keep Poise

by Larry Fox
Daily News

Fort Lauderdale—The Jets got their Super Bowl game plan today, 40 pages of plays and scouting reports in blue folders, one for each man. They will live with the booklets every other hour until Sunday's game with Baltimore. Fine for losing the top secret document—$200.

However, just as important as the plays and the defenses is Weeb Ewbank's oral warning to his players: "Don't lose your poise."

This is something he will be drilling into them from now until the final gun on Sunday. "We lost our poise once this year, in the Oakland game out there," he said today. "And this question of poise is something I will emphasize to the players the rest of the week. I don't want to happen to us what happened to the Chiefs and the Raiders in the other Super Bowls."

Ewbank pointed out that Kansas City was very much in the inaugural game against Green Bay two years ago until Len Dawson threw an interception and completely lost his cool. Then, last year, there was the turning point of Rodger Bird's fumbling a punt and a missed pass coverage that gave the Packers an easy touchdown to put Oakland out of the game.

"You just hope it doesn't happen to you," Ewbank said, referring to the critical error, "and if it does, you hope it doesn't upset you."

The Jet coach rates this Baltimore team as even stronger than the Green Bay entries that won the first two Super Bowls by wide margins. However, he also feels that his club is superior to the first two AFL representatives.

"I wouldn't have said at midyear but I think we are now the best team the AFL has sent here," Weeb said. "We've been getting progressively better every game since then and we should be better this week."

Ewbank gives several reasons for the team's last half improvement—the progress of Emerson Boozer, whom he feels showed his old flash as a runner only in the last game of the regular season; the maturation of Joe Namath at quarterback with only six interceptions in his last 10 games; the coming of age of the defense; and the all-important matter of confidence. "They all believe they're better," Weeb said.

After five games this season the Jets were only 3-2, and Namath had thrown a dozen interceptions. Since then, they won 9 out of 10, including the championship game and the last five in a row.

"This is a great Baltimore team that we are playing while we're just green and growing," Ewbank continued in his most sorrowful tone. "I know we don't have the same overall thing the Colts have built up over the years, but we're proud of what we've got and we're quite proud and happy to be a part of it."

Ewbank clearly is giving the Colts nothing to put up on their bulletin board.

After a long meeting in which they were given the game plan, the Jets capered through a brief workout at the local Yankee Stadium. The session had originally been scheduled as closed but Ewbank had to change his plan so photographers could have their turn with yesterday's three late sleepers: Namath, Boozer and Matt Snell.

YOUNG IDEAS

by Dick Young
Daily News

January 8, 1969, Golden Beach, Florida—"I haven't bet on a football game in eight years," said Sonny Werblin. "But I have to go for this."

The Jets plus 18 is what he has to go for. That's what he can get on Sunday's football game, billed as the World Professional Football Championship game.

That's what it says on the tickets, on the press kit, on the official program. Nowhere does it say Super Bowl. For some reason, Pete Rozelle and the football people never went for the Super Bowl business. Two years ago, in fact, they ran a contest to come up with a name. It was right around the time that the Proctor & Gamble people were running a contest to find a first name for Mr. Clean. If either contest produced a result, I'm not aware of it.

SAME HONOR

January 9, 1969—Earl Morrall of the Colts and Joe Namath of the Jets, the Super Bowl quarterbacks who were named the Most Valuable Players in the two major pro football leagues, will be honored by the Long Island A.C. at the Garden City Hotel, January 31.

Each will receive a 19-inch bronze statuette, the work of Jimmy Ridlon of Syracuse, former defensive back in the NFL.

COLT WATCH COLT WATCH COLT WATCH COLT WATCH COLT WATCH COLT WATCH COLT WATCH COLT

I CAN'T DO AS GOOD AS EARL CAN—UNITAS

by Norm Miller
Daily News

January 9, 1969—Fort Lauderdale—This was another routine workday for Johnny Unitas, backup quarterback. He loosened his arm with passes of 10 to 30 yards at the schoolboy field where the Colts are preparing for the Super Bowl.

He ran through play drills, mostly with the No. 2 backfield combo of Terry Cole and Tim Brown. He sat next to Earl Morrall at the offensive meeting.

Johnny Unitas looked like a man who is ready to play against the Jets Sunday. He knows there is little chance. In Johnny's frank appraisal: "I can't do it as good as Earl can."

The torn elbow muscle in the golden arm that made him pro football's top quarterback for more than 10 years has improved considerably during the past month but, by his admission, "it still isn't 100%."

"Sure, I'd love to play," he says. "I'm a competitor. But I have to be able to accept the situation. It's not because I'm not good enough to play. I was not beaten out of my position. I'm out because of an injury."

His relationship with Morrall, the Colts say, is one of complete cooperation and respect. In that area, coach Don Shula says: "It is amazing the degree to which they are alike as individuals."

January 11, 1969—Miami Beach—Pete Rozelle officially legitimized the AFL-NFL championship game by calling it the Super Bowl. Like the man who marries the gal on the child's third birthday, the commissioner conceded that the publicly accepted term, Super Bowl, "seems to have taken hold, and I think we're pretty well set with it."

Rozelle said his resistance to the name had been based on a belief that the slang word super was corny. "It was used by kids back in our junior high days", he said. He was referring to the gum popping girls who would express satisfaction about anything at all by saying 'chee, that's 'super.'"

Rozelle said that, as far as he knows, the word Super Bowl was first used by the young son of Lamar Hunt, owner of the Chiefs. The boy had one of those high-bouncing super-balls, and it evolved from that.

SUPER REF

January 11, 1969—Miami—Pro football commissioner Pete Rozelle announced today that Tom Bell of the NFL will head the officiating crew for Sunday's Super Bowl. Bell, a Lexington, Kentucky, lawyer who has officiated eight NFL seasons, will be referee.

Continuing the policy of alternating the officiating positions between NFL and AFL each year, the remainder of the crew will be made up of umpire Wal Parker, AFL; head linesman George Murphy, NFL; line judge Cal Lepore, AFL; back judge Jack Reader, AFL; and field judge Joe Gonzalez, NFL.

YOUNG IDEAS

by Dick Young
Daily News

January 10, 1969—Fort Lauderdale—Weeb Ewbank is whacking up his AFL share ($8,500 or so) equally among his four assistant coaches and Mrs. Ewbank. "My wife is an assistant coach," he says.

When in Baltimore, Weeb tossed his share into the players' pool. He has told his Jet players he's doing it differently this time because most of them make more money than the assistant coaches.

FAMILY MAN

January 11, 1969—Bob Talamini, Jets' tackle who is in Florida with his booming family, was asked how players can get up emotionally for a big game under such placid domestic conditions. It was pointed out that, in the old days, players were isolated from their families, and went into the contest as raving savages.

"Are you kidding?" said Talamini. "This one will be for blood. Have you ever been locked in a room for a week with a wife and four kids?"

⋆⋆⋆ FiNAL

DAILY ⓝ NEWS
NEW YORK'S PICTURE NEWSPAPER ®

MORE THAN TWICE
THE CIRCULATION
OF ANY OTHER
PAPER IN AMERICA

New York, N.Y. 10017. Monday, January 13, 1969

JETS SUPER CHAMPS
Snell's TD, 3 FG Shock Colts, 16-7

Jet fullback Matt Snell, head down and ball securely tucked, breaks into clear and heads for paydirt to score in second period.

Story on page 60; other pix page 1, centerfold

JANUARY 12, 1969

New York 16, Baltimore 7

New York	0	7	6	3	— 16
Baltimore	0	0	0	7	— 7

Super Bowl III

The lopsided 18-1 odds were stacked heavily against the Jets, but the underdogs prevailed in what was called "the impossible victory." After promising a win by the Jets, Broadway Joe Namath fulfilled his guarantee by leading the Jets to a 16-7 upset victory over the Colts. It was the AFL's first Super Bowl victory, and it changed the face of professional sports forever.

Fullback Matt Snell carried 30 times for 121 yards—both totals easily surpassing old Super Bowl records. After giving in to his 17 of 28 passes for 195 yards, the Colts finally conceded their praise for Joe Namath's superstar performance. Among the 75,377 fans on hand for the Jets' victory were the Apollo 8 astronauts, Vice President Spiro Agnew, and Senator Ted Kennedy.

Super Bowl Matchup

by Joe O'Day
Daily News

Jets Offense

No.	Player	Pos.	Ht.	Wt.

80 George Sauer Split End 6-2 195
One of the finest split ends in the pros, this Texan topped the Jets in pass receptions for the second straight year . . . He has only average speed but has tremendous moves and hands . . . Opponents often double-teamed him but with his fakes he still came up with the ball . . . He's been a pro four years.

75 Winston Hill Left Tackle 6-4 280
His job is to provide the pass blocking for Joe Willie and no defensive end has climbed the hill all season . . . Had tendency to hold but overcame the short-coming through hard work . . . Another debit is his lack of mobility on running plays . . . Six years in pros.

61 Bob Talamini Left Guard 6-1 255
A nine-year veteran who was acquired from the Oilers, is considered one of the better blockers in the league—especially on sweeps . . . Has title game experience off his many years in Houston.

52 John Schmitt Center 6-4 245
Local boy from Hofstra in fifth year as pro, Smitty ranks as the top pivotman in the league . . . Also provides solid protection for Namath in handling those hard-charging middle linebackers . . . Is excellent at pulling out and leading downfield blocking on running plays.

66 Randy Rasmussen Right Guard 6-2 255
Only a sophomore, he was moved into spot when Ewbank swung Dave Herman over to tackle . . . Rated an average pass blocker, Randy more than did the job as he used his speed and strength to overcome the mistakes.

67 Dave Herman Right Tackle 6-1 255
One of the premier guards after five years in the AFL . . . Herman switched to tackle to afford more pass protection for Namath . . . Move was necessitated when rookie Sam Walton broke down in the late stages of the season.

87 Pete Lammons Tight End 6-3 233
Has played in shadows of Sauer and Don Maynard for three years but is rated a fine blocker and a fine down-and-in receiver on short-yardage situations . . . Possesses fine hands.

12 Joe Namath Quarterback 6-2 195
Four years in AFL, he's one of the finest passers in pro ball . . . Broadway Joe has the quickest release . . . Despite "famed" hobbled knees, has started every game in his four years as a pro . . . Also, is a threat to throw the bomb anytime.

32 Emerson Boozer Running Back 5-11 202
Still not fully recovered from off-season knee surgery . . . Has still retained his speed after three AFL years but lost some of the balance that made him a tremendous open-field threat as a rookie.

41   Matt Snell   Running Back 6-2   219

Another knee surgery retread . . . Snell, out of Carle Place locally, rebounded strongly this season . . . Topped team in ground gaining by pounding out better than 700 yards . . . Good runner with excellent acceleration and solid pass blocker . . . Can also receive on flares.

13   Don Maynard   Flanker   6-1   179

Castoff from the NFL, this Texan really matured and holds all-time pro mark for yards gained by pass receptions . . . Has phenomenal moves and hands with great speed after 11 years in big time.

Substitutes: (11) J. Turner, (15) Parilli, (23) Rademacher, (29) B. Turner, (30) Smolinski, (31) Mathis, (33) Johnson, (71) Walton, (74) Richardson.

Colts Defense

No.	Player	Pos.	Ht.	Wt.

78   Bubba Smith   Left End   6-7   295

Tremendous speed coupled with big hands . . . Pro two years . . . Rated possibly best young lineman in league . . . Possesses great lateral motion on running plays and has nose for ball . . . An overpowering rusher, who literally runs over the opposition.

74   Billy Ray Smith   Left Tackle 6-4   250

A 10-year veteran who uses strength to manipulate opponents into making bad moves . . . Great "in fighter" who generally stays back to protect against the draw . . . Fair pass rusher but has experience and savvy to call his shots.

76   Fred Miller   Right Tackle 6-3   250

Starter for five of his six seasons in pros . . . Makes up for his shortcomings in size with cat-like moves and knowledge . . . A tough cookie who can handle the best.

81   Ordell Brasse   Right End   6-4   245

After 12 seasons in the rough, tough NFL, few, if any, foes, have found a chink in his armament . . . Has better than average speed but is solid on the pass rush and excellent on recovering for a run . . . Few turn his end . . . He and Miller complement each other brilliantly.

32   Mike Curtis   Left Linebacker 6-2 232

Fullback at Duke, this four-year pro came into his own and won All-League honors . . . Excellent speed and agility . . . Has great pursuit and is a hard-hitting tackler . . . Helps out on pass defense, too.

53   Dennis Gaubatz   Middle Linebacker 6-2 232

Called "The Animal" by his teammates, he is rough with speed and exceptional strength . . . Smart and reads plays well . . . Like Curtis, he is considered one of the hardest hitters on the team . . . A pro six years.

66   Don Shinnick   Right Linebacker 6-0 228

A 12-year veteran of the wars who knows all the answers . . . Has excellent recovery after making move to abet cornerbacks on pass coverage . . . Enjoys blitzing and reads offenses well . . . Holds NFL record for interceptions by a linebacker with 36 steals.

40   Bobby Boyd   Left Cornerback 5-10 192

Sixth sense for covering receivers and leads active defensive backs in pass interceptions . . . After nine years, has lost some speed, but makes up for it with savvy . . . Tough tackler . . . Will more than shadow Don Maynard all day.

43   Lenny Lyles   Right Cornerback 6-2 204

Another hard-hitting veteran . . . Been around 11 years . . . Rated one of the fastest cornerbacks in the NFL despite size . . . Always plays his man tight, and has power to jar any ball loose . . . He'll play George Sauer in this one.

20   Jerry Logan   Strong Safety 6-1   190

Another key in the Colts' strong secondary . . . Assets are speed and strength . . . A hard-hitting tackler tough to outrun . . . He can be outmaneuvered, but only by the good ones . . . A pro six years.

21   Rick Volk   Free Safety   6-3   195

Only a sophomore but already heralded as one of the finest safetymen in the league . . . Very fast and strong . . . Won job from veteran Alvin Haymond as rookie a year ago . . . Has football sense despite little experience.

Substitutes: (37) Austin, (47) Stukes, (49) Lee, (55) Porter, (64) S. Williams, (79) Michaels, (85) Hilton.

Mom Roots for Both Super Sons

by Phil Pepe
Daily News

Jets or Colts, Colts or Jets? For most people the choice is simple. They go where their rooting interest—or their money—is.

But for a lovely lady in the tiny coal-mining town of Swoyersville, Pennsylvania, the problem is one of mixed emotions.

"I don't know who to root for," said Mrs. Mary Michaels, 73 years young, mother of eight children (six living), grandmother of "17 or 18," great-grandmother of eight.

There were seven Michaels boys—Stanley, John, Tom, Joe, Ed, Walter Jr., John and Lou, the baby. Walter Jr. is defensive backfield coach of the Jets. Lou, the baby, is the placekicking specialist of the Colts, and they will come face to face today in the super colossal, super sensational Super Bowl in Miami and, because of it, Mrs. Mary Michaels has a dilemma.

"I have no idea," Mrs. Michaels said. "They're both good sons. I don't know who's going to win. Whoever is tougher, that's who's going to win."

It is simple logic from a woman uncomplicated by the complex world of Xs and Os. Hers is the logic of emotion, and to her, this is not a game of Joe Namath against the ferocious Colt defense; it is not a game of the veteran coach, Weeb Ewbank, against the young genius of Don Shula; it is not a game of the old league against the young league. To Mrs. Mary Michaels, it is a game of her son, Walter, against her baby, Louie.

"My Walter is a good boy . . . a good coach . . . but my Louie is playing, so maybe he's going to get it. It's luck that will decide. Whoever has the luck will win."

The football mother remembers what it was like with all those vigorous, energetic boys growing up in Swoyersville. She has lived in the same house for more than 50 years.

"All my boys were born in this house," she says.

Swoyersville, as close as Mrs. Michaels can estimate, is 100 miles from Wilkes-Barre. "It's 30 cents by bus," she says.

Mr. Michaels worked in the coal mines, and his oldest boy, Stanley, followed him there, but he was determined that his other boys would have a better life. They found it with football.

"Stanley and Thomas, my two oldest boys, played football at Swoyersville High," Mrs. Michaels recalled. "When I went to see them play, I got so sick when I saw all those other boys jumping on top of my boys. I wanted to go down and help my boys."

Now she has become an avid football fan. "I enjoy football. I always put on the television and watch it, even if it is not the Jets or the Colts. I still go to the high school games if I know any of the boys who are playing."

She has gone to New York and Baltimore to see games, and to Cleveland, when Walt played for the Browns. In 1966, she was enshrined in the Football Hall of Fame at Canton, Ohio, as Football Mother of the Year. But, today, in Miami, is the culmination of all her dreams . . . of her life.

"I can't believe it—that it came like that—two of them together," she said. "I'm glad they both made it. I'm proud of both of them, but who will I cheer for? I don't know. It's going to be tough. I guess I'll just cross my fingers for both of them and see what happens."

JETS DEFENSE

No.	Player	Pos.	Ht.	Wt.	Yr.
42	Randy Beverly	RCB	5-11	198	2
86	Verlon Biggs	RE	6-4	268	4
80	John Elliott	RT	6-4	249	2
62	Al Atkinson	MLB	6-2	230	4
72	Paul Rochester	LT	6-2	250	9
81	Gerry Philbin	LE	6-2	245	5
22	Jim Hudson	SS	6-2	210	4
60	Larry Grantham	RLB	6-0	212	9
51	Ralph Baker	LLB	6-3	235	5
24	John Sample	LCB	6-1	204	11

Substitutes: (26) Richards, (43) Dockery, (45) Christy, (47) D'Amato, (48) Gordon, (50) McAdams, (56) Crane, (63) Neidert, (85) Thompson.

COLTS OFFENSE

No.	Player	Pos.	Ht.	Wt.	Yr.
28	Jimmy Orr	SE	5-11	185	11
72	Bob Vogel	LT	6-5	250	6
62	Glenn Ressler	LG	6-3	250	3
50	Bill Curry	C	6-2	235	4
71	Dan Sullivan	RG	6-3	250	7
73	Sam Ball	RT	6-4	240	3
88	John Mackey	TE	6-2	224	6
15	Earl Morrall	QB	6-2	206	13
41	Tom Matte	RB	6-0	214	8
45	Jerry Hill	RB	5-11	215	7
87	Willie Richardson	FL	6-2	198	6

Substitutes: (16) Ward, (19) Unitas, (25) Hawkins, (26) Pearson, (27) Perkins, (34) Cole, (52) Szymanski, (61) Johnson, (75) J. Williams, (80) Cogdill, (84) Mitchell.

THE SORCERER VS. THE APPRENTICE

January 12, 1969—It will be the Sorcerer against the Apprentice with Weeb Ewbank of the Jets and the Colts' Don Shula cast in the respective roles. The roly-poly Ewbank won championships with the Colts in 1958 and '59, while Shula moved in as a defensive coach in the not-so-halcyon years that followed those back-to-back titles.

Ewbank was offered a five-year plan by new owner Sonny Werblin in 1963 and quickly accepted the challenge. Meanwhile, Colts' owner Carroll Rosenbloom figured Shula had learned his lessons well and installed the former Ewbank pupil as head coach. Neither, of course, succeeded at first, although Shula got the Colts moving to win his first conference crown in 1964 and he just missed a year ago, when the Rams caught him inside the sixteenth pole.

Ewbank, who is the only coach ever to win NFL and AFL championships, has compiled a 193-81 record in 15 years with the Colts and Jets. Shula, on the other side of the field, has an envious 63-18 mark in six seasons running the Hosses.

Jets Find Out How Super They Are Today

Colts Still 17½ Pt. Picks in Miami

by Norm Miller
Daily News

Miami—Broadway Joe takes on the Earl of Baltimore today in a mission to convince America that clean, modest living does not necessarily pay off.

It's the third Super Bowl, matching the champion Jets of the AFL vs. the champ Colts of the NFL; pitting Joe Namath roustabout and popoff, against Earl Morrall, the quiet, clean-livin' family man; stacking all the Jets plungers who have taken the unusually high speed of 17 1/2 points against the Colts' backers confident enough to lay the price.

It is without doubt the single most ballyhooed showpiece in American sport. It is a clash that will attract more than 75,000 to the Orange Bowl and countless millions to the TV and radio sets at the 3 p.m. (NBC) starting time.

Among the live watchers will be this nation's three Apollo 8 astronauts, Colonel Frank Borman, Lieutenant Colonel William Anders and Captain James A. Lovell, Jr.

It is a clash for money and for prestige. The $2.5 million TV-radio revenue sets up a jackpot of $15,000 to each winning player and $7,500 to each loser.

Just as important is the prestige battle between the 49-year-old NFL, which boasts it is the major league of pro football, and the 9-year-old AFL, which insists that claim is nonsense.

Since his arrival here a week ago, Broadway Joe has done his best to knock the Colts' Super-team reputation.

At a Miami touchdown luncheon at which he was honored, Joe "guaranteed" the guests the Jets would win.

The Colts have responded with quiet amusement to Namath's popoffs. For the most part, their reaction could be summed up: "He'd better come ready to play on Sunday."

Newsmen side with the oddsmakers. A poll at press headquarters showed a 49-6 margin favoring the Colts.

SUPER BOWL FACTS

At stake—World professional football championship.
Rivals—Baltimore Colts of the NFL and New York Jets of the AFL.
Site—Orange Bowl, Miami.
Time of Game—3:05 p.m.
Odds—Colts favored by 17 1/2 points.
Television—NBC, 3 p.m. (Miami area blacked out).
Radio—NBC, 3 p.m.
Series record—NFL won 2; AFL won 0.

Rival quarterbacks—Baltimore, Earl Morrall; New York, Joe Namath.
Winner's share—$15,000 per player.
Loser's share—$7,500 per player.
Expected attendance—75,354.
Ball used—NFL ball when Colts are in possession; AFL ball, slightly more pointed, when Jets have possession.
Extra points—NFL rule for one-point conversions will be in effect. There will be no two-point conversions as in the AFL.
Tie game—If game ends in tie, teams will play sudden-death and winner will be first to score.
Home team—Colts, in blue jerseys.
Visiting team—Jets, in white jerseys.

Pop! There's 1 Less Colt Fan

by Phil Pepe
Daily News

A small, intimate gathering of 30 or 35 watched the Super Bowl in Joe Namath's East Side bistro, Bachelors III, and among them was one misplaced person—a Colt fan. He said his name was Charlie O'Connor and he was from Worcester, Massachusetts, and he knew where he was going.

"I figured I would have fun gloating over the Colts' win," Charlie said impishly. "By the second quarter I knew I was in trouble. Now, I'm a new Jets' fan—and I'm a new fan of Joe Namath. I'm convinced."

Charlie said the rest of the crowd gave him a hard time, but was "a friendly hard time. They're a great bunch of people. They even gave me the first glass of champagne."

It was champagne on the house when the gun sounded, but in the noisy pub, nobody heard the final gun.

"I had a bottle of champagne in my hands while they were ticking off the final seconds," said Joe Dellapina, who manages the place for Namath, Bobby Van and Ray Abbruzese.

"When it went to a zero, I popped the cork. We drank a dozen bottles.

"It was a fantastic game. I knew the Jets would win. I know Joe and when he said the Jets would win, I knew he meant it. He's a fantastic guy. I heard a lot of stories about him before I started to work here. But since I've been working for him, I think he's one of the finest people and one of the finest gentlemen I've ever known."

Barbara De Snoo, a waitress, said the scene in Bachelors III was "indescribable. It was fantastic, just fantastic."

And Charlie O'Connor, the Colt fan from Worcester, sipped his champagne and said: "I'm coming back here next year."

Daily News Cover, Monday, January 13, 1969

Life Continues Exciting for Moonmen

by Norm Miller
Daily News

Miami—The Super Game brought out the super celebrities, headed by the Apollo 8 astronauts, Frank Borman, Jim Lovell and Bill Anders, who received as big a hand as the players when introduced.

At the Saturday night round of pre-Super Bowl parties, one of the astronauts wowed the guests with his remark: "We're really excited about this Super Bowl game." As if shooting the moon weren't enough excitement for one lifetime.

Other celebs at the game were Vice President-elect Spiro Agnew; Senator Ted Kennedy and his father, Joe Kennedy; Ohio governor James Rhoades; Herb Klein, aide to President-elect Richard Nixon; Bob Hope and a host of entertainment stars.

Jim Kensil, assistant to Commissioner Pete Rozelle, announced his staff issued a record 1,209 press credentials for this game. It worked down to 367 working newsmen, 235 photographers, 214 TV and radio men and 82 new media officials.

The third Superclash also brought forth the SuperScalper. A bellhop in Ft. Lauderdale claimed he arranged for the sale of a pair of tickets for $300.

For NBC, it was the super production. The eleven cameras used were four more than ever before put to work on a football game. For replays, five video tape machines were used, three of these slow motion.

The game was beamed to more than 1,000 radio and TV stations.

Talk About A Landing—Wow! Bill Gallo cartoon, Daily News, Monday, January 13, 1969.

B'way Joe Jolts Colts in Miami

by Larry Fox
Daily News

Miami—They challenged Joe Namath to put up or shut up today and Broadway Joe hasn't stopped talking yet. In one of pro football's greatest upsets, the Jets scored the AFL's first Super Bowl victory in three tries by beating the Colts, 16-7, as 75,377 fans in the Orange Bowl and millions in the TV audience marveled at the one-sided nature of the game.

The Colts had shut out four NFL opponents during their championship season but, in the end, it was Baltimore scrambling to get on the board before the finish with sore-armed Johnny Unitas trying, as a 35-year-old sub, to reach back for one more day of his youth.

Namath was the guy they said would rattle; he was the guy they said needed humility; he was the guy who threw the interceptions.

But, when they got on the field this overcast afternoon, he was the man directing the only kind of disciplined attack that can beat a team like the Colts—and he did it without throwing a single interception.

Meanwhile, the Jets' rush line was hurrying Earl Morrall, the former Giant, into three interceptions—all of them critical—and

these, plus one more steal against Unitas, were the difference.

Against what was billed as one of the greatest defensive teams in the history of football, the Jets piled up 21 first downs, rushed for 142 yards and passed for 206 more.

The Jets had thrown 49 passes in their title game victory over Oakland, and NFL boosters scoffed at the new "basketball" league. but today the Colts had to throw the ball 41 times in a desperate effort to catch up and they didn't even get on the board until only 3:19 remained in the game.

At that, it took a fourth-down completion by Unitas to start the drive, two roughness penalties to help it along and three cracks from the 1 before Jerry Hill finally carried it across. The Jets had led the AFL in defense, but nobody thought this meant anything.

Matt Snell and Jim Turner were Namath's chief accomplices on the offense. Snell, the fullback whose left knee had been aspirated only Thursday, had the greatest day of his career. Carrying an amazing 30 times, he blasted the Colt defense for 121 yards, both totals easily Super Bowl records.

He also caught four passes for

40 yards as the Jets went to a short game to counter Baltimore's feared zone defense.

Snell scored the Jets' only touchdown on a second-period four-yard sweep that capped a 12-play, 80-yard drive. When Snell went over with 5:57 elapsed in the second quarter, it marked the first time an AFL team had ever even led in the Super Bowl. It also marked the ability of this put-down AFL team to ram the ball down its favored opponent's throat.

Turner, who broke all the pro football placekicking records this year, booted three field goals from 32, 30 and 9 yards out. The last was the most difficult, from a near impossible angle to the left. Turner missed twice, from the 41 in the second quarter and the 42 in the fourth. Lou Michaels of the Colts missed from the 27 in the first quarter and the 46 in the second.

Unlike past Super Bowl games, this time the NFL team made the mistakes and the AFL entry refused to lose its poise. It was the NFL team that ended up taking swings at Johnny Sample. The Jets stuck to their game plan throughout as shown by the high rushing total and the distribution of pass receptions. In addition to Snell's four, Bill Mathis caught three for 20 yards and tight end Pete Lammons caught two for 13.

George Sauer had a big day against Lenny Lyles, catching eight for 133 yards and there is no telling how Lyles may have been affected by being forced to tackle Snell all afternoon. The Jets ran at the Colts' right side all game and eventually Ordell Brasse was relieved from the contest by rookie Roy Hilton.

Don Maynard, whose pulled hamstring was "shot" on Thursday, didn't catch a pass. But he came close to grabbing two TD bombs. On one, he made a diving catch beyond the end line; on the other he had his man clearly beaten, but Namath overthrew him.

The victory, of course, was a triumph for Weeb Ewbank, the little coach who almost lost his job last year when the Jets fell just short of winning their Eastern Division title.

When the Jets won the AFL title two weeks ago, he became the first coach ever to win it all in both leagues. By beating his old team, the Colts, today, the 61-year-old Hoosier earned himself a sure place in pro football's Hall of Fame.

"We are a great team and this is the start of a new era," said Ewbank, and the Jets awarded their game ball to the AFL as a tribute to this first victory.

"It was a victory for the entire American Football League. We overcame our critics," said Namath, who went out for one play in the third quarter. That's when he was hit by Fred Miller in the right thumb that has been bothering him all year.

Joe still ended up with a Super Bowl record of 17 completions on only 28 attempts for 206 yards. He also tied Bart Starr's 1968 record of zero interceptions.

The course of this game was determined in the closing moments of the first quarter and the first six minutes of the second once it was established that the favored Colts were not going to blow the Jets off the field.

The Jets had third-and-one on their 13 and Namath made a daring "Unitas" call. Instead of the line plunge, he called a pass to Sauer. Sauer had the first down made at the 16 but fumbled when hit by Lyles, and sub linebacker Ron Porter recovered for Baltimore at the 12.

This was the kind of error that had ruined Kansas City and Oakland in previous Super Bowls. But, after Tom Matte, a standout for the Colts all afternoon, gained seven yards, the Colts blundered right back.

Baltimore had been using two tight ends on some plays to get a physical advantage over the Jet cornermen and Morrall aimed for the other one, former Raider Tom Mitchell, in the end zone. The pass was high, but catchable, it bounced off Mitchell's fingertips and Randy Beverly, the little guy everybody said would be run out of the ballpark, had the first of his two interceptions.

Now the Jets had possession at their 20. Four straight times Namath called Snell's number and the former Ohio State fullback, first prize catch the Jets ever made in the "war" with the NFL, smashed for steady gains—one yard, seven yards, six yards and 12.

After an incomplete pass, Namath caught Baltimore in a blitz and threw to Bill Mathis for six. Then he went to Sauer for 14 (longest gain of the drive) and again for 11 as Lyles almost blew the whole TD with a futile gamble for the

Matt Snell takes a Joe Namath handoff during the Super Bowl. (Daily News photo)

interception. Only a late save by Rick Volk, who twice had to be helped from the field, saved the score.

The Jets now had first down at the 23. Emerson Boozer gained two, Namath passed to Snell for 12 and a first down on the 9. Matt then carried it over in two tries. The TD was a sweep around left end as Brasse was blocked and Volk was outrun.

The Colts had a great chance to get back in the game in the last three minutes of the first half when a 58-yard run by Matte gave them a first down at the Jet 16. Hill ran for one, then Morrall was intercepted for the second time. This time he was aiming for Willie Richardson in the end zone and underthrew his man and Sample cut in front for a steal on the goal line.

The Jets couldn't move out of danger at this point and Johnson had to punt from the end zone. The Colts started at the Jet 42 and, after Morrall passed to Hill for one, there followed the wildest play of the game.

Earl resurrected the old flea flicker, had his receiver open for a huge touchdown—but then threw to the wrong man for an interception.

The play started as a handoff to Matte, who passed back to Morrall from the right flat. Jimmy Orr, who had scored on a similar play against Atlanta earlier this year, was wide open about the 5. Nobody was near him but two officials and they were 10 yards away, too. Instead, Morrall, who said he was turned the wrong way taking the flip from Matte, went to Hill over the middle and Jim Hudson picked it off on the 12 on the last play of the half.

So the Jets went off with a 7-0 lead and they made it 10-0 easily with a Turner field goal when Ralph Baker recovered Matte's fumble on the first play of the second half. The next two times they got the ball, the Jets also were able to pick up three-pointers by Turner and they led, 16-0, after 1:34 of the final period.

Unitas, lonely and overlooked in all the pre-Super Bowl excitement, had been warming up from early in the third period. He went in, finally, with 3:51 remaining in the quarter.

The first series he ran, the Colts had to punt. On the second, he moved his team from the Colt 27 to the Jet 25, only to have Beverly pull an end-zone interception by wresting the ball away

from Orr.

Then, with 6:34 to go, Unitas shucked the age and aches. The Colts were at their 20, three straight passes missed, but, on fourth down, Unitas hit Orr for 17 and a first down. He missed two more, then threw to John Mackey for 11. Adding a personal foul call on the Jets' John Elliott for piling on, the Colts now had first down on the Jets 37.

It was Unitas of old, picking the defense, finding the sideline and fighting the clock. Down the field the Colts moved to a first down at the 2. Matte was stopped by Paul Rochester for no gain, but the Jets were offside. It was first down on the 1.

Unitas tried a sneak but was stopped by Verlon Biggs. Matte hit right guard by Al Atkinson and Hudson grabbed him. Finally, Hill went over left tackle for the TD.

Only 2:21 remained when the Jets took over and, with Snell running on six straight plays, they managed to kill all but eight seconds of it.

"VIG" BETTING

January 13, 1969—The Super Bowl was one of the biggest betting sports events in the last decade, but the books did not get hurt by the upset because of a little thing called "vigorish."
The man who got hurt was the regular bettor, the smart money boys. "They went big for Baltimore," said one football accountant. "Most of the Jets money came from first-time bettors, sentimentalists."
But the bookie was sitting pretty with money on both ends and that old "vigorish." Meaning whether you took the 17 1/2 points or gave them, you still had to put up $5.50 to win $5.

DAILY NEWS

NEW YORK'S PICTURE NEWSPAPER ®

Vol. 50. No. 182   Copr. 1969 News Syndicate Co. Inc.   New York, N.Y. 10017, Thursday, January 23, 1969★   WEATHER: Partly sunny and mild.

10¢

10,000 FANS MOB THOSE JETS

NEWS photo by Paul DeMaria

Joe's Fans Won't Let Him Pass. All alone in a crowd, with hardly any blocking, Joe Namath picks his
Super_.ts. Mayor and 10,000 other fans acclaimed heroes at City Hall. way to sports car he was given yesterday during City's hurrah for
—*Stories p. 22; other pics. centerfold and back page*

Probe Cop's Little Notebook

Story on Page 2

The New York heroes' lives certainly did not calm down after the culmination of the championship season. After being greeted at the airport by screaming fans, the Super Bowl champs were later honored at a reception in City Hall Park. Joe Namath won the George Halas Award as "most courageous" player of the year, and Weeb Ewbank was named AFL coach of the year.

Namath's life off the field continued to be the source of much attention. In a seemingly uncharacteristic move, Namath passed up the opportunity to receive his new car for being named Super Bowl MVP so that he could instead visit his mother in his home-town of Beaver Falls. Namath also signed to make a guest appearance on the Kraft Music Hall and pondered a role in a movie in his new life as Super Bowl Champion.

Super Bowl Celebration

Love Those Jets!
City Reception Set

by Joe Trimble
Daily News

Our Town has a love affair going with its first sports champion in six years. Everybody loves the Super Jets and Super Joe, and Fun City is throwing them a blowout next Wednesday.

Mayor John V. Lindsay announced yesterday that the Jolly Green Heroes who upset the $17^1/_2$ point odds and the Baltimore Colts in the Super Bowl in Miami last Sunday will be honored with an official City Hall reception. Hizzoner will meet coach Weeb Ewbank and the players on the Hall's steps at 11:45 a.m. that day.

The reception was set for Wednesday because 11 of the Jets had to remain behind in Florida to help represent the East against the West in the AFL All-Star Game Sunday in Jacksonville's Gator Bowl.

A copy of the citation that was presented to the New York Jets at City Hall for their Super Bowl victory.

THE NEWS
NEW YORK'S PICTURE NEWSPAPER

Whereas the NEW YORK JETS scored a stunning victory to win the Professional Football Championship of the World.

Whereas against seemingly overwhelming odds, our JETS' forged a 16-7 triumph over Baltimore's Colts in the SUPER BOWL.

Whereas they have given New York its first sports world title in six years, and first football crown since 1956.

Whereas the JETS' feat will be remembered as long as football is played.

Whereas their superb team effort, faith and confidence set an inspiring example to New Yorkers and the entire Nation.

The New York Daily News
proudly presents
this
CITATION
to the

New York Jets

January 22, 1969

Fans Give Jets Super Welcome at Kennedy

by Tommy Pugh and Art Mulligan
Daily News

Five hundred cheering, screaming fans gave a tumultuous Kennedy Airport welcome to coach Weeb Ewbank and 13 of his World Champion Jets yesterday when they arrived from Miami after crushing the Baltimore Colts in the Super Bowl Sunday, 16-7.

Also on hand to greet Ewbank and Jets' owner Phil Iselin were Mayor Lindsay, City Council President Francis X. Smith, Queens Borough President Sidney Leviss, and John (Bud) Palmer, the city's official greeter.

The crowd was somewhat disappointed on learning that the Jets' great quarterback, Joe Namath, was not aboard the plane and neither was the mammoth Super Bowl trophy.

Namath and 10 other Jets remained in Florida to play in the AFL Pro Bowl game at Jacksonville next Sunday. The trophy was to arrive on a later plane, according to Jean Kersey, public relations representative for Northeast Airlines.

The crowd, liberally sprinkled with children, started arriving at the Northeast Airlines terminal shoirtly after noon. The Jets' charter flight, scheduled to land at 1:30 p.m., was 45 minutes late.

When Lindsay arrived via helicopter at 1:30 p.m., the assembled crowd started chanting: "We want a parade; we want a parade."

Lindsay said, "Well, we're

Jets fans cheer as their favorite team arrives at the airport. (News photo by Gene Kappock)

going to do something for them."

Asked what he thought about Namath, the mayor said: "I'm for him."

Would you like to run against him for mayor?" Lindsay was asked.

"I don't want to run against anyone—right now," he replied.

When the Jet contingent, led by Ewbank and Iselin, entered Gate 9 in the terminal, everyone surged into the corridor. The Jet group, many of the players accompanied by their wives and

Larry Dieso of Queens with his three-year-old cousin Michael Gardini, as they wait for the Jets to arrive. (News photo by Gene Kappock)

children, finally made their way to the main lobby of the terminal for the official greeting.

After Bud Palmer introduced everyone all around, Leviss presented Ewbank with a proclamation congratulating the Jets and reasserting his declaration that Sunday January 12 was Jets' Day in Queens, whether they had won or lost.

While newsmen and television men struggled to interview Ewbank, the mayor and the others, the band kept blaring away and 125 third-grade youngsters from the Rhame Ave. school in East Rockaway, Queens, kept chanting: "We want Namath," "We want Joe," and "Two, four, six, eight, Who do we appreciate? Namath, Namath, Namath."

Walter Weltner, four, and his brother Steven, one, wait to greet the champion N.Y. Jets at Kennedy Airport. (News photo by Tom Gallagher)

THEY FORGOT TROPHY

January 14, 1969—Fort Lauderdale—The Jets headed home today minus what they came to get: the World Championship trophy.

Bob Fleischer, who helped out as a trainer during the Jets' pre-game preparations here, said that the big trophy and the game ball were forgotten when the team left its hotel headquarters. The Jets remembered them when they reached the airport, where a chartered plane was waiting.

Fleischer went back and collected the items and put them on a regular commercial flight. The team has agreed to present the game ball to the AFL.

Michele Flores shows a Joe Loonan team photo given out by the *News*. (News photo by Anthony Casale)

NEW LINE

by Larry Fox
Daily News

When you dial their offices, the telephone operators no longer answer, "Good morning, New York Jets." As of yesterday, it's "Good morning, World Champions."

MOVIES CALL

January 14, 1969, Hollywood—A movie company today offered Joe Namath a role in a new film in which the Jets' Super Bowl hero would play a French resistance fighter in World War II. Levy-Gardner-Laven Productions dispatched a television program to Namath offering him the role in "Underground," to be filmed in Ireland this spring, and requested a meeting to discuss salary and related matters.

Namath Is Signed for TVer

by George Maksian
Daily News

Pro football's superhero Joe Namath has been signed to make a guest appearance on the Wednesday, March 5, colorcast of the Kraft Music Hall over NBC from 9 to 10 p.m.

The Jets' star quarterback, who led the team to victory over Baltimore in Sunday's Super Bowl game in Miami, will be seen in a music-comedy hour entitled "Boys' Night Out."

A network spokesman said that Namath's duties on the program have not been worked out as yet. Host for the show will be Robert Goulet. Other guests include Phil Silvers, the Lettermen and ballet star Edward Villella.

Jets quarterback Joe Namath laughs it up as he models sports clothes during his show. (News photo by Jim Garrett)

EWBANK, SHULA COACHES OF YR.

January 19, 1969—Super Bowl coaches Weeb Ewbank of the Jets and Don Shula of the Baltimore Colts yesterday were named AFL and NFL coaches of the year, respectively, by the Professional Football Writers of America.

Ewbank, who guided the Jets to their first AFL championship and then to a stunning 16-7 upset over the Colts in the Super Bowl, and Shula both received about 80 percent of the votes cast by the writers, according to secretary-treasurer Bill Guthrie.

Ewbank will be presented with his award at halftime of the Jets exhibition game against the College All-Stars at Chicago next August while Shula will be honored during one of the Colts' home games next season.

NAMATH MAKES THAT CAR WAIT ON HIS MOM

by Larry Fox
Daily News

January 21, 1969—Memo to those few members of the Hate Joe Namath Club who didn't go underground on Super Sunday: Anybody who'd rather visit with his mother than pick up a free new car can't be all bad.

But that's what Joe Willie is doing. Namath was supposed to receive *Sport* magazine's Dodge Charger as MVP in the Super Bowl tomorrow. However, after playing in Sunday's AFL All-Star game in Jacksonville, Florida, Joe went back home to Beaver Falls to visit his mother. He had planned to be there Thanksgiving Day, but that trip was delayed because of the Jets' Eastern Division title clinching.

So Joe yesterday informed the magazine that he wasn't coming back to New York a day before the mayor's reception just to get a car and eat an Italian lunch at Leone's.

After all, Mom's Hungarian goulash always tastes better and, besides, Joe leaves Friday for a two-week tour of service installations in Japan, Okinawa, Guam, the Philippines and Hawaii.

So *Sport* called an automatic at the line of scrimmage and changed the play. Namath goes into the driver's seat tomorrow afternoon following the City Hall affair.

Grateful City Says Thanks to Jets

by Larry Fox
Daily News

Before an enthusiastic crowd of 10,000 fans—most of them teenagers—New York's Super Bowl champs were honored by the City of New York in ceremonies on the steps of City Hall. Joe Namath and his teammates and coach Weeb Ewbank were the heroes.

Jet fans began assembling in City Hall Park at 8 in the morning for ceremonies that began 25 minutes late at 2:10 p.m.

As time for the kickoff approached, youngsters even climbed trees to get a better view of their heroes, and city officials noted that the crowd was even bigger, by five times or more, than the recent throng greeting the Apollo 8 Astronauts.

The News had 10,000 team pictures of the Jets and several thousand buttons to distribute and these were all handed out within 15 minutes.

Included among the early arrivals was pretty Susan Faiella, 18, of Livingston, N.J., president of the Joe Namath Fan Club. It was she who pinned a "We Love Our Jets" button on the mayor.

The mayor, who read a proclamation calling this "New York Jets Championship Day," called the Jets "our conquering team."

Then he added, between catcalls: "It's a privilige to have the greatest city in the world pay tribute to the greatest football team in the world—and Joe Namath."

Phil Iselin, president of the Jets, received the proclamation and held up the Jets' Super Bowl Trophy for display. "This trophy wasn't easy to come by, but it's a tribute to our loyal fans," he said.

The mayor then presented bronze city medallions to Jet coach Weeb Ewbank, offensive captain Namath and defensive captain Johnny Sample.

Namath, who was shortly to receive a car as MVP in the Super Bowl, made sure to recognize fullback Matt Snell, who set ground-gaining records as he shredded the Colt defense, as "the most valuable offensive man in the Super Bowl." He then motioned to the other Jets on the platform and said: "I want those 20 guys to stand up ... they're our football team."

Sample played with Ewbank's earlier Baltimore champs in 1958 and '59. He said: "It's great to be part of a world championship team. This is my third and the greatest of them all. Our fans, the people who supported this club since 1960, they're responsible for us winning the world championship."

Later Bob Anderson, sports editor of *The News*, lauded the Jets' "Super Year" as he presented a special citation to Iselin and the Jets. He then gave the mayor a Leroy Neiman portrait of Namath in action.

NAMATH "MOST COURAGEOUS"

January 24, 1969—Joe Namath today was named winner of the George Halas Award as the "most courageous" player of the year by the Football Writers of America. Namath, who played on weak knees and was bothered by a dislocated thumb on his throwing hand, never missed a game while leading the Jets to the AFL championship and Super Bowl victory. Namath beat out Sonny Jurgensen of the Redskins, who played with a plastic cast around his rib cage.

Some fans turned out to the celebration specifically to see Joe Namath. (News photo by Bill Meurer)

Fans mob the stage where souvenir "Jets Our Champs" buttons were handed out. (News photo by Anthony Casale)

Fans cheer the Jets after their stunning Super Bowl upset of the Baltimore Colts. New York's first winners in six years were saluted at City Hall. (News photo by Bill Meurer)

Jets QB Joe Namath speaks during a rally for the Jets' Super Bowl win at City Hall. (News photo by Anthony Casale)

New Yorkers and Jets
players Matt Snell of
Locust Valley, Long
Island, and East Sider
Joe Namath hear the
Jets praised at City Hall.

Joe Namath examines his medal
while out on the platform during
the celebration at City Hall.
(News photo by Anthony Casale)

DAILY NEWS

NEW YORK'S PICTURE NEWSPAPER ®

New York, N.Y. 10017, Monday, August 18, 1969

JETS 37, GIANTS 14

Broadway Joe, 14-for-16, Hurls 3 TD Passes

METS SWEEP; YANKEES WIN

Stories Pages 70, 71

Titans of New York

NEWS photo by Frank Hurley

Clutching the pigskin under his arm, Jets' Bill Mathis—one of three original Titans still on team—scores on a first-period plunge in game against Giants at Yale Bowl yesterday. Giants' Tom Longo (44) is too late with the stop and the ref signals a score. Super Joe Namath, hitting on 14 of 16 passes for three TDs (one to Mathis), and Jets showed 70,874 fans who's boss in New York with 37-14 win. —*Stories p. 70; other pics centerfold*

Following the Super Bowl excitement, it was announced that Weeb Ewbank would return for another year of coaching the Jets. A repeat Super Bowl victory was to be the task at hand for the upcoming season. Before they could start working on that, though, the champion Jets had one more job to finish. The much-anticipated Yale Bowl between the Jets and the Giants was set for August 17, 1969. For many New Yorkers, this pre-season clash between the cross-town rivals was the "real" Super Bowl.

The game was a blowout, as the Jets easily ousted the Giants, 37-14. Once again, Joe Namath was the star, hitting 14 of 16 passes for 188 yards and three touchdowns. Ewbank had planned to pull Namath and the other starters prior to the end of the game, but they pleaded with him to leave them in for one last scoring drive. He did, and the end result was the lopsided victory. The Jets now officially owned the Big Town.

Bookies Love Those Jets, Too; Peg 'em 6 1/2 Over Jints

by Larry Fox
Daily News

Presenting one of the earliest morning lines in history, betting agents revealed yesterday that the Super Bowl champion Jets would be 6 1/2 point favorites over the Giants if their long-awaited exhibition game were to be played this weekend instead of August 17 in New Haven.

The News Charities Inc. will share in the proceeds of the contest that is expected to draw a capacity 70,000 at Yale Bowl . . . and two stadiums could be filled if they were available.

Ironically, oddsmakers consider the Jets' 16-7 Super Bowl victory over the Colts a factor in holding down the spread.

"After that game, the Giants may be playing a little 'scared' while the Jets might be complacent. It's pretty tough to get 'up' for an exhibition game after winning the Super Bowl," one said.

"There's a question of whether the Jets can be high enough to keep the Giants from scoring," said another.

The two oddsmakers—who concurred exactly in independently making the line—agreed that the Jets would be hungry for this game. Some of the American Leaguers have been waiting nine years for this chance, fellows like Don Maynard, Larry Grantham and Bill Mathis.

However, they feel the Giants will be hearing plenty this winter and spring about how lousy they must be compared to the Super Bowl champs and they will respond with fire, too.

"This will be a grudge game, and that's another reason you can't go too far out on the points. It's like the Giants and the Dodgers in baseball, and I wouldn't be surprised if there were some fights on the field," the slender wizard of odds said.

"This," said one, licking his lips over the vigorish to come, "is going to be some action game, especially if there's live TV. Just wait till those two factions start heating up. You'll think it was the Super Bowl all over again, not just an exhibition game."

ONE BIG ONE

by Larry Fox
Daily News

January 24, 1969—The Jets will play at least four NFL teams in exhibitions next summer, and Weeb Ewbank yesterday said that's just how he'll play them—with one exception. He said that the August 17 Yale Bowl game with the Giants, from which The News Charities Inc. will benefit, is different. "I'll play it by ear and it's really up to Allie (Sherman). If he plays Tarkenton half the game I'll play Namath half the game. If he uses Tarkenton all the way, I'll do the same with Namath," Weeb promised.

WEEB STAYS AS COACH; SECOND SUPER BOWL HIS GOAL

January 24, 1969—Weeb Ewbank, spry and smiling at 61, will be back to coach the Jets next year and, he anticipates, for as many more years as he feels up to it.

"I've never given any thought to anything but to coach as long as I felt good," Ewbank said yesterday when the Jets announced their Super Bowl coach was coming back to try to make it two in a row.

Although Ewbank and club president Phil Iselin apparently had reached an understanding several days ago, the decision wasn't formalized until a board of directors meeting yesterday morning.

Asked why he decided to remain in the middle of the arena instead of stepping upstairs to the sole post of GM, the gray-haired grandfather said, "I knew I would be lost if I wasn't close to it."

Ewbank said his wife, Lucy, had concurred in his decision to stay on the field because "she knew I'd go crazy if I wasn't coaching."

Ewbank this past season became the first coach in pro history to win titles in both the NFL and AFL. He did it back-to-back (1958-59) in the old league and he'd like to do the same in the new.

"In the back of my mind, I'd like to win two Super Bowls," he admitted when reminded he had a chance to equal Green Bay's super double of 1967 and '68.

Supercoach Weeb Ewbank displays his championship ring. (News photo by Frank Hurley)

Three Namath TDs Crush Giants, 37-14

70,874 in Bowl See Super Jets Roll

by Norm Miller
Daily News

New Haven, Conn.— Broadway Joe and the Jets won the city of New York today in a poker game in New Haven. With all the prestige of the championship of the city as table stakes, Joe Namath and the Jets cleaned out the Giants and left 'em for broke, 37-14.

Before an SRO crowd of 70,874 at steaming Yale Bowl, the wise guy from Beaver Falls, Pennsylvania, made this first Fun City Bowl 60 minutes of misery for the fall guys in Giant uniforms.

In his best Super Bowl form, Namath hit on 14 of 16 passes for 188 yards and three touchdowns before trotting off the field with hands raised joyously in triumph after his third scoring toss with 7:10 left in the game.

This exhibition showdown to determine who owns the Big Town turned out to be no contest. It was 17-0 Jets after 14 minutes, 24-0 Jets at halftime, and as the Giants floundered hopelessly in the closing minutes, disgruntled Giant rooters and jubilant Jets fans took it out on Allie Sherman with the old chorus of "Goodbye, Allie."

Joe Namath's belt presented by Ray Hickok for Professional Athlete of the Year. (News photo by Judd Mehiman)

With the tremendous incentives to win this one, the Jets played it like the Super Bowl; the Giants played it like the Daze Bowl.

The Jets played it smart, with good execution and few mistakes. The Giants blew opportunities right at the start, pulled a colossal boner that gave the Jets a touchdown, showed all their sloppiest fundamentals when Jets rookie Mike Battle raced 85 yards with a punt for another TD, and finally, with a chance to make it close, they lost their poise in the final quarter with a rash of silly penalties.

Besides Namath and the defenders, another Jet hero was Billy Mathis, one of the three original Titans named co-captain for this game in a Weeb Ewbank gesture commemorating the team's nine-year rise to the pinnacle of pro football.

Mathis scored two Jet TDs, one on a two-yard smash and the other on a 20-yard pass from Namath. Broadway Joe's two other TD tosses sailed 29 yards to George Sauer and just one yard to Pete Lammons for the final score.

The crowd, almost equally split between Giants and Jets fans, was the first sellout here since 1955. The game, arranged through the efforts of *The News* more than a year ago, was played for the benefit of four charities: The N.Y. News charities; the John V. Mara fund for Cancer Research at St. Vincent's Hospital; the Albie Booth Memorial Fund; and the New Haven Register Fresh Air Fund.

So sharp was Broadway Joe that he missed only two of his tosses, one when Giant rookie Fred Dryer got in to deflect the ball and the other when he missed Sauer along the sidelines.

The game was won in the first half when Namath threw 8-for-9 and 119 yards, when Henry Dyer pulled the rock that gave the Jets their gift TD, when Battle made his beautiful punt return and when the Giants were blanked on the scoreboard.

The Jets' Emerson Boozer, Curley Johnson, John Elliot and Carl McAdams proudly display their World Champion rings. (News photo by Frank Hurley)

JOE BEGGED FOR LAST TD: WEEB

August 18, 1969, New Haven—Weeb Ewbank wanted to relieve Joe Namath and his regulars before they got their final touchdown in today's rout of the Giants but the players wouldn't have it that way, he revealed afterward.

"Let me go one more series," Namath pleaded with his coach. Ewbank said, "All the players were coming at me, especially guys like (John) Schmitt, who live in the city. They said 'Weeb, let's don't take any chances.'"

And so the regulars stayed in for another touchdown.

How important was this? Just an exhibition game?

"Naturally we wanted to win the ballgame, anything up to hurting Joe," Ewbank said.

The Jets escaped apparent injury today and Ewbank was pleased with his offense.

He also gave warning to his future AFL opponents in games that will count. "This game didn't necessarily prove anything. We have a fine football team, and potentially a great team. It will be better than last year," the coach of the Super Bowl champions declared. "There are some people who played last year who won't make our team this season."

by Larry Fox
Daily News

A Fitting Farewell to Ewbank

Hank Gola
Daily News

OXFORD, Ohio—Weeb Ewbank was laid to rest here yesterday, just over the state border from where he was born, in the town where he began his coaching career, not far from the Hall where he is enshrined and close by forever in the hearts of the men who played for him.

At the Oxford Presbyterian Church, in a moving celebration of his 91 years of life, Ewbank was remembered by townspeople as a humble everyman, by former players as a skilled, caring coach and by his family as a boundlessly giving person.

His life, said his granddaughter, Cinda Carron, ended as perfectly as one could end, two days after watching the Jets and Colts, the two teams he guided to World Championships, do battle in Indianapolis.

"On Tuesday, his last day, he went down to his trophy room and spent some time there," Carron told the packed church. "He was looking at his life, his history, his legacy . . . all the memories from high school days all the way to now.

Weeb Ewbank
May 6, 1907–November 17, 1998

"It was an incredible room, filled with so much for him. He grabbed a special playbook. He spent some time with (his wife Lucy) and said he wasn't feeling quite well. So he laid down on the couch and she was with him.

"He closed his eyes and left us. After seeing his memories, after thinking of his family, after holding the playbook . . .What could be better than that? Nobody could write that ending."

As Rev. Robert Foster, a longtime friend of the old coach, said in his eulogy, "Weeb won it all."

There were many on hand to attest to that. Joe Namath made it up from Florida and sat in the second row behind Jets owner Leon Hess and president Steve Gutman. Namath's Super Bowl III teammates Winston Hill, Sam DeLuca, Dave Herman and Billy Mathis were also there.

A wreath in the shape of a horseshoe was placed on the altar next to Ewbank's casket, along with the banner, "1958-1959 World Champions." It represented Ewbank's Colts, who beat the Giants in the widely proclaimed "Greatest Game Ever Played." Legends from that team, including Johnny Unitas, Raymond Berry and Art Donovan, paid their respects yesterday.

Coaches Chuck Knox, Buddy Ryan and Ewbank's son-in-law Charlie Winner were present. Supervisor of officials Art McNally represented the NFL, even though Weeb once chased an official clear across the field after he thought he blew a call on Namath.

"Weeb led by example. Weeb led by being accountable," Hill said.

His insight remained keen.

"He was a teacher more than a coach," Unitas said. "He gave me my chance."

"I never would have had a career in professional football if it wasn't for Weeb," said Berry.

"The longer I was in coaching the more I was able to recognize the tremendous ability he had," Berry said.

Ewbank's legacy, which is so tied into Oxford and Miami University, the so-called cradle of coaches, extends to his many years on the high school sidelines. Murray Peters played for Ewbank as a schoolboy and remained his friend until the old coach's death. He said Ewbank used to start the second team to give everyone a chance.

"We weren't all-stars by any means," Peters said. "But in 1937, we were undefeated, untied and unscored upon."

Getting the most out of his teams was a trademark of Ewbank's two decades as an NFL head coach. "He took rinka-dinks. We were a lousy football team," Donovan said. "In my first four years, I was at four winning games. He came there in 1954 and it got serious. He took all the fun out of it. He was clever. Myself, I'd have to put him up there with the best who ever coached in the NFL. And I think he brought Paul Brown's theory of football one step further."

That was the message yesterday, that Ewbank took everyone one step further.

And so, on a perfect football weekend, in a perfect football town, with another football chill in the air, he was bid farewell.

Said Mary Brown, Paul's widow, "It's the closing of another era for football."

> "He closed his eyes and left us. After seeing his memories, after thinking of his family, after holding the playbook . . .What could be better than that? Nobody could write that ending."
> —Cinda Carron, granddaughter of Weeb Ewbank

A WINNING COMBINATION...

the
New York Jets
and the
United States
Postal Service